King Matthew the First

JANUSZ KORCZAK

King Matthew the First

Illustrations by
Jerzy Srokowski

Translation and Adaptation by
Adam Fisher, Ben Torrent

Tom eMusic

Title of original Polish edition
Król Maciuś pierwszy

Author's photo on the cover
Wikimedia Commons

Edition by
Ben Torrent

Proofreading by
Dena Angevin

Typesetting by
Blake Bendezar

All rights reserved. No part of this publication may be reproduced, stored in a retrieval system, or transmitted in any form or by any means electronic, mechanical, photocopying, recording or otherwise without the prior permission of the publisher.

© Copyright for this edition by Tom eMusic
© Copyright for the illustrations by successors of Jerzy Srokowski
© Copyright for the text by Instytut Książki

ISBN 979-8-3493-8997-9

Published by
Tom eMusic

www.tomemusic.com

New York 2021

When I was a boy, as you can see in this photograph, I wanted to do everything that is written below. Then, it somehow slipped my mind, and now I have grown too old. With my youth left far behind, I have neither the time nor the energy to wage wars or visit cannibals. The photo I have included will show you what I was like when I really did want to be king, and not what I look like now as I write about King Matthew. I believe it is far better to show photos of kings, travelers and writers when they were still children, because otherwise you might think they had always been wise adults without ever being once small. Kids might think they are unfit to be ministers, travelers and writers, which is absolutely not true.

The point is that grownups should not read my novel at all, as there are chapters in it they will never understand. They will inevitably try, but to no avail; in the end, they will only make fun of it. However, should they insist on reading this book, let them do so. After all, they are grownups and we cannot stop them. Even if you tried to forbid them, they simply would not pay heed, and you could not do anything about it…could you?

And this is how it happened…

The doctor said that if the king did not pull through in three days, we had better prepare for the worst.

In fact, what the doctor said was this:

"The King is seriously ill, and if he does not pull through in three days, we can expect the worst."

In the wake of this statement, the court was rife with worry. The eldest minister put on his spectacles and asked:

"So, what will happen if the king does not recover?"

The doctor was rather evasive, but everybody understood that the king was dying. The eldest minister, distraught, summoned the Council of Ministers.

They gathered together in an enormous hall, seating themselves in comfortable armchairs around a long table. Each minister had a sheet of paper and two pencils in front of him: one ordinary pencil and a second one with one blue and one red end. A bell was also placed in front of the eldest minister.

Once the door had been locked to prevent disturbances and the electric lamps were switched on, a hush fell over the hall.

Finally, the eldest minister rang the bell and said:

"A grave matter for debate is before us. The king is sick and cannot rule any longer."

"I propose," said the Minister of War, "that we summon the doctor and demand to know in no uncertain terms whether he believes the king can be cured or not."

Everybody was afraid of the Minister of War, who always carried a sword and a pistol so that no one would ever dare to defy him.

"Yes! Let's summon the doctor!" agreed the ministers.

The doctor was sent for then and there, but he could not come as he was cupping His Royal Highness (24 cupping glasses in all).

"There is nothing to do but wait," said the eldest minister. "But now, tell me what we will do if the king dies."

"I know," said the Minister of Justice. "According to the law, after the king's death, his eldest son accedes to the throne. That's why he's referred to as the heir to the throne. If the king dies, his eldest son will become his successor."

"But the king has only one son!"

"There's no need for more…"

"Well, yes and no. The point is that Matthew, the royal successor, is but a small boy. How could he possibly become king? He cannot even write!"

"Well, it really can't be helped," replied the Minister of Justice. "There has been no such precedent in our country; but in Spain, Belgium and some other countries, kings have died leaving underage heirs, and those children simply had to wear the crown."

"True enough," said the Post and Telegraph Minister. "I have even seen stamps with the image of such a small king depicted on them."

"But my dear sirs," said the Minister of Education, "a ruler who is unable to read or count is almost unheard of. To be utterly ignorant of geography and grammar…"

"I fully agree," said the Finance Minister. "How is the king to make out checks and invoices? How is he to decide how much money to print if he does not know the multiplication tables?"

"And to make things worse, my dear colleagues," exclaimed the Minister of War, "nobody will ever fear such a tiny king. How could he possibly cope with soldiers and generals?"

"Frankly speaking," said the Minister of the Interior, "not only the soldiers, but virtually no one will be afraid of such a small king. So, if he does become king, we are bound to face endless strikes, riots and many other forms of civil and political unrest. I can vouch for nothing if you make Matthew king."

"I know next to nothing about what's going to happen," said the Minister of Justice, red-hot with anger. "All I do know is that the law spells it out categorically enough: after the death of the king, no person other than his legitimate son shall succeed him on the throne."

"But Matthew is too small!" exclaimed all the remaining ministers in unison.

A great argument would certainly have ensued, but for the appearance of a foreign ambassador, who could not have arrived at a more opportune moment. His arrival took everyone by surprise, certain as they were that the door had been securely locked. After the doctor was sent for, they had simply forgotten to relock it. That is why the ambassador was able to enter the hall while the ministers were having a Cabinet meeting. Some insisted that the Minister of Justice had deliberately left the door unlocked because he knew the ambassador was coming.

"Good evening!" the ambassador greeted the ministers. "I'm here on behalf of the king, who demands your acceptance of Matthew the First as the next king. Your refusal of his decision in this matter will be tantamount to war."

The Prime Minister (the eldest one) was frightened but pretended disinterest. On the sheet of paper in front of him, he wrote using his blue pencil:

Then let there be war, and handed the paper over to the foreign ambassador.

The latter took the paper in his hand, glancing at it briefly, then bowed and said:

"Good, I will notify my government."

At that moment, the doctor entered the hall to a chorus of voices as the ministers beseeched him to save the king, averting certain war and indescribable disaster.

"I have already given the king all the medications known to me—I have even applied cupping glasses. There is nothing else I can do, but send for other doctors throughout the kingdom if it will ease your minds."

The ministers followed his advice, summoning the most eminent doctors in the capital to confer on a cure for the sick king. The entire fleet of royal vehicles was dispatched in all directions and, this feat accomplished, the ministers asked the royal cook to prepare a great supper. Not expecting the meeting to last so long, few had dined at home and all were starving.

The cook spared no haste in laying the table, fetching the best silverware and filling the gentlemen's glasses with the most delicious wine. He knew that this supper might help to retain his position in the court after the death of the old king.

Oblivious to the drama in the king's bedroom where the doctors gathered around the royal patient, the ministers wined and dined, growing merrier with every glass of wine.

"I think," said an old doctor with a long beard, "that what the patient needs is skillful surgery."

"In my opinion," declared another doctor, "I would opt instead for a hot compress and a salt-water gargle."

"A powder for indigestion—that's the thing!" said an eminent professor.

"Drops would undoubtedly be better," disagreed still another.

Each of the doctors had brought a massive book of medicine and was all too eager to show that his sources recommended not only a different, but the very best of treatments for that particular illness.

Outside night had fallen, and though the ministers were bleary-eyed and desperate for their beds, they could not leave until hearing what the doctors had to say. There was so much noise in the royal palace that the young heir, Matthew, the king's only child, had already woken up twice.

I need to see what's going on there, thought the boy.

He got out of bed, dressed hurriedly and went out into the corridor.

He stopped before the door to the conference hall, not to eavesdrop, but because the boy was too short to reach the handles of the doors in the royal palace.

"The royal wine is delicious!" shouted the Finance Minister. "Let's drink some more, gents! If Matthew becomes king, he will have no need of it!"

"Children cannot smoke cigars either. We can take some cigars home, can we not?!" chimed in the Commerce Minister.

"And in the event of war, my friends, mark my words—this palace will cease to exist. King Matthew the First will never defend us."

Everyone burst out laughing, and cries of 'Let's drink a toast to our savior and master, great King Matthew the First!' rang out.

Matthew was hard pressed to understand exactly what they were talking about, but he knew that his father was ill and that the ministers met regularly to discuss his condition. But why were they laughing at him? Why were they calling him king, and what war were they referring to? These were questions he could not answer.

Half asleep and stomach in knots, he continued along the corridor, and passing by another door to the conference hall, overheard a random snippet of conversation.

"And don't be deceived; the king is going to die. You can dose him with powders and other medicines, but the truth is: there's no hope."

"I bet my life he'll be dead before the week is done!"

Matthew had had enough. He raced along the corridor, passing two royal halls, and finally arrived, trembling and out of breath, in his father's bedroom.

The king was lying in bed, very pale and breathing with difficulty. By his side sat the same old and faithful doctor who also treated Matthew whenever the boy was ill.

"Daddy, daddy," cried Matthew, tears streaming down his cheeks. "I don't want you to die!"

The king opened his eyes and looked at his son sadly.

"I don't want to die," said the king softly. "It pains me to think of leaving you alone in this world."

Matthew climbed onto the doctor's lap, and they did not speak anymore.

Then Matthew had a sudden recollection of another bedside vigil. His father had held him tight as they looked upon the prince's mother, as pale as his father was now, her breath just as labored.

My father will die just as my mother did, thought the boy.

Sorrow welled up in his heart, joined by a growing hatred for the ministers who were laughing at him and at the king on his deathbed.

When I'm king, I'll make them pay for this! thought the future ruler.

The king's funeral was a stately occasion, one of indescribable grandeur. Lanterns were wrapped in black silk. All the bells in the kingdom tolled while the orchestra played the funeral march. In the burial procession, the coffin was followed by elite troops and heavy artillery. Flowers had been transported to the capital by rail from the warmest countries. Sadness prevailed and newspapers wrote about a country in mourning for its beloved king.

Matthew, filled with a profound sadness he had never felt before, sat motionlessly in his room, his eyes fixed on the ceiling. Although he was to become king of a whole nation, every time he thought about his father, he felt absolutely alone with no kindred spirit to comfort him.

He remembered his mother: she had named him Matthew. Even though she was queen, she was not self-important in the least; she could always find time to play with him, make toy houses with building blocks, tell him bedside stories or browse languidly through the pages of those beautifully illustrated books.

The boy's encounters with his father were, in contrast, far and few between. If the king was not inspecting the army, he was abroad visiting foreign rulers or entertaining them in his palace. He often had to attend Cabinet meetings and conferences. But even the king, as busy as he always was, found the time to play ninepins or ride along the paths of the royal garden: His Majesty on horseback and Matthew on a pony.

What did he have to look forward to now? The same boring tutor from overseas, who invariably looked as if he had just swallowed a glass of strong vinegar! Was it really such a joy to be king? Probably not... If there was really to be a war, you could at least fight bravely. But what was the king supposed to do in times of peace?

Matthew felt really overwhelmed by melancholy, sitting in his room all by himself, even more so as he looked out beyond the royal garden at the children of the palace servants, frolicking merrily in a park.

There were seven boys, all told, and their favorite game by far was soldiers. They were always commanded by a small and very cheerful boy named Felix; at least that's what the other boys called him.

Matthew had always wanted to call out to Felix and talk to him, but he was never sure if he was allowed, whether such an association was seemly for a member of the royal family... Most of all, he worried about what to say. How would he initiate such an awkward conversation?

In the meantime, large posters announcing his ascendancy to the throne had been hung on each and every street of the kingdom. The sign included a greeting from the new king for his subjects, his wishes for their prosperity and assurances that the ministers of the former king's Cabinet would be retained to assist the young ruler.

Shops displayed hundreds of pictures of King Matthew the First: Matthew on a pony, Matthew in a sailor suit, Matthew in a military uniform, Matthew at a military review! Matthew was also presented in newsreels and special film supplements in cinemas. All the illustrated weeklies at home and abroad featured countless photos of the new king.

Truth be told, the boy was well-liked throughout the kingdom. The elders felt sorry for him, a boy who had lost both his parents at such a young age. Boys rejoiced that one of their own was finally in charge, someone whose orders must be obeyed without question at all times, before whom even generals must stand to attention and regular soldiers present arms. Girls were fond of the sight of the small king on a striking, little pony. But it was orphans who admired him most, seeing a kindred soul in him.

When Matthew's mother was still alive, she always remembered to send sweets to orphanages at Christmas and Easter. When she died, the king had ordered that the late queen's custom be observed and, unbeknownst to Matthew, sweets and toys had been sent there ever since in his name. It was not until later that King Matthew came to understand that there was no item more important in the budget than giving the people pleasure.

About six months after his accession, King Matthew won great popularity by sheer coincidence. All at once he was on everybody's lips, and not because he was king, but because he had done something which was met with widespread approval.

Let me tell you what happened.

Having obtained permission to take walks around the city, the young ruler continuously pestered the doctor to escort him, even if only once a week, to the park where all the children played.

"It is quite nice in the royal garden, but if you are alone, even the most beautiful place under the sun loses its charm," said Matthew.

At long last the doctor agreed, and through the agency of the chamberlain was able to address the palace administration with the urgent request that the royal guardian 'ad litem' go to the Cabinet meeting and wheedle the ministers into granting Matthew permission to take three walks at two-week intervals.

Strange as it may seem, it was really not that simple for the king to go for an ordinary walk. I should add that the chamberlain only consented to help because the doctor had recently cured him of food poisoning after he had eaten some bad fish. The palace administration had been trying for quite some time to get funds from the Finance ministry to have a stable built, but to no avail. So, the Minister of the Interior agreed to Matthew's request just to spite the Finance Minister; for each walk, the royal police were paid three thousand ducats, while the sanitary department received a barrel of cologne and a thousand pieces of gold.

Before each of King Matthew's walks, two hundred men and one hundred women cleaned the park thoroughly. The paths were brushed, the benches were painted green, all the alleys were sprayed with cologne and dust was wiped off the trees and leaves. The doctors made sure everything was clean, knowing that dirt and dust could be harmful to the health of the young king. The police made sure that there were no urchins in the park, who could throw stones, start brawls or make noise.

King Matthew was having a great time. He was dressed in ordinary clothes so no one would recognize him. No one would have expected the king to visit a 'common' park anyway. King Matthew had circled the entire playground twice before he asked permission to sit on a bench in a square where children were playing. No sooner had he sat down than a girl invited him to join them. Of course, Matthew didn't mind. Hand in hand they twirled until the other girls joined the circle, laughing and singing all the while. Before embarking on a new game, the girls engaged Matthew in conversation.

"Do you have a sister?"

"No, I'm afraid I don't," answered the king.

"And what does your father do?"

"My father died recently. He was king."

The girl thought Matthew was only joking because she started to laugh and said:

"If my father were king, he would have to buy me a doll as tall as a house."

Matthew soon learned that the girl's father was a fire department captain, and her name was Irene. The girl liked the firemen, who occasionally let her ride their horses.

Matthew would have liked to stay with the children, but his excursion was scheduled to end at twenty minutes and forty-three seconds past four o'clock.

Matthew waited impatiently for another visit to the garden, but it was postponed owing to heavy rain. The decision was not an easy one, but the entire court feared for his health.

When the day of the second visit finally arrived, Matthew suffered an accident. He was playing the same circle game with the girls when a couple of boys approached. One of them called out:

"Look, a boy who plays with girls!" And he doubled over in laughter.

"You'd better come and play with us!" shouted the boy.

Matthew had a closer look at him.

There was no doubt about it—it was Felix! The very same Felix Matthew had wanted to make friends with for so long.

Now it was Felix's turn to be surprised. He gazed at the young king for a while and exclaimed:

"Hey, boys! Unbelievable! He's the spitting image of King Matthew!"

Matthew was suddenly ashamed at their staring, so he started running towards his adjutant, who was also dressed in plain clothes to avoid recognition. But whether through haste or a moment's carelessness, he fell down and grazed his knee…

At the Cabinet meeting, it was decided that the king would no longer be permitted to visit the park. The ministers were ready to do whatever he wished, but visits to an ordinary park were now forbidden. The Cabinet could not accept the risk that the king could be bullied, not to mention the possibility that someone could laugh at the head of state—this was simply unpardonable!

The Cabinet's decision worried Matthew a great deal. He thought often about his two visits to the garden and all the fun he was missing out on now. Suddenly, he remembered Irene's wish.

She wants to have a doll as tall as a house!

The very thought of such a doll made him feel uneasy.

I'm king after all, so I have the right to give orders to people, but I also have to follow everyone's orders. I'm learning to read and write just like all the other children, and I have to wash my ears, neck and teeth like all the other children. The multiplication table is the same for kings and everyone else. Why then should I be king?

Although still unsure of his reading skills, King Matthew decided it was time to read his ministers the 'Riot Act'. During the audience, he demanded that the Prime Minister buy the largest doll in the world and send it to Irene.

"His Royal Highness will deign to note that…" the Prime Minister began.

Matthew knew at once what was about to follow: this unbearable man would use a lot of words he had never heard before, and his plan to buy the doll would come to nothing.

The king vaguely remembered hearing this very politician explain something to his father, using the same twisted language. The king had stomped his foot in anger and cried:

"I'm not asking you; I'm demanding!"

So, Matthew stomped his foot just like his father and, feigning anger, said very loudly:

"Minister, this is not a request; this is an order!"

The Prime Minister looked at the young king in disbelief. Then he jotted down a few words in his notebook.

"OK. I will present this demand from His Royal Highness at the Cabinet meeting."

What words were exchanged at the meeting remains unknown since the debate took place behind closed doors. In the end it was decided to buy the doll, and the Commerce Minister toured all of the capital's shop in search of the largest doll, but two days later declared the task to be impossible —a doll of such size was nowhere to be found. So, the Commerce Minister called together all the tradesmen in the country, and one manufacturer agreed to make the doll in his factory in four weeks' time, for an exorbitant price. When the doll was ready, he displayed it in his shop window with a sign, which read:

THIS DOLL HAS BEEN MANUFACTURED BY THE ROYAL COURT SUPPLIER FOR IRENE, THE DAUGHTER OF THE FIRE DEPARTMENT CAPTAIN.

The moment the doll appeared in the shop window, all the newspapers in the country, in an attempt to outdo one another, began printing photos of the fire brigade at work and later of Irene and the doll. It was widely rumored that King Matthew was very fond of watching fires burn as well as seeing the fire brigade in action. In a letter to the press, an anonymous reader declared that if their beloved king liked fires, he was ready to set fire to his own house. Many a girl wrote to the king that she would also enjoy having such a doll. But the court secretary did not read those letters to Matthew, forbidden to do so by the Prime Minister, who was still angry with the young king.

Crowds of people stood in front of the shop, admiring the royal gift for three full days. But on the fourth day, by decree of the Police Prefect, the doll was taken out of the window since the crowd was blocking the flow of cars and trams.

So, now you see how King Matthew earned such a good opinion among his subjects—all because of the beautiful present he gave to Irene.

Matthew got up at seven o'clock every morning. He washed, dressed, polished his shoes and made his bed all by himself. This was a custom introduced by Matthew's great-grandfather, valiant Paul the Conqueror. Once his morning routine was done, Matthew drank a wineglass of cod-liver oil and sat down to breakfast, but for no longer than sixteen minutes and thirty-five seconds—that was how long Matthew's ancestor, great King Julius the Innocent, ate his breakfast. Then Matthew went to the throne room, a very cold room in more ways than one, to receive the ministers. The throne room had neither a tiled stove nor a fireplace because Matthew's grandmother, Ann the Pious, a woman of infinite wisdom, had nearly suffocated from the fumes of a faulty stove as a child. To commemorate her fortuitous survival, palatial etiquette was expanded to include a rule that the throne room would remain without a stove for the next five hundred years.

Matthew sat on the throne, his teeth chattering loudly while the ministers discussed the most important problems facing the kingdom. It was rather unpleasant because there was hardly ever any good news.

The Foreign Minister talked about who was cross with Matthew's kingdom and who was unfriendly towards his rule, and…Matthew could hardly understand what he was saying.

The Minister of War would enumerate all the fortresses that needed a complete overhaul and all the cannons that were out of order and could not be fired anymore. Finally, he would quote the number of soldiers on sick leave.

The Minister of Transport would explain that locomotives were in short supply and that there was an urgent need for new ones.

The Minister of Education would complain that children were not doing their best at school and arrived late for their lessons. Boys were smoking cigarettes on the sly and tearing pages out of their exercise books. Girls were sulking and quarreling about one thing or another, while the boys were always fighting and throwing stones and breaking windows.

Last but not least, the Finance Minister was always angry as there was not enough money and refused to buy new cannons and new machines, for they all cost far too much.

Then Matthew would go down to the royal garden where he could run and play for an hour. But it wasn't much fun playing all alone.

Given all this, it's no wonder he willingly returned to his lessons. Matthew was a diligent pupil, for he knew that without a proper education you could hardly pass for a decent king. So, he studied and in practically no time, he knew how to sign a document with an elongated flourish. He also had to learn French and various other languages so that he could talk to other kings whenever on a foreign visit.

Matthew would have applied himself even more eagerly if only he were given permission to ask all the questions that occupied his mind.

For a long time, Matthew racked his brains, wondering if it was possible to invent a type of remote-controlled glass that would ignite gunpowder. Were Matthew to invent such a glass, he would declare war on all the kings the world over, and on the eve of the decisive battle, he would blow up all the enemy powder magazines! He would win the war hands down as the sole possessor of gunpowder. Then, even though still very small, he would all at once become a great emperor. Hearing his ideas, his tutor only shrugged his shoulders, winced as if in pain and said nothing.

On another occasion, Matthew asked whether a dying father could leave all his knowledge and wisdom to his son. Matthew's father, Stephen the Sensible, was very knowledgeable and wise indeed. Now Matthew sat on his throne and was destined to wear the same crown, but had to learn everything from scratch, and he did not know if he would ever gain as much insight as his late father once possessed. If his wishes came true, he would, along with the throne and crown, acquire the valor of his great-grandfather, Paul the Conqueror, the piety of his grandmother and the immense intelligence of his father.

But this question was not received well either.

The next question our hero puzzled over was 'the cap of invisibility'. It took him even longer to figure out what it would be like to wear such a cap. No matter which way you looked at it—a great idea! Matthew could go around unseen as much as he wanted to. By day he would say he had a headache and could stay in bed and get some decent sleep, and at night he would put on his cap of invisibility and spend a night on the town. He would walk the length and breadth of the capital window-shopping, and he would certainly go to the theater, too.

Matthew had been to the theater to see a special gala performance when both his parents were still alive. He had only a dim recollection of the play as he was very little then, but he did remember that the performance was magnificent.

If Matthew had the cap of invisibility, he would escape the royal garden to the palace backyard and make friends with Felix. He could move at will through the palace and its grounds: He would have a look-see at the kitchen as royal food was being prepared. Then he would visit the stable to see the horses and all those buildings and outbuildings he was not allowed to enter.

Strange as it may seem, the number of dos and don'ts that the king had to follow was mind-boggling. I should explain to you that court etiquette is very strict—here, there and everywhere. Etiquette is what kings have always done and what each new king must follow, because if he wanted to do something of his own and not the traditional way, he would immediately lose his honor and nobody would respect or fear him. It would mean that he did not respect his powerful father-king, or grandfather, or great-grandfather. If a king wants to do something in a different way than the time-honored way, he has to ask the Grand Master of Ceremonies, who knows the rules that kings have always followed and oversees court etiquette.

As I have said before, King Matthew's breakfast always lasted sixteen minutes and thirty-five seconds just because his grandfather had done so, and that the throne room had no stove in it because Matthew's grandmother had insisted on it and since she died a long time ago, there was no way of asking her permission to have a stove put back in.

Occasionally the king can change one thing or another but each and every such alteration must be thoroughly discussed at long Cabinet meetings, as was the case with Matthew's walks in the outside park. So, it was quite unpleasant to ask for something and then have to wait for it indefinitely.

King Matthew the First happened to be in a more difficult situation than other kings since etiquette was meant for adult kings, whereas Matthew was just a small child. So, etiquette had to be altered a little. That's why King Matthew, instead of delicious wine, drank daily two wineglasses of cod-liver oil, which he abhorred. By the same token, instead of reading newspapers, the king only looked at the pictures as he still had problems with reading.

It would be quite a different story if he had his father's wisdom and the cap of invisibility: he would then be a real king! But as it was, he often wondered whether it would not have been better if he had been born an ordinary boy, went to school, tore pages out of his exercise books and threw stones.

One day it dawned on Matthew that if he learned to write, he could send a message to Felix, and perhaps Felix would answer his letter. This would be almost as if the two boys had had a chat.

This was a crucial realization. From that moment on, Matthew was a model student:

learning to write became his top priority. Day in and day out he practiced by rewriting poems and tales from his handbook. If he had been allowed, he would not have gone to the royal garden, choosing to write from sunrise to sunset, but this would have gone against the rule of etiquette—etiquette and court ceremony required that the king should leave the throne room and go straight to the royal garden. The moment he rose from the throne, twenty lackeys were ready to open the French windows for him. If Matthew refused to enter the royal garden, those twenty lackeys would have nothing to do and would be bored stiff.

You might be thinking that it is no big deal to open a door for someone, but that is only because you do not know court etiquette. I should also tell you that those lackeys, because of that door business, were kept occupied for five solid hours. Each of them took a cold shower in the morning, then had his hair set by the royal barber, who also trimmed the lackeys' beards and moustaches. Their livery had to be impeccably clean, without a single speck of dust. Some three hundred years ago, during the reign of Henry the Impetuous, a flea jumped straight onto the king's scepter from one of his lackeys. The king, of course, had the slovenly subject beheaded, and the chamberlain escaped the headman's axe by a hair's breadth. From then on, the supervisor checked each lackey personally for cleanliness. Once washed, dressed and clean as a whistle, the lackeys stood in the corridor, waiting from seven minutes past eleven until seventeen minutes past one o'clock to be inspected by the Grand Master of Ceremonies. This was no simply formality—a single button undone resulted in six years imprisonment, the wrong haircut earned its wearer four years of hard labor, and an ungainly bow four months in jail with bread and water rations.

Matthew knew a little of all of this, so it would never have occurred to him not to go for a walk in the garden. Who knows—there may have been a ruler who had never walked through the royal garden; if historians had discovered this, it would have set a precedent for Matthew to follow, and his newly-acquired writing skills would have been all for naught, for how else could Matthew pass a letter to Felix than through the garden bars?

But despite his tendency to fantasize, Matthew was able to focus and had strong willpower, so he resolved:

"In a month, I will write my first letter to Felix."

Difficult as the task was, Matthew pressed on with his work, and after a month he completed the letter to Felix singlehandedly.

Dear Felix—wrote Matt—*it has been a long time since I began watching you play in the royal backyard. I would also love to play with you. But I am king so I can't. I like you very much, so please write something about yourself. I would like to make friends with you. If you are from a military family, you can be allowed to visit the royal garden from time to time.*

Matthew, the King

Matthew's heart was pounding like a pneumatic hammer as he called out to Felix through the bars and handed him the letter. His heart was also hammering in his chest the following day when he received a reply via the same route.

Your Majesty—wrote Felix—*my father is a platoon commander in the palace guard and therefore a military man. I would like very much enjoy a visit to the royal garden. I am, Your Highness, your faithful servant, and I would defend you with my life. If ever you are in need of my help, just whistle, and I will answer your call.*

Felix

Matthew put the letter in his bottom drawer under a stack of books, and he threw himself into mastering the art of whistling. Matthew, however, took a very cautious approach. He did not want to put all his cards on the table too soon. Were he to demand that Felix be allowed into the royal garden, long debates would ensue: why, how did he know Felix's name, how did they meet? And so on and so forth. What would happen if they saw through his scheme and did not approve? A platoon commander's son?! Why not at least a lieutenant's? An officer's son might be permitted, but as it was, they would certainly refuse…

"I'd better wait and see," decided Matthew. "In the meantime, I'll have to learn to whistle."

It is not such a simple thing to learn to whistle, especially if you have nobody to show you how to do it. But Matthew was a strong-willed boy.

Fixing his mind to the task, he took a stab to see if he could do it. Can you imagine his astonishment when…who should appear before him, but Felix in the flesh, standing at attention as stiff as a poker?

"How did you get here?"

"I climbed over the railings."

The royal garden was home to a plot of very dense raspberry bushes, and that is where the boys hid to decide what to do next.

Listen Felix, I'm a very unhappy ruler. Ever since I learned to write, I have been signing all the papers they put under my nose, which should mean that I rule this country. But in fact, all I do is carry out their orders—the most boring things in the world—and I'm forbidden from doing anything pleasant."

"Who could forbid Your Highness from doing pleasant things and order you about?"

"The ministers," replied Matthew. "When my daddy was alive, I did what he told me to do."

"I see. You were Crown Prince, heir to the throne, and your father was His Royal Highness—the King. And now…"

"Well now, it is a hundred times worse. There are so many ministers in the court that I've lost count of them."

"Military or civilian?"

"Only one of them is a military man: the Minister of War!"

"And the rest are civilians?"

"I don't know what the word 'civilian' means."

"Civilians are those fellows who wear neither uniform nor swords."

"Oh yes, I see—they are civilians."

Felix put a handful of raspberries into his mouth and fell into deep thought. Then slowly and not without hesitation, he asked:

"Are there any cherry trees in the royal garden?"

Matthew was slightly baffled by the question, but he trusted his new friend completely and admitted that there were pears and cherries galore. The king agreed to hand the fruit to Felix through the bars. Any quantity he wanted.

"OK, we can't see each other too often as we might be caught. In public we will pretend to be perfect strangers, yet we will exchange letters. Let's place the letters on the fence…with cherries if possible. As soon as the correspondence is in its place, His Royal Highness will whistle, and I'll collect it instantly."

"And as soon as you write back, you will whistle. Won't you?" exclaimed Matthew joyfully.

"Oh, no! You can't whistle at the king!" protested Felix vehemently. "I can send a different signal. I will stand in the shade and imitate the call of the cuckoo from afar for Your Highness."

"It's a deal!" agreed King Matthew. "And when are you coming next?"

Felix hesitated for a moment and said at last:

"I can't come here without permission. My father is a platoon commander and has perfect eyesight. He won't even allow me to approach the railings around the royal garden and has warned me several times. 'Felix,' he said, 'let's get this straight—God have mercy on you if you're ever caught sneaking into the royal garden and stealing cherries. You are my son, my own flesh and blood, but were you caught stealing, I would skin you alive and let you bleed to death.'"

All of a sudden, Matthew felt ill at ease.

It would be a travesty—it had taken so much effort to find a friend and now that friend, through no fault of his own, but with Matthew to blame, could be skinned alive. Oh, no! This danger was far too great.

"But how will you return home safely?" asked Matthew anxiously.

"I think His Royal Highness had better go now, and I will manage one way or another."

Without thinking twice Matthew left the thicket. It was high time, for the foreign tutor, agitated by the prolonged absence of his charge, was peering warily around the royal garden.

From that moment on, Matthew and Felix, although separated by railings, worked in tandem. Matthew often sighed in the presence of his doctor, who weighed and measured him once a week to see if the small king was growing and when he would be big enough to wear the crown. King Matthew complained of loneliness and isolation, and once even mentioned to the Minister of War that he would very much like to master a military drill.

"Do you happen to know, Mister Minister, a platoon commander who could give me lessons?"

"I fully appreciate Your Highness's desire to acquire military knowledge. But why must it be a platoon commander?"

"It could even be a platoon commander's son!" exclaimed Matthew joyfully.

The minister frowned and took down the king's demand.

Matthew sighed as he already knew what the minister was going to say.

"I will raise this demand of yours, Royal Highness, at the earliest convenience, possibly at the next Cabinet meeting."

Once again this will all be for nothing, thought Matthew. I bet they will send me some old general!

What actually happened was something quite different!

The Cabinet meeting in question was entirety devoted to one problem—namely, the fact that three countries had just jointly declared war on King Matthew.

War!

Meanwhile Matthew was waiting for the outcome of his request. The evening passed with no news. He still hadn't heard anything by the afternoon of the following day. News of the impending war finally came to him by way of Felix. With all the previous letters, the boy had each time made the cuckoo's call only three times, but on this occasion, it was probably as many as one hundred! Matthew understood that the new letter would contain some extraordinary news. But he did not know how extraordinarily extraordinary. There had been no war for quite some time, for Stephen the Sensible always knew how to steer clear of military conflicts. Although there had been little love lost between his country and the neighboring kingdoms, he had never aspired to open war, and nobody had ever dared to declare war on him.

Now it was plain that they were taking advantage of Matthew's young age and inexperience; this just made Matthew want to prove them wrong. He wanted to show that, despite his age, he was perfectly capable of defending his people. Felix's letter read:

Yesterday three countries declared war on His Royal Highness. My father has always said that he would get drunk out of joy at the first news of war. I am waiting for this because we must meet urgently.

Felix

It was not for nothing that Matthew was the great-grandson of that brave king, Paul the Conqueror. The news made his blood boil.

"I wish I had that remote-controlled glass for igniting gunpowder and the cap of invisibility!"

So now, Matthew waited, thinking that he would be summoned to hear an emergency report at a special session, and that now he, the legitimate head of the country, would take the helm of the state. A session really did take place that night, but nobody bothered to call the king.

The following day, it was business as usual as far as Matthew was concerned. There was no change in the timetable, and the foreign tutor behaved as if nothing had happened.

Matthew knew court etiquette, knew that the king could not pick and choose, be obstinate, sulk or get angry, and he did not want to do anything to compromise the king's dignity and honor at such a historic moment. His eyebrows were drawn together and his forehead creased, and when he looked at himself in the mirror during the lesson, one thought entered his head:

I look very much like Henry the Impetuous!

There was nothing to do but wait for the audience.

However, when the Grand Master of Ceremonies announced that the audience was cancelled, Matthew, impassive but very pale, said decisively:

"I demand that the Minister of War be summoned to the throne room. Now!"

The word 'war' was said with such emphasis that the Master of Ceremonies understood at once that Matthew already knew everything.

"The Minister of War is attending the Cabinet meeting."

"And so will I!" retorted King Matthew, directing his steps towards the conference hall.

"Your Royal Highness will deign to wait just one moment. Your Royal Highness will have mercy on me. I'm not permitted… I'm responsible for…"

The old man burst out crying.

Matthew felt a surge of pity for the Grand Master of Ceremonies, who knew what the king could do and what was unbecoming. More than once, they had sat together by the fire late into the night, and it was very pleasant to hear the old man's stories about his father the king, his mother the queen, court etiquette, foreign balls, gala performances in theaters and military maneuvers attended by the king.

Matthew felt pangs of conscience. Writing letters to a platoon commander's son was a serious infringement of court etiquette, but it was picking cherries and raspberries in secret that tormented him most. Admittedly, the royal garden belonged to him, and although he did not pick the fruit for himself, he did it secretly, and who could tell whether he was not staining the honor of his great and valiant ancestors?

To be sure, it was not for nothing that Matthew was the grandson of the saintly Ann the Pious. Matthew had a heart of gold, and he was deeply moved by the old man's tears. He could have continued behaving improperly, letting his emotions rule him, but he regained his composure and said impassively:

"I will wait ten minutes."

The Master of Ceremonies shot off like a bullet, and soon all hell broke loose in the palace.

"How did Matthew find out?" cried the Minister of the Interior angrily.

"What is the 'brat' going to do now?" exclaimed the Prime Minister.

Hearing this, the Minister of Justice dressed him down immediately:

"Mister Prime Minister, it is against the law to use such abusive language when referring to the king. In private you can say what you please, but our session is official. Think what you like, but you must watch your language."

"The meeting had been temporarily adjourned!" stammered the Prime Minister, frightened and in an attempt to defend himself.

"Then you should have announced that the session was adjourned. And you didn't."

"I forgot. I am truly sorry!" said the Prime Minister, chastened.

The Minister of War glanced at his watch.

"Dear sirs, the king gave us ten minutes. Four minutes have already passed, so let's not quarrel. Since I'm a military man, I must carry out this order issued by the king."

The poor Prime Minister had much more to be afraid of, for on the table a sheet of paper with a sentence written in blue was placed:

Then let there be war.

It was easy to play the hero then, but now the time had come to face the music. Careless words might prove costly.

What should I say if the king asks why I wrote those words? thought the Prime Minister. *Everything started because we did not want Matthew as king after the death of his father.*

All the ministers knew how it had started, and now they sat smugly, for they were not very fond of the Prime Minister with all his pride and his habit of throwing his weight around.

For their part, the ministers were thinking how to pass the buck to a colleague and avoid the king's anger for withholding such important information.

"One minute to go," announced the Minister of War.

He did up a button, straightened the array of medals on his chest, tweaked his moustache, took his pistol off the table, and a minute later he was standing at attention before the king.

"There is to be war, then?" asked the king in a quiet voice.

"That's right, Your Royal Highness."

For Matthew, it was a load off his mind, for—to be perfectly clear—he had spent the past ten minutes in a state of great uncertainty.

Perhaps Felix meant to write something else? Perhaps it was not true? Perhaps he was only joking?

The war minister's words left no room for doubt. There would be war, and war on a grand scale to boot. They wanted to fight it without him. But Matthew, in a manner known only to him, had discovered what they were trying so desperately to hide.

An hour later, newspaper boys were heard shouting at the top of their voices in the streets of the capital:

"Extra, extra! Special edition! Cabinet reshuffle!"

Clearly, the ministers had had a serious row…

The Cabinet reshuffle happened like this: The Prime Minister led everyone to believe that he was offended and wanted to resign his position. The Minister of Transport said the rail could not carry the troops because he was short on locomotives. The Minister of Education said that the teachers would surely go to war, leading to more window-breaking and vandalism by youth, and therefore he was tendering his resignation.

Another special session was convened for four o'clock. King Matthew, taking advantage of the chaos, snuck into the royal garden, whistled once shrilly and then a second time, but to no avail. Felix did not appear.

Whose advice should I seek at such an important moment? Matthew felt that with him rested great responsibility, but he had doubts whether he could rise to the occasion.

Suddenly, he remembered that any difficult task should be preceded by a prayer—his mother had taught him that.

King Matthew strode purposefully into the thicket where he first talked to Felix and directed an ardent prayer to God.

"I'm a little boy," prayed Matthew, "and without Your help, Almighty God, I won't manage. It was by your grace that I received the crown of my country, but so great is my heartache that I need your guidance."

The longer Matthew prayed to God for help, the more hot tears rolled down his cheeks—but it is not shameful, even for a king, to cry in front of Almighty God…

So, King Matthew prayed and cried in turns until, thoroughly exhausted, he fell asleep, resting his head on the stump of a felled birch tree.

He dreamed that his father was sitting on the throne, before him all his ministers standing to attention. Suddenly, the grandfather clock in the throne room—wound for the last time four hundred years ago—chimed like a church bell. The Grand Master of Ceremonies, followed by twenty lackeys, entered the hall. The lackeys were carrying a gold coffin. At this moment, his father rose from the throne and lay down in the coffin. The Grand Master of Ceremonies removed the crown from Matthew's father's temples and rested it on Matthew's head. Now the young king wanted to sit on the throne, but much to his surprise, it was still occupied by his father, but to make things still more bizarre: crownless and a mere shadow of his former self. Then his father said:

"My little Matthew, the Grand Master of Ceremonies has given you my crown, and I hereby give you my wisdom."

At that, the king's shadow took Matthew's head in his hands—the boy's heart jumped painfully into his throat.

AND NOW WHAT? he thought.

Suddenly, Matthew felt a tug at his sleeve and he woke up.

"Your Royal Highness, it is almost four o'clock."

King Matthew rose from the grass where he was sleeping, feeling more rested than after a night in his own bed. Little did he know that, from that moment on, he would spend many a night sleeping roughly, parting with his royal bed for quite some time.

As in his dream, the Grand Master of Ceremonies handed Matthew the crown. At four o'clock on the dot, King Matthew rang the bell in the conference hall and said:

"Gentlemen, let this session begin."

"I request permission to speak," said the Prime Minister.

He embarked on a long and windy speech in which he explained why he could not do his work anymore. He felt sorry to have to leave the young monarch unassisted in such tragic circumstances, but his ill health simply left him no alternative.

The same speech was repeated by four other ministers. Yet Matthew remained undaunted and said by way of an answer:

"This is all very well, but now that the war is going on, we have no time for weakness and fatigue. You, Mister Prime Minister, know how things are in the country, so you will simply have to remain in office. The moment I win the war, we'll discuss the conditions of your retirement."

"But it says in the newspapers that I'm resigning."

"And now they will say that you are staying, because I've asked you to."

King Matthew wanted to say 'I've ordered you to' at first, but his father's shadow seemed to be advising him to tone down his language at such a crucial moment.

"Gentlemen, we have to defend our fatherland; we have to defend our honor."

"So, Your Royal Highness will be fighting three countries?" asked the Minister of War.

"Do you want me to beg them for peace, Mister Minister? I'm the great-grandson of Paul the Conqueror. God will help us defeat the invaders."

The ministers liked the brave words of the new king, and the Prime Minister was tickled pink that the king was asking him to remain. He was still playing hard to get, but at the end of the day he finally agreed.

The debate lasted for hours on end. But when it was finally over, the newspaper boys shouted in the streets:

"Extra, extra! Special Edition! Crisis averted!"

This meant that the ministers had already settled their differences.

Matthew was mildly surprised that no speaker raised the question of the king's speech to his faithful people, nor did anybody mention that, mounted on his white steed, he, Matthew the First, would be riding at the head of his brave army. They talked about rail transport, money, biscuits, shoes for the infantry, about hay, oats, oxen and pigs, as if they were not talking about the impending war, but about something entirely different.

Though Matthew had heard a lot about past wars, he knew very little about modern warfare. He was about to learn what it was like and understand what biscuits and heavy-duty shoes were for, and what they had to do with war.

Matthew's anxiety increased when on the following day, his foreign tutor came for his lessons punctually as if nothing had happened.

No sooner had half of the lesson passed than the king was called to the throne room.

"These are the envoys of the countries which declared war on us; they will be leaving shortly," said the Grand Master of Ceremonies.

"I see. And where are they going?"

"Returning to their homelands."

It seemed strange to Matthew that they should be allowed to travel freely despite the impending war. But he preferred this to having them impaled or tortured.

"And why have these envoys come before me?"

"To say their farewells to Your Royal Highness."

"Am I supposed to look offended?" asked Matthew softly so that the lackeys would not hear, since they would have lost all respect for him.

"No, Your Royal Highness should bid them a courteous goodbye. They are fully trained in such delicate matters."

The envoys were not bound nor were they shackled at wrists or ankles.

"We have come here to bid farewell to Your Royal Highness. We are very sorry that this war has to be fought. We have been doing all in our power to prevent it, but in vain. We are forced to return Your Highness the medals we were once awarded, because it would be contrary to etiquette to wear the medals of a country our governments are currently at war with."

The Grand Master of Ceremonies collected the medals.

"We thank Your Royal Highness for the hospitality that has been shown to us in your magnificent capital. We leave your kingdom with many pleasant remembrances. We hope that this trivial conflict will soon come to an end and that our once cordial friendship will unite our governments anew."

Matthew rose to his feet and said in a quiet voice:

"Tell your governments that I'm truly glad war has broken out. I will make every effort to defeat your armies as quickly as possible, and the conditions of the peace treaty that I will set won't be too demanding. That is what my ancestors have always done."

One of the envoys gave an awkward smile followed by a deep bow. The Grand Master of Ceremonies tapped his silver mace against the floor three times and said:

"The audience is over."

King Matthew's speech, printed in all the newspapers and magazines, filled everybody with admiration.

An enormous crowd had gathered before the royal palace. There was no end to the cheers and hurrahs.

Three days passed. King Matthew waited and waited to be called to the throne room, but no summons came.

Well, if war is good for anything, it certainly does not teach kings to learn grammar, write dictations or solve mathematical problems.

Deeply preoccupied with such thoughts, Matthew was strolling through the royal garden when he heard a familiar signal:

"Cuckoo! Cuckoo!"

A moment later, he held another precious letter from Felix.

I am going to the front. Father got drunk, just as he promised, but instead of going to bed, he began getting things ready for the journey. He did not find his canteen, Swiss army knife and cartridge belt. He thought I had taken them and gave me a good hiding. Tonight or tomorrow night, I am running away from home. I've already been at the railroad / railway station and talked to some soldiers. They promised to take me with them. If His Royal Highness wishes to give me some order, I'll be waiting at 7 p.m. I could do with a pound of sausage (dried if possible), a bottle of vodka and a small sack of tobacco for the road.

Felix

It is a sad turn of events when a king has to slip out of his own palace as if he were a burglar…and worse still if this errand is preceded by an equally mysterious foray into the drawing room where three things—a bottle of cognac, half a yard of dried sausage and a hefty chunk of smoked salmon—would be listed as missing in action.

War is war, thought Matthew. *In war you can even kill your enemy.*

Matthew was very sad, but Felix was positively beaming with pleasure:

"Cognac is even better than vodka, and it does not matter that there is no tobacco, for I've managed to dry some leaves for myself, and then, at the front, I'll be given regular military rations. So far, so good! It's a pity, however, that the commander-in-chief is said to be such a duffer."

"How come he's a duffer? Who is he?"

Matthew felt a rush of blood to his head. Yet again he had been outwitted by his ministers. As it turned out, the troops had been on the road for a week and had already fought two not so successful battles. The army was commanded by an old and incompetent general, whom even Felix's father had called a blockhead.

So, that's how it was: Matthew would visit the front, perhaps once, and in a place where there would be no danger. Matthew would study while his people defended him. When the wounded were brought to the capital, he would pay them a visit in the hospital and if a general was killed, Matthew would attend his funeral.

How on earth is it possible? I won't be defending my people, but my people will be defending me? he thought. *How would my royal honor feel about this; what would Irene think of that? So, I'm only king to learn grammar and give enormous dolls to girls who ask for them. Oh no! If that's what the ministers think, they simply don't know me.*

Felix was just finishing his fifth handful of raspberries when Matthew tugged at his arm and said:

"Felix!"

"Yes, Sir! Yes, Your Royal Highness!"

"Do you want to be my friend?"

"Yes, Sir! Yes, Your Royal Highness!"

"Felix, what I'm going to tell you now is a secret. Remember, you mustn't betray me."

"Yes, Sir! Yes, Your Royal Highness!"

"Tonight I'm running away to the front with you."

"Yes, Sir! Yes, Your Royal Highness!"

"We must seal it with a handshake."

"Yes, Your Royal Highness!"

"And let us call one another by our Christian names, OK?"

"Yes, Sir! Yes, Your Royal Highness!"

"I'm no longer king. I'm… Wait, I don't know what name to call myself. OK! From now on I'm Tom Thumb. I'll call you Felix, and you'll call me Tom."

"Yes, Sir!" shouted Felix, swallowing a sizable bite of the smoked salmon.

They made a joint decision: tonight at two o'clock, Matthew, or rather Tom, would be waiting beside the railings.

"Listen, Tom, if there are to be two of us, then we'll have to have more provisions."

"Well…alright," replied Matthew reluctantly, because it seemed to him that at such an important moment, it just did not do to think about one's stomach.

His foreign tutor winced when he saw a trace of raspberries on Matthew's cuff, a memento of the handshake with Felix, but since the maelstrom of war had already reached the palace, he chose to turn a blind eye.

But something unbelievable had happened: someone had snitched a freshly opened bottle of cognac, a chunk of excellent sausage and a half a smoked salmon from the royal sideboard. These were the three delicacies the foreign tutor had specified in advance as his terms for teaching the heir to the throne. The deal was clinched when Matthew's father was still alive, and today, quite out of the blue, he was deprived of his wages in one fell swoop. Although the cook did his best to make up for the tutor's loss, new orders had to be written out for the missing things. Each order had to be stamped by the head of the palace administration, signed by the court chamberlain, and then and only then, at the order of the cellar master, was a new bottle issued. Should someone insist and suspend permission until the inquiry was completed, it meant a wait of a month or longer for the beloved cognac…

Visibly perturbed, the tutor poured the king a glass of cod-liver oil, and five seconds earlier than foreseen by the regulations, he gave Matthew the signal to go to bed.

"Tom, are you there?"

"Is that you, Felix?"

"Of course, it's me. Let's get going and we'd better watch out for the guards."

Not without difficulty, Matthew climbed a tree, clambered onto the railings, and climbed down to the ground.

"The king he may be, but he's as clumsy as a bull in a china shop," whispered Felix to himself, when Matthew finally jumped to the ground from the height of two feet.

From afar they heard the voice of a palace guard:

"Who's there?"

"Don't say a word!" Felix warned him.

In falling to the ground, Matthew had scratched the skin on his hand—the first wound he sustained in the war.

Gingerly, they crossed the road to the ditch, and there, crawling on all fours right under the guard's nose, they managed to reach the poplar alley which led up to the barracks unseen. They passed the barracks along the left wall, guided by the light of an enormous lamp in the guardhouse. Then they crossed a small bridge and found themselves on the road leading straight to the central military railway station.

What Matthew saw now reminded him of stories of olden times. Yes, it was a camp. As far as the eye could reach, campfires were burning, warming the soldiers and heating water for tea.

It never occurred to Matthew to admire Felix for the expertise with which he had led them to their unit, unmistakably choosing the shortest path. Matthew simply thought that all boys—except kings—were like that. However, Felix was an exception, even among the bravest boys of the kingdom. In this state of chaos, where every sixty minutes or so a new train disgorged hundreds of fresh troops, where detachments of infantry and artillery changed positions ceaselessly, it was very easy to get lost. Even Felix had to stop a few times to think where they were. He had been here by day, but since then much had changed. A few hours ago he had seen several cannons in one place, but now they seemed to have been carried away in a train.

A field hospital had been erected. Sappers and bomb disarming experts had moved up to the forefront, their positions now occupied by radiotelegraph operators. Part of the camp was lit by gigantic floodlights and the rest was lost in darkness. To make things worse, it began to rain, and as the grass was thoroughly worn down by thousands of military shoes; their feet began to get stuck and squelch in the sticky mud.

Matthew did not dare to lag behind and risk losing his friend, but he was soon short of breath. Felix was not so much walking as running, jostling and being jostled by soldiers passing by.

"It seems like it should be here," said Felix unexpectedly, narrowing his eyes. Suddenly, his eye fell on Matthew.

"Haven't you brought your overcoat?" he asked.

"No, my overcoat is hanging in the royal cloakroom."

"And you haven't brought you rucksack, either? You know, it takes a sissy to go to war equipped like you are!" Felix let that ugly comment slip quite unwittingly.

"Or a hero," retorted Matthew, hurt to the quick.

Felix bit his tongue. He had momentarily forgotten that Matthew was king. But he was overcome with anger in the face of a persistent downpour and the fact that his friendly soldiers had gone AWOL: the soldiers had promised Felix that they would take him as stowaway on their train and now they were nowhere to be found. On top of it all, he had brought Matthew along with him without ever briefing him what might come in handy on the road. For the price of a good flogging, he had a canteen, a Swiss penknife and a cartridge belt, without which you could hardly go to war. On the other hand, Matthew—can you beat that—was wearing patent-leather shoes and a green tie, badly done up in haste and muddied, which gave his face an even more pitiful appearance. Felix would have laughed if it were not for the fearful thoughts that suddenly occurred to him.

"Felix, Felix!" the boys suddenly heard from close quarters.

A moment later, Felix and Matthew were approached by a tall boy, also a volunteer, who wore a military trench coat and looked very nearly like a regular soldier.

"I was waiting for you. Our soldiers are already at the train station. They are boarding their train in an hour. Hurry! Faster!"

Faster still? The mere thought made Matthew wince.

"And who's that pretty boy behind you?" asked the boy, pointing at Matthew.

"Uh, well. It's a long story. I will tell you later. I had to take him. I had no choice."

"I've no doubt. But remember, without my backing, they wouldn't have agreed to take you. And now you arrive with this pup…?"

"Don't give me any of your lip!" answered Felix angrily. Then he whispered so that Matthew did not hear:

"Thanks to him, I've got a bottle of real cognac."

"You'll give me a sip, won't you?"

"We'll see."

The three volunteers walked for what seemed like hours in silence: The eldest, angry that Felix had not listened to him; Felix, restless for he was sensing that he had really stirred up trouble for himself, and Matthew, mortally offended.

If I didn't have to keep my mouth shut, I would put this lout in his place. I would teach him how to address the king, thought Matthew.

"Listen, Felix!" Their guide suddenly stopped. "If you don't give me some cognac, you can keep going on your own. I got the soldiers to agree to take you with them and you promised to obey and you haven't. If you're cheeky now, what's next?"

This was a clear invitation to a fight, but as soon as the quarrel broke out, there was a far louder noise. A whole box of flares blew up with a deafening bang. Apparently, a carelessly discarded cigarette butt was to blame. Two frightened artillery horses bolted. All hell broke loose: a prolonged, pained moan pierced the air, followed by a moment of panic, and when the smoke cleared, the boys saw their guide lying down in a pool of blood, his leg shattered.

Felix and Matthew stood there gazing helplessly at their wounded companion. They were absolutely stunned. What should they do now? They were prepared for death, blood and wounds in the battlefield—but later rather than sooner.

"Why the hell are you kids hanging around here?" growled an elderly gentleman, apparently a doctor, who pushed the boys aside. "I'm guessing he's a volunteer… Couldn't he have remained at home, clinging to his mother's skirts?" muttered the doctor under his breath, cutting through the material of the boy's trouser leg with scissors taken out of his rucksack.

"Tom, let's get out of here!" cried Felix, catching sight of two field gendarmes walking beside stretcher-bearers who were obviously headed for the unfortunate volunteer.

"Shall we leave him like this?" asked Matthew bashfully.

"Of course, he will end up in hospital. He's unfit to fight."

They hid in the shade of a tent. A moment later, the place was deserted, except for a single shoe, traces of blood in the mud and the boy's trench coat which the stretcher-bearers discarded when placing the wounded youth on the stretcher.

"The trench coat will come in handy," said Felix. "I will return it when he recovers," he added by way of an excuse. "Let's hurry to the station. There's no time to lose. We've wasted a good ten minutes."

Their unit was just being checked when they squeezed onto a platform.

"Stick around, soldiers!" shouted a young lieutenant. "I'll be back in two minutes."

Felix gave a vivid account of what had happened to the volunteer and—not without trepidation—introduced Matthew, or rather Tom, to the soldiers.

"What will the lieutenant say when he sees me?" Matthew wondered out loud.

"The lieutenant will chuck you out of the railway car at the first station," said one of the soldiers. "We've already mentioned Felix to him—he said nothing but wrinkled his nose."

"Hey little soldier, how old are you?"

"Ten."

"Nothing good can come of this, but if you're sure, get into the car. Mark my words, the lieutenant will chuck you out; there are no two ways about it. No matter what, we will be given a solid tongue-lashing."

"If the lieutenant chucks me out, I will go to the front on foot!" exclaimed Matthew rebelliously.

He was on the verge of tears. How ironic that the king, who should have been leaving the capital at the head of his army on a white steed and showered with flowers, was sneaking out to the front to fulfill his holy duty to defend his country and his subjects—and instead of flowers, he was treated to a hail of deadly insults.

Cognac and salmon worked miracles, and the soldiers soon cheered up.

"Royal cognac and royal salmon," they roared, extolling the court cuisine.

Matthew watched his comrades-in-arms treating themselves to the delicacies from the tutor's sideboard with no small amount of joy.

"Hey, little comrade, help yourself. Let's see if you're a true warrior."

At last Matthew was drinking what kings drank.

"Down with the tyrant!" he yelled.

"Ha-ha-ha! This is some revolutionary," observed a young corporal. "And who are you calling the tyrant? Surely not King Matthew. You'd better watch your language. You might get a bullet in a most unwelcome place."

"You're right: King Matthew the First isn't a tyrant," admitted Matthew.

"He's still little, and you never know what a child will grow up to be," replied the corporal.

Matthew was about to add something, but Felix deftly changed the subject.

"I tell you, we were walking up a badly lit path and then we heard a BANG. I thought it was a bomb dropped from an airplane. But it was only a box of flares. Then the stars seemed to fall down around us…"

"And why the hell do they need flares on the battlefield?"

"To light up the road where there are no searchlights."

"The heavy artillery was over there. The horses bolted and galloped straight at us. Both of us managed to step aside, but he didn't.

"Was he badly hurt?"

"There was a lot of blood, and the stretcher-bearers took him away almost in a flash."

"War is war," sighed one of the revelers. "Is there still a drop of that cognac left? No sign of our train yet?"

Just at that moment, the train pulled into the station, hissing like some gigantic boa constrictor. Noise, rush and confusion followed.

"Don't get on yet!" called the lieutenant, running towards them.

But his voice was drowned out by the overwhelming tumult. Matthew and Felix were thrown into the car like two bundles of clothes. Another pair of horses spooked, and rearing up violently, refused to climb into the train. Some cars were set to be coupled up or uncoupled—nobody knew for certain. The train had barely pulled out of the station when they heard a loud knock and the engine driver decided to return to the station.

Someone with a torch entered their car and took roll call. Then the soldiers jumped out of the car with a cauldron in hopes of filling it with some soup.

Matthew may have seen and heard what was happening, but through a veil, for he was overcome with sleep. When the train finally and irrevocably left the station, King Matthew was already fast asleep. When he woke up, the monotonous rhythm of the wheels clicking on the rails told him that the train was in motion.

I'm going to the front, he thought, and soon the rhythmic rattling of the train's wheels lulled him back to sleep.

The train consisted of thirty covered cars in which the soldiers traveled and a few platform cars carrying vehicles and heavy machine guns as well as one passenger coach for the officers.

Matthew woke up with a slight headache and a distinct pain in his leg and back. His eyes hurt whenever he opened them. His hands were intolerably dirty, and he had a nasty itch all over his body.

"Get up, rookies, or your soup will get cold!" called one of the privates.

Unaccustomed to soldier's food, Matthew managed to swallow only a couple of spoonfuls.

"Dig in, brother! You won't get anything else," Felix encouraged him.

"I have a headache," moaned Matthew.

"Listen, Tom, don't you dare get sick!" whispered Felix, visibly worried. "At war you can be wounded, but not sick!"

All of a sudden, Felix started to scratch himself.

"I hate to say this, but the old man was right. Oh Gosh! They've got me already! Are they biting you?"

"Who?" asked Matthew.

"Who? Fleas, that's who! Or perhaps something worse. The old man told me that at war, fleas are worse than bullets."

Matthew remembered the story of the unfortunate royal lackey and thought:

I wonder what the insect that once made the king so angry looks like?

But there was no time to continue that train of thought, for they suddenly heard the corporal's voice:

"Hide! The lieutenant's coming!"

The boys were pushed into the corner of the car and covered with trench coats.

The inspection revealed that the soldiers had a few things to spare, and a tailor happened to be traveling with them on the same car. He was a nice man, and just to kill time, he made a couple of uniforms for the two volunteers from the things the soldiers gave away. However, shoes were a different kettle of fish; they posed a real problem.

"Listen, boys, are you really thinking of fighting the enemy?"

"That's why we're going to the front!"

"Yes, yes, but marches are no child's play. They're pretty tough business. A soldier's shoes are his most important piece of equipment, just as important as a rifle. As long as your feet are in good shape, you're an effective soldier; but once you develop blisters, you're a dead dog. A next to nothing! Gone with the wind!"

Forward they chugged, dawdling at station after station, sometimes pausing the journey for an hour or so. They were occasionally put on a side-track to let more important trains pass, or turned back to stations they had already called at, or had to wait for their turn at the station.

The soldiers started singing when someone played the concertina in the neighboring car. A few even danced on the platform during numerous stopovers. But for Matthew and Felix, time dragged terribly, especially since they were not allowed to leave the train car.

"Keep your heads down, or the lieutenant will see you!"

Matthew felt as tired as if he had fought at least five battles. The more he wanted to go to sleep, the less he was able, kept awake by a nasty itch and lack of fresh air in the car.

"Do you know why we've been here so long?"

A soldier had approached them. He was a jolly and lively man, an expert at obtaining information which he was rarely averse to sharing.

"Why? The enemy must have blown up a bridge or destroyed the track somewhere along the line."

"Wrong! Our men are keeping a close watch on bridges and the railroad network."

"We must have run out of coal. No one could have foreseen how many supplies were needed for so many trains."

"Try again…"

"A spy may have damaged the train."

"Wrong again! All the transports have been stopped to let the royal train pass!"

"And who on earth is traveling on it? Surely not King Matthew?"

"But he's so badly needed there, isn't he?"

"Badly needed or not, he's our king!"

"Nowadays kings don't fight wars."

"Perhaps other kings don't, but Matthew will," butted in the king suddenly, ignoring Felix who was tugging furiously on his sleeve.

"All kings are the same. There is no one to admire among royalty today. Maybe it used to be different…"

"How can we know how things used to be? They might also have been hiding under a comforter, and since nobody remembers, they might as well be lying."

"Why should they lie?"

"Tell me: how many kings have died in wars and how many soldiers?"

"What a stupid question. There's only one king and there're thousands of soldiers."

"And you think we need more kings? As if one wasn't enough trouble…"

Matthew could not believe his ears. He had been hearing day in and day out about the nation's love for the king and especially about the army's admiration for its commander-in-chief. And now this?! Only yesterday he thought he would have to hide to avoid an overenthusiastic reception, and now he saw that if they discovered who he really was, they might not even care.

It was strange: the army was going to fight for a king it did not even like. Matthew feared the soldiers might say something ugly about his father, but there was no cause for concern, for they praised the late king.

"He didn't like wars. He didn't want to fight himself and didn't force his people into something he didn't like himself."

The remark brought some comfort to the aching heart of the young king.

"And to be quite frank, what would a king do in a war? A nap on the grass and he'll have a runny nose. Fleas will make it hard for him to sleep. The smell of sweaty uniforms will give him a headache. And his skin is so delicate and nose so sensitive…"

Matthew's sense of justice forced him to admit that they were absolutely right. Yesterday's sleep on the ground had brought on a nasty catarrh, and he did have a headache and itchy skin.

"Hey boys, what's the point of this idle talk? We won't reinvent gunpowder. We're better off singing a cheerful song."

"We're moving again!" someone shouted.

Indeed, the train started to move at a fast clip. Strange as it may seem, it invariably happened that whenever someone said that the train would be stuck in one place for a long time, it invariably got under way without any warning, and soldiers had to jump into the moving cars. Some of them weren't fast enough and were left behind.

"They are conditioning us to be constantly on the look-out," observed someone quite rightly.

The train pulled into a larger station where a train with some very important people aboard would be heading in the same direction. There were national flags, the guard of honor, some ladies dressed in white satin and two children with beautiful bouquets.

"The Minister of War himself is on the royal train. He's going to the front."

Their train was once again put on the side-track where it stood the whole night. This time Matthew slept like a log. Hungry, tired and sad—he did not dream.

Since dawn the soldiers had been washing and cleaning the entire train, car by car. The lieutenant kept running to and fro, overseeing the clean-up in person.

"We will have to hide you somewhere," said the corporal, "or there will be trouble."

So, Felix and Matthew landed in a small hut belonging to the switchman, where his wife, a kind-hearted woman, took care of them. Hungry for news, she hoped that the children would be able to give her some snippets of information.

"Oh, children," lamented the woman, "why in heaven's name are you here? Wouldn't it have been better to go to school? When did you become soldiers? Where have you been so far? And where are you heading?"

"Dear lady," retorted Felix coolly, "our father is a platoon commander, and he told us before our departure: 'A good soldiers has legs to march, hands to use his rifle, eyes to watch out for the enemy, ears to hear and a tongue to keep behind his teeth until a spoonful of soup opens his mouth. A soldier defends his head with his rifle, but he can—thanks to a wagging tongue—lose his head and his entire unit.' Where we've been and where we're going is a military secret. We know nothing and that's as much as we'll tell you."

The switchman's wife stood for several moments with her mouth agape. When she got over the shock, she managed to give quite a speech:

"Who would have thought? Such a small child and such adult talk. You're absolutely right. There are so many spies about. Some sharp-eared fellow dressed as a soldier will try to fool you into telling him secrets and run straight to the enemy."

Out of respect for the two valiant comrades-in-arms, the woman treated them to tea and some excellent hunter's sausage.

Even the king appreciated the tasty breakfast, but most of all, he was grateful to be able to wash properly for the first time since leaving the palace.

"The royal train! The royal train!" the boys suddenly heard.

To get a better view, Felix and Matthew climbed a ladder leaning against the cowshed in the switchman's yard.

A beautiful passenger train with large windows was chugging into the station. The orchestra was playing the national anthem. In the window, Matthew spied the face of the Minister of War he knew so well.

Their eyes met momentarily.

Matthew's head twitched involuntarily, and he shrank back against the wall: what would happen if the minister recognized him?

However, the Minister of War could not have had recognized the king, firstly because he was lost in thought, and secondly because immediately after Matthew's escape, about which the Prime Minister kept the entire kingdom in the dark—which will be discussed in more detail later on—a new fake king had bid farewell to the Minister of War as he was leaving the capital. To make things worse, the Foreign Minister had told him to prepare for war with one king, and now he found out that he had to fight three of them and all at the same time.

So, the Minister of War already had plenty of food for thought:

Go and fight! Easier said than done when three of them are coming at you. Even if you defeat one or even two of them, the odds are ten to one that the third will do you in. We might have enough soldiers, but we are short of rifles, heavy guns and clothing.

Hence, the Minister of War worked out the following plan: he would carry out an unexpected attack on the first enemy, destroying its army completely, take possession of what the enemy had prepared for the war, and only then fall on the second force.

It was a sorry sight for Matthew's eyes when he watched the troops standing at attention, the minister being given flowers to the accompaniment of music played by a military orchestra.

This acclaim should be mine while he stands behind me, thought Matthew.

But since justice was his middle name, he immediately told himself:

OK, it's easy just to walk and salute, and listen to music and receive bouquets of flowers. But tell me, Matthew, would you know where to send troops when you don't know geography?

What did the poor boy know? He knew a few names of rivers, mountain ranges and islands, knew that the planet Earth was round and revolved around the sun in a nearly circular orbit. The point is that such a minister needed to know all the fortresses and roads and even every path in the woods. Matthew's great-grandfather once won a great battle, for when the enemy was leading his forces into battle, his great-grandfather ordered his regiments to hide among the trees. There they waited until the enemy plunged deeper into the woods. Then, using a network of paths unknown to the foe, they launched a fierce attack from the rear, which virtually destroyed the unsuspecting invaders. The enemy had thought he would attack the king's army head-on. Instead, he himself was attacked from behind and pushed into a quagmire.

Did Matthew know the location of every wood and quagmire?

He did not, but he knew he would learn it all now. If he were sitting in the capital, he would know only his royal garden. But now he would see his entire kingdom.

The soldiers were right in laughing at Matthew. Matthew was a very small and still poorly-educated boy thrust into the role of king. Perhaps it was not so good that the war had broken out so early after all. At this moment, Matthew wished he had had another year or two to prepare.

Now let me tell you what happened in the palace when Matthew's disappearance was discovered.

At seven o'clock in the morning, the eldest lackey entered Matthew's bedroom and could not believe his eyes: the window was wide-open, the bed unmade and of Matthew, there wasn't even the slightest sign.

The royal lackey was no fool. He locked the bedroom and rushed to the Master of Ceremonies, who was still sleeping. The lackey woke him up and said:

"Honorable Master of Ceremonies, the king has disappeared!"

The Master of Ceremonies telephoned the Prime Minister.

No sooner had ten minutes passed when three cars pulled up in front of the royal palace at breakneck speed.

The cars belonged to: the Prime Minister, the Minister of the Interior and the Police Prefect.

"The king has been stolen!"

It was as plain as the noses on their faces. The enemy must have had a vested interest in stealing the king. The moment the army learned that there was no king, they would lay down their arms and the enemy would capture the capital without a shot fired.

"Who knows that the king has disappeared?"

"Nobody."

"That's good."

"We must find out whether Matthew has been abducted or murdered. Mister Prefect, will you please find out? I need to know in an hour!"

There was a pond in the royal garden. Perhaps the king had been drowned? A diving suit was brought from the Ministry of Marine Affairs. The diving suit looked like an iron lampshade with small windows and a pipe through which air was pumped. The Police Prefect put the lampshade on his head and lowered himself to the bottom of the pond to search for the king while up above, on the edge of the pond, seamen pumped air down to him. But Matthew was not to be found on the bed of the pond…

Now it was time to call the royal doctor and the Commerce Minister. It was all done in the utmost secrecy, but some explanation or other had to be given, for the servants knew that something had happened, seeing that the ministers had been tearing around like scalded cats since early morning.

So, they said that Matthew was feeling slightly under the weather and since the doctor had prescribed him crayfish for breakfast, the Prefect had performed his dive in the pond.

The foreign tutor was told that Matthew would not be having lessons as he was bedridden. The presence of the royal doctor convinced everybody that Matthew was truly unwell.

"OK, so far, so good—for today, that is. But what shall we do tomorrow?"

"I'm the Prime Minister, and believe me…I have a good head on my shoulders. You'll see in a short while."

The Commerce Minister arrived.

"Do you remember that doll Matthew ordered you to buy for the girl named Irene?"

"Yes, I remember perfectly. I still remember the fuss the Finance Minister made over my trifling away the money."

"Go and find the manufacturer who made the doll. Tell him to make one based on the king's photo. It must be the spitting image of King Matthew so that nobody will see through the deception and no one will differentiate the doll from our king. Hop to it!"

In the meanwhile, the Police Prefect had gotten out of the pond, and to make the deceit still more believable caught ten crayfish, which were instantly sent to the royal kitchen with much pomp and circumstance. The doctor wrote out, under dictation, this prescription:

Recipe
Crayfish soup
ex 10 crayfish dosis una
S. One spoonful every two hours.

When the manufacturer heard that the Commerce Minister himself was waiting in his office, he rubbed his hands with joy.

"So, Matthew came up with yet another crazy idea."

The order was a real godsend, for from the moment the war broke out, nearly all able men had gone to the front, and now no one wanted to buy dolls or even order them.

"Mr. Manufacturer, this is a shotgun order if you know what I mean: the doll must be ready for tomorrow," said the minister.

"That won't be easy, sir. Almost all my male employees have gone to war. I'm left with women and the sick. What's more, I'm up to my ears in work, for nearly every father going to the front has ordered a doll for his children so that they don't cry and miss him and, of course, remember to behave themselves."

The manufacturer was clearly lying through his teeth. None of his workers had gone to war. They were paid so badly that they were all sick from malnutrition and unfit for military service. He had not had any orders in months. He said what he said because he wanted to charge as much as possible for the doll.

He was all smiles and nods when he learned that the doll was to represent none other than the young king.

"You know how it is," said the minister. "The king has to appear in public. He will be riding in his coach around the capital so that nobody thinks he's scared of the war and hiding somewhere from the enemy. And what's the point of dragging the child all over the city? He may get caught up in a storm or a heavy shower and come down with the flu. And when, if not now, should we take the best care of the king's health?"

The manufacturer was not an honest man, but he was not stupid either. He smelled a rat on the spot. He could not put his finger on it but knew that something was just not right. The minister could not have been telling the truth.

"So, it is necessary for tomorrow?"

"Tomorrow at nine in the morning," was the answer.

The manufacturer reached for a pen and pretended to be counting something—King Matthew had to be made of the best porcelain, and this was always in short supply. Of course, it would cost a lot, no doubt about that. The workers would have to be given some money to keep them quiet. Of all the rotten luck, the machine had just broken down. How much would the repair cost? he wondered… Last but not least, he would have to put off a few urgent orders. He counted and counted and at long last said:

"Mister Commerce Minister, if it weren't for the war—I fully appreciate that great sums of money have to be spent on the war, on heavy guns… In a nutshell, were it not for the war, you would have to pay twice as much. Hell, I'll even give you a discount, but this is final—the price is non-negotiable. I can't possibly charge less…"

As he named the price, the minister nearly fainted.

"But this is outright robbery!"

"Mister Minister, you have just slandered our national trade."

The minister telephoned the Prime Minister as he was afraid to shoulder such an enormous expense. Fearing that the line might be tapped, instead of 'doll' he used the word 'cannon'.

"Mister Prime Minister, they want to charge a fortune for that cannon!"

The Prime Minister decoded the message at once and said:

"Do not haggle, but tell him that the cannon must be able to salute at a pull of a string."

The telephone operator could not believe her ears, hearing that there would be new cannons capable of saluting.

Now the manufacturer began to rant and rave.

With this new, outrageous demand, it would be hard for him to break even. This was not his cup of tea.

"Ask the royal mechanic or a watchmaker. I'm a respectable industrialist and not some magician. Matthew will open and close his eyes, but he won't be saluting. End of story!"

At long last, the respectable industrialist agreed to the palace's demand as well. But he refused to knock off a penny!

The Commerce Minister, bathed in sweat and thoroughly exhausted, returned home, while the Police Perfect, also perspiring heavily and thoroughly exhausted, returned to the palace and declared:

"I know how Matthew was stolen. I had the most-thorough look possible at the crime scene. Here's how it happened: when Matthew was sleeping, he had a cloth sack placed over his head and was then carried to that corner of the garden where raspberries grow. There's a well-trodden spot among the raspberry bushes. There the boy fainted. He was given cherries and raspberries to bring him around. I found six cherry stones there. When Matthew was carried over the railings, he must have been fighting to free himself, for on the bark of a tree growing there, I detected traces of his 'blue' blood. To baffle future investigators, the kidnappers put Matthew on a cow's back. I saw myself a number of hoof prints leading to the wood where the sack was found. Then they must have hidden Matthew still alive, but where, I don't know, for I had too little time to find out. I could not ask any witnesses so as not to reveal the secret. One more thing: the foreign tutor should be taken special care of as he's a rather shady character: he has asked to pay Matthew a visit. Oh…and here are the cherry stones and the sack."

The Prime Minister put the sack and the stones into a wooden box, padlocked it and sealed it with red wax. On top of the box, he wrote in Latin: corpus delicti[1]. It is a generally accepted practice that if one does not know something and does not want anybody else to know it either, then one writes in Latin.

The following day the Minister of War submitted a farewell report and Matthew-the-Doll said nothing but saluted by way of an answer. On every street corner, there was a notice that everything was business as usual, that the inhabitants of the capital could work peacefully now that King Matthew the First could ride in an open limousine on a daily basis.

---

[1] Corpus delicti ('**body of crime**' in Latin): material evidence.

The scheme conceived by the Minister of War was executed to perfection. All three enemies thought that King Matthew's armies would attack them with one stroke. In fact, he concentrated all his forces in one place; he attacked but a single foe, created a swath of carnage and took huge spoils as well as thousands of good-quality rifles, hundreds of heavy guns, boots and rucksacks with precious contents.

The spoils were being divided when Matthew and Felix reached the frontlines.

"And which army are these valiant warriors from?" asked the quartermaster general mockingly.

"We're the same soldiers as everybody else here," said Felix, "except we're slightly smaller."

Everybody chose a pair of shoes, a revolver, a rifle and a rucksack. Felix even regretted having taken his father's cartridge belt and the Swiss penknife. He could have avoided the spanking. But you never know with wars; it is impossible to foresee what surprises they hold in store for you.

It was not for nothing that the commander-in-chief was said to be a nutcase. Having scored such a victory, instead of withdrawing and entrenching, he moved forward. He managed to capture some five or six towns of little or no importance and only then ordered his troops to entrench. But it was too late because the two other armies, idle until now, hastened to the rescue of their defeated ally.

This became common knowledge only later. At the time Matthew's unit was unaware of these movements because this information was kept secret.

The order was given to march hither and thither; the order came to do this or that. Go and do it. Don't ask any questions. Mum's the word.

When they walked into one captured foreign town, Matthew had no cause to complain. They slept in comfortable and spacious rooms, albeit on the floor, but it was far better than a cramped country cottage or a field of stubble.

Matthew was looking forward to the first battle because so far he had seen and heard a lot of interesting things, witnessed everything except for a real battle. It was such a pity that they were too late for the victorious one.

They spent only one night in the town and moved on the following day.

Soon they were ordered to stand and dig.

Matthew knew next to nothing of modern warfare. He thought that all the army did was fight, mount their horses and chase the enemy until it could trample the survivors underfoot. That soldiers also dug trenches, drove stakes with barbed wire into the ground and sat in those trenches for weeks had never occurred to Matthew. Not even once. No wonder that he rather unwillingly put his hand to the plough. He was very tired and pretty weak—every part of his body ached. He was here to fight and this was his royal vocation. But digging was not his cup of tea—anyone else could do that better than him.

One order followed another, always insisting on haste as the enemy approached. Distant cannon fire could now be heard.

Suddenly, a car carrying a colonel, the commandant of sappers, came roaring down the road. The colonel was yelling at the top of his voice, threatening to shoot anyone who wasn't pulling their weight and digging properly.

"There will be a battle tomorrow, and those fools are idling about! And what are those two heroes doing here?" he shouted, clearly at the end of his tether. "Where did you get these giants from? Goliath and Cyclops, if I'm not mistaken?"

The full weight of the colonel's anger now seemed centered on our two friends, but fortunately a moment later, they heard the whirr of an enemy airplane engine overhead.

The colonel reached for his binoculars. He scanned the sky anxiously, then jumped back into his car and drove off as quickly as he could. Soon, three bombs had fallen in the vicinity—bang, bang, BANG! Fortunately, no one was harmed, but everybody jumped into the trenches, assuming it was the safest place to be on such occasions.

Bombs and cannon balls are created in such a manner that once they hit the aim or meet a solid object, they burst into thousands of deadly metal pieces, which play havoc with human lives. But those who are lucky enough to be sitting in a trench usually only hear the whistle of metal bits flying overhead. Of course, it sometimes happens that a bomb or missile falls into a ditch full of soldiers, but such occurrences are very few and far between since bombs are dropped and rockets fired from afar, and it is not easy to achieve deadly accuracy from great heights or long distances.

Those three bombs taught Matthew a lot. He stopped sulking and instantly put his shoulder to the wheel, calling a spade a spade while he began digging. He nearly worked himself into the ground, and when he was too tired to lift a finger, he fell in a heap at the bottom of the newly-dug trench and slept like a log. His comrades-in-arms did not wake him up but went on working overnight by the light of the flares. At the crack of dawn, they came under enemy attack for the first time. At first, four horsemen appeared: these must have been scouts in search of Matthew's unit. The soldiers opened fire at them all at once, hitting one rider in the chest. He fell off his horse, seemingly dead, while his companions wheeled their horses around and escaped.

"We're in for a bloody battle!" cried the lieutenant. "It's only a matter of minutes now. Stay put, and don't stick your noses out of the trench, only your rifles, and wait for orders!" roared the lieutenant.

Sure enough, pretty soon the enemy troops appeared on the horizon, and a few minutes later, the exchange of fire began. But Matthew's unit was hidden in the trench while the attackers were approaching them through an open field. The enemy bullets whistled and swished over the ditch, above the heads of the hidden soldiers, doing virtually no harm to them, while those fired from the trench wreaked havoc upon the attackers.

What was not immediately obvious to Matthew yesterday clicked into place now. The boy realized that the commandant of sappers was absolutely right in shouting at them yesterday. During a war, orders must be carried out unquestionably. There are no 'ifs', 'buts', 'either…or'; the only acceptable reply is 'Yes, sir!'

Yes, civilians can decide whether they listen or not, take their own sweet time or argue, but the soldier knows one thing: orders must be respected and carried out no matter what and right away.

"Forward!" means "forward", "about turn!" means "about turn" and "shoulder arms!" is "shoulder arms!"

The battle raged all day before the enemy realized that they were fighting a losing battle. All they could achieve was to double or triple their losses. Barbed wire prevented them from fighting at close quarters, so they changed strategies, withdrawing to entrench themselves. But to dig undisturbed is one thing, and to entrench yourself under heavy fire with bullets whistling and zipping by is quite another.

In the night, flares were set off periodically, creating the illusion of daylight. The exchange of fire slowed audibly as some shooters settled in for a well-earned rest, but the battle was still underway.

"We have stood our ground!" said the soldiers with satisfaction.

"We have stood our ground!" the lieutenant reported when he telephoned the chief-of-staff.

The signal corps had already established telephone networks for the army leaders to communicate.

Little wonder that the order to withdraw, which came the following morning, left them in stunned surprise.

"How can this be? We have entrenched ourselves and held off the enemy; we are more than able to defend ourselves."

If Matthew had been in the lieutenant's position, he would have never obeyed that order. This had to be a mistake. If only the colonel had come to see how his subordinates had succeeded... There were so many attackers killed and here, on Matthew's side, just one private with a wounded hand. When he was shooting from the trench, a stray bullet grazed his lower arm which was sticking out recklessly. How could the colonel know from afar what was going on here?

There was a moment when Matthew felt he could not resist shouting at the top of his voice:

"I'm King Matthew! Let the colonel give his orders, but I won't allow my soldiers to withdraw! A king always outranks a colonel."

In the end, Matthew controlled his initial impulse because he doubted whether anyone would believe him. Even more likely, he was afraid that he might be laughed out of camp.

It was the second time in the past few hours that the king became convinced that, while in the army, instead of reasoning with your superiors, you should promptly obey their orders.

It was with heavy hearts that the soldiers parted with the trenches they had spent so much time and effort digging, even leaving behind supplies of bread, sugar and bacon. It was a humiliating experience returning through the village where peasants asked them why they were retreating.

They were already well over ten miles from their trenches when a mounted messenger caught up with them and handed a letter to the lieutenant. The letter ordered a retreat at full speed, wasting no time for unnecessary stopovers.

It was easier said than done: after two sleepless nights, one spent digging and the other fighting, you could hardly march without a moment's rest. Moreover, they had little food and they were both angry and worried. When they were advancing and chasing the enemy soldiers, they seemed to have never-ending reserves of energy and lightning speed, but during the retreat they couldn't stop stumbling over their own feet.

They continued to fall back—plodding step by plodding step—and all of a sudden, they were caught in crossfire, bullets zinging towards them from two directions.

"Now I understand!" shouted the lieutenant. "We went too far forward and the enemy attacked us from behind. The colonel was right when he told us to retreat as fast as possible. They could have taken us prisoner."

"And now it's do or die; we'll have to fight our way through!" said one of the soldiers angrily.

So, war is not always plain sailing. Now the enemy had them in their crosshairs and they would be hard-pressed to escape.

Matthew now knew why, at the Cabinet meeting, the ministers had discussed the question of shoes, oats for the horses and biscuits.

If they had had no biscuits in their rucksacks, they would be starving now—it was as plain as the nose on your face. For three days, biscuits had been all they had to eat. But for them, Matthew and his comrades-in-arms would have starved. They took turns sleeping, each for just a few hours at a time. Their feet were so badly injured that blood squelched in their boots.

Silent as shadows, they retreated through the woods as the lieutenant continued desperately to consult his ordnance survey map in hopes of finding a hiding place, be it a ravine or a thicket.

Every now and again, enemy scouts approached on horseback to see which way they were retreating and send a signal to those in the lead of the pursuit.

If only you could have seen Matthew! Over the past few days, he had become as thin as a rake; he had even begun to walk with a stoop and looked even smaller than he actually was. Many a soldier, panic-stricken, dropped their rifles, but Matthew held onto his for dear life, despite the pain and numbness in his tiny royal fingers. Rarely in the field of human conflict had one suffered so much in so few days, being so young and innocent.

My father, my dear father, thought Matthew, *it's no breeze to be a king who fights wars. It was all very well to say '…because we are scared to death'. But I'm no longer scared. Not in the least. I will beat the enemy just as my valiant great-grandfather did. But it's easier said than done. Oh, what a naïve child I was then. All I thought of was leaving the capital on a white horse showered in flowers by my subjects. I never once spared a thought for those who would lose their lives.*

All around him men were going down like ninepins in a hail of bullets, and Matthew survived mainly due to being so much smaller than the average soldier. Knee-high to a grasshopper, he was no sitting duck for the enemy.

How glad they were to meet their fellow soldiers and the safety of a trench line able to hold twice as many soldiers as there were.

Pretty soon we'll be the laughing stock of the entire army! thought Matthew.

But he was soon to learn that even in war justice exists.

When they had slept off the hardships of the past few days and sated their hunger, they were sent from combat zones to the rear. Fresh soldiers replaced them in the trench and immediately opened fire at the enemy. Meanwhile Matthew, Felix and the remnants of his unit had covered at least five versts[2] to find themselves in the rear.

In the square of a small town, the boys were approached by the commandant of sappers. No longer cross with them, he said:

"Tell me, lads, now you know what trenches are for, don't you?"

They understood, and how!

Then he separated those soldiers who had dropped their riffles from those who had not, addressing the latter as follows:

"My deepest respect to you for retaining your arms. True heroes distinguish themselves not so much in victory as in defeat."

"Look, there are those two tiny children!" called the colonel. "Long live the brave-hearted brothers, Goliath and Cyclops!"

From then on Matthew was known as Goliath, and Felix as Cyclops; from then on, nobody ever called them Tom or Felix.

"Hey, Cyclops! Go and fetch some water!"

"Listen, Goliath! Add some sticks to the fire!"

The whole unit loved the boys, both as mascots and younger brothers.

Here, far from the madding armies, they learned that the Minister of War and the Commander-in-Chief had had a terrible row, only reconciled due to King Matthew's intervention.

Matthew, of course, knew absolutely nothing of the doll that was now the acting king in the capital and could not understand why there was no word of his disappearance. Whenever he was mentioned, it was always as if he were at home. Matthew was still a very young king, and he had little idea that diplomacy meant telling as many lies as possible so that the enemy had no idea what the actual truth was.

When they had rested and eaten, they were sent back to the trenches for another helping of trench warfare. This military term referred to a rather useless exchange of bullets, which completely missed their targets because both sides were sitting below ground level.

From time to time, bored by the ineffectiveness of this tactic, the soldiers left the trenches to launch an attack. Both sides took turns gaining and losing ground.

---

2   Verst: an obsolete Russian unit of length, equivalent to about 0.67 miles / 1.07 kilometres.

In the trenches, the soldiers paced to and fro, played the guitar and sang, or played cards, while Matthew spent a lot of time on his studies.

Their lieutenant, who was also bored stiff, helped Matthew with math, history and grammar. All he had to do was post guards to watch out for enemy movements, or telephone headquarters to check if everything was all right—life could not have been any easier, war notwithstanding, but it could have been more interesting. That is why the lieutenant agreed to teach the small Goliath. These lessons were surprisingly pleasant. Imagine Matthew sitting in a trench and learning geography with skylarks singing all around, or resting calmly while the bullets flew overhead.

Now, all of a sudden, that calm was broken by a sound akin to howling dogs. The war was back in full swing. This new music was produced by small field cannons, echoed by the 'BANG, BANG' of heavy guns that did pose a danger to soldiers huddled in the trenches.

All hell broke loose, accompanied by a cacophony of sound: the frog-like croaking of machine guns, whistles, hisses, booms and bangs, the clap, peal and rumble of explosions. Smoke and the smell of burnt gunpowder hung heavily in the air.

Time seemed to stand still and then race by. Occasionally, a cannon ball dropped into the trench, killing a few and maiming others. But their companions had grown accustomed to the sight of blood and death.

"Well, it can't be helped. He was a jolly good fellow!"

"May he rest in peace!" someone would say, crossing himself in a sign of respect.

The doctor attended to those who were badly hit, dressing their wounds and sending them to the field hospital to recuperate.

What a wretched thing war is!

Luck was not with Matthew when a deflected bullet hit him in the arm. With the bones intact, the wound did not seem very serious, but the doctor was adamant: deaf to Matthew's pleadings, he sent him to the field hospital.

It was the first time in four months that Matthew could enjoy a real bed. What pleasure! A genuine straw mattress, a pillow, a continental quilt and white sheet, a linen towel, a white bedside table, a mug, a plate and a spoon similar to the ones he ate with at the royal palace.

Matthew's health improved in leaps and bounds. The nurses and doctors were very kind, and Matthew would have felt quite comfortable were it not for one serious danger.

"Look at the boy. Isn't he a dead ringer for King Matthew?" said the colonel's wife.

"That's it. His face rang a bell, but I just couldn't think where we might have met."

They wanted to take some photos of him for a newspaper, but Matthew would not agree—not for all the tea in China.

They tried to convince him that King Matthew would send him a medal if he chanced to come across a photo of such a small soldier in the newspapers. But it was all in vain.

"You will send your father a photo, you silly boy, and he will jump for joy."

"No, no and no!"

Matthew had heard enough talk of photographs, and even the thought was making him ill. What if they recognized him and guessed what had happened.

"Leave the boy alone. If he doesn't want his picture taken, that's his business, not ours. Maybe he's right. King Matthew might take it amiss and have a guilty conscience that he's riding in his limousine around the capital while his peers are wounded on the front."

Who the hell is this Matthew they are always talking about?

Matthew's language had strayed far from the niceties of court etiquette in favor of military slang.

It is just as well that I escaped to the front, thought Matthew, just to reassure himself.

They did not want to discharge Matthew from the hospital; he was even asked to remain to serve tea to the wounded and sick and work as kitchen help. But Matthew wouldn't hear of it. No way was he going to sit on the sidelines! Let Let figurehead kings give away presents...killed in action. As a real king, King Matthew the first would return to the trenches.

And so he did.

"Where is Felix?"

"Felix is gone."

Felix had become bored with trench warfare. He was the restless type and could not sit in one place for long.

All you did in the trench was sit for weeks, keeping your head down. If you disobeyed orders and looked out of the ditch, you risked being shot at, or at best a scolding from the lieutenant.

"Will you keep your stupid skull down?" shouted the lieutenant. "They will shoot that fool in the head, and then we will have to dress the wound and drive him from hospital to hospital. We have enough to do without this."

For the first and second time, just a telling off would do, but more persistent offenders landed up in jail on bread and water rations…and that's how it was with Felix:

In the enemy trenches, new troops appeared, replacing the previous unit. The old one was sent to the rear, and the fresh one took up its position. It was all done under the cover of darkness. The trenches were now so close to each other that one side heard what the other was shouting. So, they began, apart from exchanging fire, to exchange angry words, adding insult to injury.

"Your king is a snot!"

"And yours is an old klutz."

"You silly mongrels in leaky shoes!"

"And you hungry mugs get pigswill to drink instead of coffee."

"Come over here and try it!"

"Whenever we take one of you prisoner, he's as hungry as a wolf."

"And your men are raggedy and starving."

"The only thing you are really good at is escaping from us."

"But we'll kick your butts in the end!"

"You can't shoot. None of you would hit the moon from five yards."

"And you would?"

"Of course, we can! Stick your stupid heads out."

Felix got very angry and jumped out of the trench. Turned his back on the enemy, bent his head close to his knees, and tucked up his coat.

"Now you can shoot!" he shouted.

Four shots were fired but none of them hit their target.

"Some marksmen they are!" commented Felix's comrades.

What was a barrel of laughs for the soldiers angered the lieutenant beyond endurance. He clapped Felix in jail.

The prison was a deep hole with a roof made of wooden planks. It was common practice then for soldiers to bring any wood available, especially from cottages demolished by bombs, to make walls and floors in the ditches and even sheds for shelter from the rain.

Felix spent only two days in the pit because the lieutenant forgave him. But even those two days proved too much for him.

"I don't want to serve in the infantry!" he declared.

"Where will you go then?"

"To the air force."

The country happened to be suffering from severe petrol shortages, and with little fuel, airplanes could hardly fly with heavy cargo. So, the order was issued to take only very light soldiers on board. Everyone was sure that Felix would do well in the air force. Who could weigh less than a twelve-year-old child? The pilot would fly the airplane while Felix dropped bombs.

Matthew became a bit worried when he learned that Felix was no longer in their unit. But on second thought, he came to see it as a blessing in disguise. Felix was the only one who knew who Matthew actually was. True, Matthew himself had asked to be called Tom. But the way that Felix had treated him as his equal was never alright. In fact, Felix looked on him as someone less important than himself. Since Matthew was two years younger, Felix actually looked down at him. Felix drank vodka and smoked cigarettes, and if someone wanted to offer Matthew a glass or a cigarette, he would say:

"Oh, no! Don't give him the strong stuff. He's too young."

Matthew cared neither for cigarettes nor for vodka, but he felt he was grown-up enough to say 'thanks, but no thanks' by himself, and not be protected by Felix.

Whenever they were leaving the trenches for night reconnaissance, Felix always managed to put his best foot forward and be chosen.

"Don't take Tom—he will only be a burden to you."

Reconnaissance errands were no child's play. They were also dangerous. You had to crawl stealthily up to the enemy barbed wires, cut them with special scissors or look for the enemy guardsmen hideouts. Sometimes you had to lie still for an hour or more, listening for anything suspicious. On the other hand, when your presence was detected, flares were set off instantly, and you were lucky to get away unscathed in a hail of bullets. So, the soldiers always took pity on Matthew and more often than not chose Felix. Matthew felt passed over and unwanted—like a fifth wheel on a wagon.

Now with his 'brother Cyclops' gone, Matthew's role in his unit gained importance. If he did not supply the guards with ammunition, he made forays into the enemy trenches, slipping under the barbed wire entanglement, and twice he managed to sneak deep into enemy territory.

Dressed up as a shepherd, he wormed his way through the barbed wire. Then he covered a distance of two versts and sat in front of a bombed-out cottage, pretending deep sorrow.

"Why are you crying?" asked a soldier passing by.

"How could I not when our cottage has burned down and I can't find my mother anywhere? I don't know where she's gone."

They took Matthew to their headquarters, where hot coffee was waiting for him.

Good-hearted people, they fed Matthew and gave him some old overalls as he was shivering from the cold. He was dressed as a shepherd, but a very poor one. Now he met fine people, whom he was deceiving. He had come here to spy on them.

A number of thoughts began to catapult around the boy's head: he decided not to say anything upon his return to his unit, even if they thought him to be a stupid and good-for-nothing snot unsuited for intelligence tasks.

I don't want to be a spy. Let the colonel and lieutenant call me what they will. I won't be sent on spy errands anymore.

No sooner had he made up his mind than he was summoned to appear before the staff officer.

"Listen kid, what's your name?"

"My name's Tom," answered King Matthew.

"So listen carefully. You can stay with us here until your mother turns up. You will get some clothes, a canteen and a military kettle, soup and money. But in return for all of this, you will have to sneak into their positions and see where they keep their powder magazine."

"And what is this powder magazine?" Matthew pretended not to know.

So, the officer led him to their own magazine. There Matthew was shown where cannon balls, bombs and hand-grenades, gunpowder and ammunition were kept.

"Do you know now?"

"Sure thing."

"Then you will go and find out where they keep theirs, and after a lucky return, you will give us a detailed account."

"OK!" agreed Matthew readily.

The staff officer, glad to have recruited a spy so easily, gave King Matthew a whole bar of chocolate.

So that's where the shoe pinches, thought the boy, *greatly relieved. If I really have to be an intelligence agent, I prefer to spy for my side and not for theirs.*

Now our hero was sent to the trenches and then, he continued on his new mission. To divert attention, Matthew's 'new' companions fired a few shots—not at him but into the air. Matthew was now returning to his true comrades, very pleased with himself despite all the crawling and sneaking, and with a chocolate bar to munch on.

Now what the hell was this?! He heard the BANG-BANG-BANG of friendly fire. His comrades-in-arms might have killed him, seeing someone crawling but having no idea who it was.

"Set off three flares in that direction!" commanded the lieutenant.

He got hold of his binoculars and shuddered to see that they had almost killed their own secret agent.

"Hold your fire!" he cried. "It seems that Goliath is coming back."

Now out of danger, Goliath landed in the trench. He gave a full account of what had happened to him. Without further ado, the lieutenant phoned the artillery command. Their heavy guns began to shoot at the enemy powder magazine. The first twelve shots were off the mark, but the baker's dozen proved a lucky number. There was a deafening explosion and a gigantic fireball lit up the entire sky. There was so much pungent smoke in the air that everyone was gasping for breath. The blast caused quite a commotion in the enemy trenches.

The lieutenant raised Matthew up and repeated three times:

"Attaboy! Attaboy! Attaboy!"

So far, so good. They loved him even more. That was how it should be.

Meanwhile in reward for destroying the enemy's powder magazine, the unit received a whole barrel of vodka. Since the enemy had no gunpowder now, Matthew and his friends could sleep safely for three days. The lieutenant did not even forbid them to leave the trenches and stretch their limbs, while their enemies were left swearing and seething with anger.

For a while things returned to normal. By day, Matthew, taught by the lieutenant, worked hard not to drop behind in his studies. This was, of course, quite apart from his regular duties: digging—for continual rains damaged the trenches—standing sentry, or shooting at the enemy.

Not once did Matthew think:

How strange! I thought so much about inventing a remote-controlled glass that would ignite gunpowder to blow up enemy powder magazines, and in a way my wish has come true.

Thus, autumn came to an end and winter arrived in its full glory. They were sent winter clothing. It was peaceful and white all around. The ground was carpeted with a pristine blanket of snow.

Yet again, Matthew was learning an important lesson. The troops could not just sit in the trenches forever. Something had to give. But how would the war end?

While silence fell on the front and in the trenches, enormous work was underway in the capital to draw up a plan for concentrating all the kingdom's forces in one place in order to carry out an all-out attack to break through the enemy's defenses. As soon as such an operation was achieved, the defenders would have to beat a hasty retreat, for the attackers would enter through the gap and begin to shoot from the rear.

Over the winter, the lieutenant was promoted to the rank of captain, and Matthew was awarded a medal in recognition of his heroic service. He jumped up and down for joy. Their company was given an honorable mention twice for great military valor.

The general came to their trench in person to read the order:

"In the name of King Matthew the First, let me thank you for blowing up the enemy powder magazine and for your brave and faithful services in defense of your fatherland and fellow countrymen. Now I give you this secret order: to break through the enemy frontlines as soon as warm weather allows."

It was a great honor to be rewarded in this way.

But war isn't all fun and games. The moment the general left, grand scale preparations began for the offensive. Dozens of heavy guns with ammunition were brought forward. In the rear, the cavalry had already gathered.

The soldiers, ready for combat, were looking forward to warmer days, turning often to gaze at the sun. They hoped for spring to break the boredom and monotony of a long winter.

The waiting was unbearable despite all the preparations that needed to be made. Little did they know, however, what lay in store—what an ordeal they would have to go through. Their captain worked out a pretty risky stratagem: on the first day, a small section of their forces would launch an attack on enemy positions. They were to move forward and fall back quickly no matter what resistance the enemy offered, making the enemy think that they posed no real threat. Only then would the captain thrust all his forces forward and break through the enemy defenses.

And he kept to the original plan.

The captain ordered half of his troops to launch an attack. The action was preceded by heavy gunfire to shatter the barbed wire entanglements and make way for the infantry.

"FORWARD!"

Oh! What relief it was to get out of those unbearable wet and moldy trenches and run forward shouting 'Hurrah!', 'Forward!', 'Long live the king!'. The enemy was terrified by such a bold bayonet charge. The defenders were so shocked that they almost forgot to fire. The enemy's shots were few and far between and could not stop the charge. King Matthew's soldiers were approaching what remained of the barbed wire when the captain gave the order to withdraw.

But Matthew and a few other soldiers either did not hear the order or got too far ahead. Whatever the case, they were soon surrounded by enemy guards, and had no choice but to surrender.

The soldiers, who just moments earlier were too stunned to shoot, now taunted them mercilessly.

"Your valiant comrades-in-arms chickened out; didn't they? They ran so far and made so much noise, but they got cold feet when they reached our positions. There aren't so many of you after all."

For the second time, Matthew was on his way to enemy headquarters: the first time disguised and as an enemy spy, and now in a military coat as a prisoner of war.

"Gotcha!" yelled the staff officer triumphantly. "You're the reason our powder magazine was blown up. You won't escape us this time. Take the older soldiers to the POW camp; as for the little scoundrel, he'll be hanged for espionage."

"I'm a soldier!" cried Matthew. "You have every right to put me before the firing squad, but I won't be hanged."

"Don't be such a wise guy!" yelled the officer. "Ha! Look who's making demands! You may be a soldier now, but when you betrayed us, you were Tom the shepherd. And we'll hang you."

"You can't do that!" insisted Matthew. "I was still a soldier when I came here before. I was in disguise, and I sat down in front of that cottage on purpose."

"Enough of this idle talk! Escort the prisoner to his cell under guard. Make sure he doesn't escape. Step to it! Tomorrow, the court martial will try his case. If you were really a soldier, you stand a good chance of being shot. Though personally, I favor the hangman's noose to a bullet in your case."

The following day, King Matthew was court-martialed for espionage.

"I accuse this boy," said the military prosecutor, "of spying for the enemy. In winter he identified the location of our powder magazine and passed this information to the enemy artillery. They fired twelve times without success, hitting the target with the thirteenth shot and blowing up the magazine."

"Is what the prosecutor said true? Do you plead guilty or not guilty?" asked a grey-haired judge-general.

"I'm afraid I have to disagree with the prosecutor. It was the staff officer who led me to the magazine, showed me what it looked like and told me to find out where our powder magazine was. He even gave me a bar of chocolate in exchange. Isn't that the truth?"

The staff officer's face went beetroot red, because he knew he had made a terrible blunder. He should not have disclosed such sensitive information to a perfect stranger.

"I was a soldier, and I had been sent on a reconnaissance mission. It was your officer who wanted to make me into your spy," Matthew continued, undaunted.

"How was I to know?" retorted the staff officer in an attempt to defend himself.

But the general did not let him finish:

"Shame on you, officer. This child has managed to make a fool of you. Everyone has to pay for their mistakes, and you are no exception to this rule. On the other hand, this boy cannot be excused. What are your thoughts, Mr. Counsel for the Defense?"

The Counsel began to defend Matt:

"My learned colleagues, the accused, known to us either as Tom Thumb or Goliath, is not guilty. He was a soldier and had to carry out orders. He went on the 'recon' mission because he was ordered to. I think he should be sent to the POW camp just like the other soldiers."

The general was relieved because he felt genuinely sorry for the boy. But he did not say anything because as an officer, he had no right to show pity, especially for an enemy soldier.

So, he bent his head over the book where all the military laws were listed and began looking for paragraphs on war espionage.

"Oh, here it is," he said at last. "Civil spies are to be hanged summarily, while military prisoners may either be executed summarily by firing squad or—if the Counsel for the Defense objects to an execution—all the relevant papers should be sent to a higher court and the execution suspended."

"I demand that the case be reviewed by a higher court," said the Counsel for the Defense.

"I concur!" said the general, and the other judges followed suit.

So, once again Matthew was escorted to his cell.

The prison was an ordinary country cottage. As often happens in the field, the front usually has no regular prisons with barred windows—such 'luxuries' can only be found in towns and not off the beaten track. So, Matthew was led to a cottage where even the windows had no bars in them. Before each window and door, two soldiers stood with loaded rifles and revolvers.

In prison, Matthew had plenty of time to think. Strange as it may seem, he did not lose hope at all. On the contrary, he was beginning to take heart.

"They were about to hang me, but they didn't. So, chances are I will avoid the firing squad as well. So many have already fallen around me, and I'm still alive."

Although Matthew was sentenced to death, he had not lost his appetite. When they brought him his supper, he dove in with both a knife and fork. Prisoners condemned to die were actually really well fed, and Matthew was certainly considered to be on death row.

Once, sitting by the window, our prisoner saw three airplanes. Though they were flying low, it was not easy to see whether they were friendly or unfriendly. Before he could decide, three bombs fell nearby with a tremendous triple BANG!

Thanks to the pumpkin-size bombs, Matthew did not remember what happened next. One apparently had hit the cottage—there was a gigantic flash of light, followed by a deafening noise, pungent smoke and moans of the wounded. Someone grabbed hold of Matthew, whose head dangled limply. Then, something began to rattle around slowly, leading its owner back to consciousness. Matthew woke up to find himself in a comfortable bed in a beautifully furnished room.

"And how is Your Royal Highness Feeling?" asked the general anxiously (the same one who had decorated Matthew with a medal for blowing up the powder magazine the previous winter).

"I'm Tom Thumb, aka Goliath, an infantry private, general, sir!" shouted Matthew, jumping to his feet.

"Of course, you are!" the old general burst out laughing. "We will see in a minute. Hey, bring Felix here. Right away!"

Felix walked into the room, dressed as an aviator.

"Tell me, Felix, who is this?!"

"This is His Royal Highness, King Matthew the First," answered Felix.

Matthew could no longer deny the obvious, and there was no need now to hide his true identity. Quite on the contrary, the situation on the front called for a decisive step. This seemed to be the best moment to come out and say convincingly:

"King Matthew the First is alive, fighting on the front!"

"Is Your Royal Highness well enough to take part in the Council of War?"

"Of course!"

Now the general tied up a few loose ends for the young monarch. He told Matthew how they had had a porcelain doll made in place of him, and how this doll was driven all over the capital, and how the Prime Minister had it placed on the throne during audiences, and how the doll was able to salute and nod its head at the pull of a string.

The doll was always carried in the royal car, since—according to the newspapers—King Matthew had said his foot would not step on his native soil until his land was free of the last enemy soldier.

The hoax was successful for a long time—and people believed it even though it seemed strange to some that King Matthew always sat in the same position, be it on the throne or in his limousine. He also never smiled or said anything, but occasionally nodded his head or saluted.

Some felt that there was something fishy going on, and there were many who knew about the king's disappearance.

The king's enemies, warned by their spies, also began to suspect something, but pretended indifference. It was winter and all the soldiers did was sit in their trenches.

It was not until they learned that King Matthew's troops were planning to break through their defenses that they did some more serious investigating and discovered the truth.

Can you believe that they actually hired some rascal to hurl a stone at the porcelain doll?

Matthew 'the fragile' was no more. The head did not withstand the impact; the porcelain broke into pieces while the doll continued its traditional salute. Some began to despair, others were angry at how they had been duped and threatened to start an armed uprising, and there were also those who just had a good laugh.

The day after, that is after the day of the feigned attack when King Matthew was taken prisoner and shortly before the true offensive, the skies suddenly filled with airplanes that, instead of bombs, dropped tens of thousands of leaflets, all bearing the same message:

Soldiers! Your generals and ministers have lied to you. King Matthew is dead. Since the beginning of the war, the king we have seen being driven around the capital has actually been a porcelain doll. Today the doll was broken into pieces by a stone thrown by a miscreant. Cease fire, stop fighting and return home.

It was not easy to persuade the soldiers to wait and see if the news was really true. But they did refuse to go on the offensive. It was only then that Felix decided to tell the whole story.

The generals greeted this news with indescribable joy. Over the phone, they ordered the captain to send Matthew to headquarters. Can you imagine the generals' dismay when they heard that the king had been taken captive while leading an attack?

Nobody knew what to do.

To tell the rebellious soldiers, who had already been lied to once, that the king was in captivity did not seem a good idea. So, an emergency meeting was held during which it was decided that an airstrike should be carried out to rescue the king.

Four squadrons of airplanes were to take part. One would attack the POW camp, one would bombard the jail, another would blow up the powder magazine and the fourth the officers' headquarters.

The airmen followed their orders. They bombarded the building in which all the officers were stationed so nobody could issue orders. A hail of bombs was dropped where the powder magazine was supposed to be, but it was not there. The third squadron descended on the POW camp, but they did not find the king. It was only the fourth unit that managed to set Matthew free. The young monarch fainted of minor injuries sustained during the explosion but was otherwise OK.

"You did good work, gents. How many airplanes have we lost?"

"We sent out thirty-four and fifteen returned."

"How long did the whole operation last?" asked King Matthew.

"Forty minutes, all told. From take-off to touchdown."

"Well done!" he said. "So, tomorrow we're launching the general offensive!"

The high-ranking officers clapped their hands.

"That's great! The sooner the better."

In no time, the soldiers along the entire frontline learned that King Matthew was alive, and—surprise, surprise—was now among them and would ask them in person to launch the offensive. The boys rejoiced at the news and, needless to say, were now determined to fight like cornered tigers.

Telephones throughout the capital started to buzz, and telegraphs began to click. Special newspaper supplements were printed overnight.

Two proclamations written by King Matthew the First were issued. One was addressed to the army and the second to the nation. Thoughts of revolution were far from everyone's minds, save for teenagers and children who were protesting uncivilly outside the Prime Minister's palace.

All at once, an emergency Cabinet meeting was called to issue a proclamation in which the ministers let it be known that all of these events had been staged to fool the enemy.

In the army, spirits were so high that the soldiers could not wait to begin the morning offensive; they kept asking what time it was.

At long last, they were given the signal to attack.

Three kings were fighting King Matthew. The army of the first had been thoroughly destroyed and their king taken captive. The second king was also thoroughly defeated, and would be unable to wage war for at least three months since Matthew's soldiers had captured nearly all of his heavy artillery and over half of his soldiers. Only one king remained.

When the battle was over, yet another Council of War was held with the Commander-in-Chief and the Minister of War, who managed to reach the front on a special train from the capital.

"Shall we pursue the enemy?"

"Chase the scoundrels!" yelled the Commander-in-Chief. "If we were able to beat them when they had three armies, we should have no trouble to beat just one."

"I say no!" objected the Minister of War. "We were taught a lesson when we recklessly insisted on chasing the enemy too far."

"This is an unfair comparison, Mister Minister," said the Commander-in-Chief.

Everybody was waiting to hear what the king had to say.

Matthew dreamed of putting their foe to flight, a foe that had been so eager to hang him.

After all, it was the cavalry that would chase the enemy, and the king had yet to ride a horse in the war. Matthew had heard so much about kings mounted on white steeds defeating invaders, achieving brilliant victories over hostile armies with a forward charge, while he really only knew how to crawl on his tummy or crouch down in the trenches. If only he could ride a horse like a true cavalryman…

Matthew recalled that at the beginning of the war, they had been extended too far into enemy territory and were very close to losing the entire campaign. He remembered that the Commander-in-Chief was said to be a dumbbell. Matthew also remembered what he had promised to the envoys leaving his capital, that he would make every effort to defeat them and that the conditions of the peace treaty he would set would not be too demanding.

It was a long time before he began to speak, and no one assembled before the king dared to prompt him.

"Where is our royal prisoner?" asked the king unexpectedly.

"Not far from here."

"Go and fetch him please!"

They led in the enemy ruler, his wrists in iron shackles.

"Unshackle the king!" ordered Matthew.

The order was carried out instantly, and the guards surrounded the prisoner so that he would not run away.

"Vanquished king," began Matthew, "I know what captivity is. I will give you your freedom. You have been defeated, but the only wish I have is that you take the remnants of your army and leave my kingdom."

The king was driven to the frontlines and set free to return to his country.

The following day, a letter arrived signed by all three enemy kings.

King Matt—they wrote—*you are brave, wise and noble. Why should we continue to fight? We wish to restore friendly relations between our kingdoms and are returning to our countries. We await your agreement on establishing a lasting peace.*

King Matthew agreed, and just like that, peace was restored.

Soldiers rejoiced that the war was over, along with their wives, mothers and children. There were perhaps those less pleased—those for whom war meant business, such as robbers and looters who took advantage of abandoned property. But fortunately, there weren't many people in this camp.

Wherever his royal train called on the way to the capital, the victorious monarch was greeted enthusiastically by his grateful subjects.

At one particular station, the king ordered the train to stop. He got off and went to visit the switchman's wife.

"I have come back for a cup of coffee," said Matthew smiling.

The kind-hearted woman was stunned and overwhelmed.

"You honor me, Your Highness!" she repeated, tearfully.

In the capital, a luxurious limousine was waiting for him, but Matthew demanded a white horse instead.

"What a clever boy!" exclaimed the Grand Master of Ceremonies, shaking his head in disbelief. "That's how it should be. The king returns on a white horse and not inside a metal box."

King Matthew the First led his horse at a walk along the streets of the capital amid deafening cheers from thousands of people in the windows, mostly children and young people. The loudest and most sincere cheers came from the children, who also threw him flowers.

"Long live King Matthew! Three cheers!" shouted the children while their elders clapped their hands and ladies wiped away discrete tears.

Matthew maintained a stately appearance, even though he was absolutely exhausted. The offensive, his captivity, the escape, the Council of War, another battle, the long journey to the capital and now the unending ovation—they had all taken their toll. Matthew felt that the lack of sleep was finally catching up with him. His head was

buzzing, and red and black specks began to appear before his eyes. Sometimes they looked like tiny stars.

Suddenly, a cap thrown into the air from the crowd fell right on the head of Matthew's horse. The poor animal, a border in the royal stable, was very sensitive and unaccustomed to such silliness. He hurled himself sideways, tossing his rider in the process.

The boy was carried instantly to an ambulance and transported at full speed to the palace. Although Matthew landed with a bump, he did not suffer any serious injury. He did not even faint. Believe it or not: once on the ground, he fell asleep on the spot. He slept through the evening, night and the following morning, waking only at noon.

"Damn you! I'm dying of hunger! Gimme some grub. Step to it!" roared the boy while his lackeys turned white with fear.

Hardly a minute had passed when a hundred plates of the most exquisite delicacies appeared as if by magic, covering the bed, the table and every other available surface in the king's bedroom.

"Take that outlandish rubbish away at once!" cried Matthew angrily. "What I want are sausages with sauerkraut and beer."

What horrible luck! Not even the tiniest bit of sausage was to be found in the royal pantry! Fortunately, a corporal in the palace guard had a ring of sausage.

"You sad sack mamma's boys!" yelled Matthew, showing off his military vocabulary. "Believe me! I'm going to show you your place in the pecking order."

Matthew wolfed down the sausage and thought:

Now they know who is boss and who gives the orders around here.

Matthew had a hunch that after the victorious war he would have to fight another, even more relentless, with his ministers.

Already on the front, the news reached Matthew's ears that the Finance Minister was seething with anger.

"Some victor he is!" he repeated. "Why the hell didn't he demand war damages? It has been like this for ages: the winner takes everything…and the loser pays. Acts of nobility will not fill up the royal treasury. Let him run the economy with an empty coffer. Let him pay cannon manufacturers for heavy artillery, shoemakers for military shoes, suppliers for oats, peas and groats. As long as the war was fought, everybody waited patiently; but now that the bill is due, how will we pay it?"

The Foreign Minister was also as angry as a raging bull.

"Never has a peace treaty been signed without the Foreign Minister. Am I really a paper minister? My clerks are laughing at me."

The Commerce Minister was being pestered by the doll manufacturer:

"When will you pay me for the porcelain doll?"

The Prime Minister's conscience was not so clear, and the Police Prefect could also have been criticized for his awkward handling of Matthew's escape.

Matthew knew little, but enough to guess the rest. He decided not to leave anything to chance, but sort things out himself.

"Enough is enough!" he determined. "It's about time I put a stop to the rule of ministers in my kingdom. Either you listen to me, or get lost, dear ministers. Now I won't negotiate with the Prime Minister whenever he pleads sickness. End of story!"

Matthew licked his lips after the sausage, spat on the carpet and ordered that a bucket of ice-cold water be dumped over his head.

"This is a real soldier's bath," he said cheerfully. He put on his crown and went to the conference hall. The only person he found there was the Minister of War.

"Where are the others?" he asked.

"They did not know if Your Royal Highness would deign to meet with them."

"They might have thought that, upon my return from the war, I would resume lessons with my foreign tutor. And that they could keep on doing what and how they please. Over my dead body! They couldn't have been more wrong. Mister Minister, I will convene a Cabinet meeting today at two o'clock. When we have gathered, a platoon of soldiers will report for duty outside the conference hall. They will be waiting there in readiness for action. The platoon commander is to stand close to the conference hall door listening for my signal. The moment I clap my hands, the platoon will enter the hall. I'll make an exception, Minister, and tell you my intentions: if the misters should insist on, 'business as usual' and oppose the reforms I plan to propose, I will have them arrested. I order you to keep this secret."

"Yes, Your Royal Highness!" said the Minister of War with a bow.

Matthew took off his crown and went to the royal garden. He had not been there for ages.

"Oh my God!" he called. "I completely forgot about Felix!"

He whistled, and soon heard in return the familiar cuckoo call.

"Come over here, Felix. Now there is nothing to be afraid of. Now I'm a real king, and I don't need to explain myself to anybody."

"That makes two of us with new-found confidence, and my father may not like that at all. I don't know what he'll say."

"Tell him that you're the king's confidant, and I forbid him to touch you with even a single finger."

"If Your Royal Highness would put that in writing…"

"I'll do it with pleasure! Let's go to my study."

Felix beamed with joy.

"Mister Secretary, please draw up a document stating that Felix is my new confidant."

"Your Royal Highness, there has never been such a post in the royal court."

"Even so, there is now, because such is my will!"

"Your Royal Highness, perhaps you could postpone your order until the Cabinet meeting. This is not a long delay, but it would be more in agreement with court etiquette."

Matthew was ready to give in until Felix tugged discreetly on his sleeve.

"Damn it! I demand that the document be drawn up at once!"

The court secretary scratched his head twice and prepared two documents. The first paper read as follows:

I, King Matthew, demand irrevocably that this promptly drafted document appointing Felix to the post of royal court confidant, sealed after being submitted for signature, be handed to me. Anyone who flouts this categorical order of mine will be prosecuted and severely punished. I let it be known to the court secretary and confirm it with my own signature.

The court secretary explained that only after Matthew had signed the first document would he be given the second one.

The moment Matthew signed the document, the secretary handed him the second one appointing Felix to the post of court confidant.

Then the boys visited the royal recreation room where they played with the toys and browsed through the books, talked and reflected on their adventures at the front and dined together. Then they went into the garden. Felix beckoned a few of his peers to the railings, and they had a good time together until it was time for Matthew to go to the Cabinet meeting.

"I have to go," said Matthew, reluctant to part company with the boys.

"If I were king, I would never have to do anything."

"You don't understand. Even kings cannot always do what they want."

Felix shrugged his shoulders—clearly he did not agree with His Royal Highness. Knowing that the document signed by the king gave him every justification to stay, he returned home reluctantly, knowing that his father was waiting to lay into him, an attack always preceded by the question:

"Where have you been, you silly mongrel?!"

Felix knew exactly what always followed, but this time things would be different.

The meeting began with the ministers giving full vent to their grievances.

The Finance Minister said that he had no money. The Commerce Minister said that due to the war all the merchants had incurred serious losses and were unable to pay their taxes. The Minister of Transport said that the trains had to transport so much to the front that most railroad cars needed a major overhaul, which would be costly. The Minister of Education said in turn that during the war the discipline in schools had become so lax that standards of behavior had hit rock bottom. With fathers away fighting for their country, mothers were left alone to cope with their unruly children. Now teachers were on strike, demanding pay raises and the replacement of broken windows. Also owing to the war, fields were left fallow, and there were painful shortages of consumer goods. The list of impending tragedies continued in this vein for a good hour.

The Prime Minister gulped down a glass of water. Matthew did not like it when the Prime Minister drank water because it meant he was about to make a very long speech.

"Dear Sirs, I find this meeting quite strange, indeed. If someone listening to the speakers did not know the truth, he would have thought that we were defeated. But in point of fact, we won the war. Historically, the defeated have always paid war damages, leaving the victorious country richer as a result. It stands to reason that the winning state cannot achieve that victory by scrimping and saving, but by spending large sums on cannons, gunpowder and food for its soldiers. We outspent our rivals to win this war. Our heroic King Matthew saw with his own eyes that our soldiers wanted for nothing. But why should we be the ones to pay? It was they who attacked us, they who began the war; we have forgiven them as a demonstration of our generosity and magnanimity. But why should they not reimburse us for our costs? We don't want to take anything that belongs to them outside of what is our due. Heroic King Matthew, apparently driven by a spontaneous overflow of noble feelings, gave our enemies this peace offer—which was both a wise and beautiful deed—but a peace that has created financial problems that are unheard of in our history. We shall overcome these difficulties, because we have the necessary experience, because we are prudent, because we have so much knowledge and resolve, and if only King Matthew will honor us with the same trust as we enjoyed before the war, and will follow our advice…"

"Mr. Prime Minister," interrupted King Matthew, "that is quite enough. You could talk the hind legs off a donkey. Your argument cuts no ice with me. In truth, you want to rule, and as for me—well, if I'm to be a porcelain doll, I'll be damned if I agree to that. My only reply is: no, no, and once again no!"

"Your Royal Highness…"

"I do not agree, and that's final! I am king and so I will remain!"

"I request leave to speak," said the Minister of Justice.

"Make it quick!"

"According to the law—amendment five to paragraph 777,555 of book XII, tome 814, under Inventory of Rules and Regulations, page five, line fourteen, it reads: 'If the heir to the throne has not attained the age of majority (20 years of age)…'"

"Mr. Minister of Justice, I couldn't care less!" exclaimed Matthew.

"I see that Your Royal Highness is determined to break the law. I'm ready to quote the paragraph which applies in such a case. It is paragraph 105,486."

"Mr. Minister of Justice, allow me to tell you again. I don't give a damn!"

"We even have a paragraph for this: 'If the king disregards the laws contained in these paragraphs…'"

"Will you stop, or shall I show you how choleric I can get?"

"There is also a separate law on cholera. 'In the event of the outbreak of cholera…'"

Matthew, vexed beyond reason, clapped his hands, and the conference hall filled with green uniforms.

"You are under arrest!" exclaimed Matthew. "Escort them to prison."

"There is a law which provides for that as well," pointed out the minister triumphantly. "This is called a military dictatorship… This is open lawlessness!" he cried when a soldier hit him with his rifle butt.

Pale and trembling, the ministers were escorted to jail in single file. Only the Minister of War avoided arrest. He made a deep bow and left the hall a free man.

Dead silence fell as Matthew remained alone in the conference hall. He put his hands behind his back, pacing to and fro in the spacious room. Whenever he walked past the mirror, he asked himself the same question:

Do I resemble Napoleon Bonaparte? Napoleon would certainly know what to do, but I don't.

On the table was a scattered pile of government documents. Was Matthew to sign them all? What was in them? Why on some of them should you write 'allow', on others 'postpone' and still others 'forbid'?

Perhaps not all the ministers should have been arrested. Perhaps Matthew should not have done it at all. What would happen now? What should they be charged with? What crimes had they committed? To be quite frank, Matthew had made a very serious mistake. Why did he insist on such a hasty peace? He could have summoned all the ministers—the Finance Minister would have told him about war damages. How could he have known about those repayments? It seemed obvious that whoever began the war and lost should pay up. There were no two ways about it.

Perhaps he should write to the defeated kings. After all, there were three of them, and it would be easier for three monarchs to pay the debts than one.

But how should he write such letters? The minister had mentioned tome 814. There were so many of those books! Matthew had read two collections of short stories and Napoleon Bonaparte's biography. Those wouldn't be much help...

Poor Matthew was in a spiral of agonizing thoughts when he heard a cuckoo call through the door, which was slightly ajar.

At least he was not alone.

"Listen Felix, what would you do if you were in my place?"

"If I were in Your Royal Highness's place, I would go on playing in the garden and wouldn't attend any Cabinet meetings. I would do what I like when I like and would let them do whatever they like."

Matthew could not help thinking that Felix was not as bright as he had once thought. He obviously did not understand that the king must rule for the good of his people, leaving aside such simple pleasures as playing tag or hide-and-seek. But Matthew didn't say what he was thinking.

"What's done is done. They're already in prison."

"Let them stay there if this is Your Royal Highness's will."

"Well, but look at all those unsigned papers. If I don't sign them, there will be no new trains, or factories, or anything at all."

"It looks as if you have to sign them, then."

"The trouble is that without those ministers, I don't know anything. Even a king needs ministers."

"So, perhaps you could let them out."

Matthew was so relieved that he nearly flung his arms around Felix's neck. Such a simple solution, and yet it had not entered his royal head. Of course, he could release them at any moment. But he would drive a hard bargain. They would no longer be allowed to throw their weight around—they would have to obey his orders. They would never see the day when he, the king, would have to steal from the royal pantry or from his own garden, or look jealously through the bars at his peers. What was wrong with the fact that he also wanted to play? From now on, Matthew wanted the captain under whom he served in the army during the war to be his tutor. What was wrong with him wanting to be a happy boy? Matthew, just like every other child, yearned to be carefree.

Felix could not stay long as he had some important business to attend to in town. He came to borrow some money, not too much, just for the tram fare and perhaps for a pack of cigarettes and a chocolate bar.

"Why, of course, Felix. Here you are. Have a good time."

Again he was left to his own devices.

For reasons known only to him, the Grand Master of Ceremonies tried to avoid Matthew at every turn. Every time the king appeared, the foreign tutor vanished into thin air. Even the lackeys steered clear of him, as silent as the grave.

Suddenly, it dawned on Matthew that they all probably regarded him as a tyrant. At this thought, he felt a powerful pang of fear. Nothing could be more terrible than this. After all, Matthew was the great-great-grandson of Henry the Impetuous, who killed people like flies… What could he do to fix the situation? If only Felix would come to the rescue, or someone else…

As if in answer to Matthew's pleadings, his old doctor entered his room. Matthew was genuinely pleased to see him.

"I'm here to ask a favor in a matter of great importance. But I suspect that Your Royal Highness will refuse."

"Why? Do you think me a tyrant?" asked Matthew, looking warily into the doctor's eyes.

"Eh, a tyrant? Where did you get that from? No, but the matter I wish to discuss is of a very delicate nature."

"Could you be more specific?"

"I would like you, on behalf of our ministers, to take a few steps with a view to making their stay in prison a bit more bearable."

"I'm all ears, doctor. Tell me what the problem is, but in principle I agree. I'm no longer cross with them. I'll set them free as long as they promise not to throw their weight around so much."

"Oh, these are words worthy of a king!" exclaimed the doctor in jubilant relief, and proceeded to enumerate the requests of the prisoners:

"The Prime Minister asks for a continental quilt, a pillow and a mattress, for he cannot sleep on hay and complains that his bones ache."

"I slept on the bare ground," interrupted Matthew.

"The Health Minister asks for a toothbrush and toothpaste. The Commerce Minister wants white bread as he cannot eat black bread. The Minister of Education would be grateful for a book to read. The Minister of the Interior asks for a painkiller, for his whole body is aching from despair."

"How about the Minister of Justice?"

"He has not asked for anything since he read in tome 745 of our laws that the ministers have the right to ask the king's favor after three days, and they have only been imprisoned for a mere three hours."

Matthew ordered that palace bedclothes should be sent to the ministers as well as the royal dinner and—in the evening—the royal supper with wine. Then he had the Minister of Justice brought back to the palace under guard.

When the Minister of Justice arrived, Matthew asked him kindly to take a seat and then said:

"Would it be legitimate if I were to release you from prison tomorrow?"

"Perhaps not, Your Royal Highness, but if we were to recognize a military dictatorship as such, we would apply the fast track procedures it foresees and everything would thus be by the book."

"Mister Minister, if I set the ministers free, will they then legally clap me in jail?"

"Hardly! Though on the other hand, tome 949 discusses the legal aspects of a so-called coup d'état."

"I don't understand," admitted King Matthew humbly. "How long would I need to understand it all?"

"Probably no less than fifty years," answered the minister.

Matthew sighed resignedly. The crown had always seemed heavy to him, but now it felt like a cannon ball..

The shackles of the ministers were removed, and they were led to the prison canteen. The Minister of War and the Minister of Justice also joined them there of their own accord and as free men—guards with their swords drawn took their places—and the powwow began.

During the night, Matthew had thought up the following plan:

You'll deal with the grownups while I'll be the children's king. When I'm twelve years old, I'll rule children up to twelve years of age; when I'm fifteen—children up to fifteen. Since I'm small myself, I know what's good for small children. I must be free to do as I please, for I'm the king. As for the rest, let it remain the same.

"We were also small at one time," observed the Prime Minister with a smile.

"No doubt about that, and how old are you now?"

"Forty-three," replied the Prime Minister.

"Why do you rule your elders? The Minister of Transport is also young, and yet there are many older people who travel by train."

The ministers answered:

"Hmm, that's true."

"So, what do you think, Minister of Justice: is this acceptable?"

"On no account!" answered the Minister of Justice. "According to the law (tome 1,349) children belong to their parents. There is only one possibility."

"Namely?" everybody pricked up their ears.

"King Matthew must assume the title: King Matthew I the Reformer (tome 1764 p. 377)."

"What does that mean?"

"It means that he's a king who changes laws. If the king says: 'I want to introduce such and such law,' I will say to this: 'It is not permitted because there is already another law to the same effect.' If, however, the king says: 'I want to introduce such and such reform,' I will say: 'Please do.'"

Everybody agreed. The hardest nut to crack was Felix.

"He cannot be your confidant."

"Why?"

"Because it is contrary to court etiquette."

The Grand Master of Ceremonies was absent from the meeting, and the ministers were unable to explain properly what court etiquette was. One thing, however, was clear beyond a shadow of a doubt: the document given to Felix had to be taken back, by hook or by crook.

"This is not a legal document," confirmed the Minister of Justice. "Felix can visit the king and certainly be his bosom pal, but this relationship cannot be codified in writing, or worse still, sealed."

"OK, OK," Matthew nodded, and just to test them he said: "let's assume that I don't give in and leave you behind bars. Then what?"

"That's an absolutely different kettle of fish," smiled the Minister of Justice. "Kings can do anything."

Much to Matthew's astonishment, all of the prisoners were ready to do time for this trivial document.

"Your Royal Highness," began the Minister of Justice, "we mean no offence, but the law provides for such a situation as well. There is a word on that in tome 235. The king can appoint his confidants in his lifetime, but he must then assume the title of non-reformer."

"But how?" asked Matthew anxiously, for he was beginning to see the point.

"He must become a king-tyrant."

Matthew got to his feet, the guards raised their swords and dead silence fell. The ministers paled with fright, unsure of what the king would say. Even the flies stopped buzzing.

Matthew said slowly and distinctly:

"From today on, I'm King Matthew I the Reformer, and you, fine gentlemen, are free to go home."

The jailer at once carried out the shackles for storage in the closet as they were no longer of any use. The guards put away their swords, and the jailer opened the massive iron prison gates. The ministers rubbed their hands together jubilantly.

"Wait, wait gentlemen. As the reformer, I have to introduce at least one small reform. Let each school-aged child receive a pound of chocolate, first thing tomorrow morning."

"That's far too much, Your Royal Highness!" protested the Minister of Health. "A quarter of a pound at the most."

"Deal! Let it be a quarter of a pound."

"There are five million pupils in the entire kingdom," said the Minister of Education. "If all the urchins and underachievers were to be given chocolate…"

"Everybody," cried Matthew. "I don't want any exceptions to be made."

"Our factories can only produce such a quantity of chocolate in fourteen days."

"And the rail can deliver it to every corner of the kingdom in a week."

"As Your Royal Highness sees, the order cannot be carried out sooner than in three weeks."

"Well, if it can't be helped, it can't," said Matthew resignedly, but deep down his soul admitted:

It's just as well that I have such experienced aides. If not for them, I wouldn't even know how much chocolate is needed. Without the Commerce Minister, I would have no idea who was to produce the chocolate. It never dawned on me that the chocolate would need to be transported to each and every place in the country.

But he did not say this aloud. The king even pretended to be mildly annoyed, and he added:

"Please make sure that this business with the chocolate is printed in the newspapers tomorrow."

"I'm very sorry," said the Minister of Justice. "This is all very well, but it has little to do with true reform. It's just a royal gift to the schoolchildren. If His Royal Highness issued a law that each pupil be given chocolate by the State Treasury on a daily basis, it would be a different story. This would be a law. Otherwise, this is nothing more than a gift, a surprise, a treat."

"OK, I give up. Let it be a new law," agreed Matthew, as he was very tired and afraid that there would be no end to the minister's torrent of words.

"The meeting is over. Thank you very much. It's been a pleasure to speak to you, gents. Goodnight."

Matthew was driven to his palace in the royal limousine. Upon arrival, he rushed to the royal garden and whistled for Felix.

"You see, my friend, now I'm a real king. Everything is alright now."

"Perhaps everything is fine with Your Royal Highness, but not with me."

"Why?" asked the king, a little surprised.

"My father gave me one hell of a spanking for that paper of yours. I really did see stars."

"He gave you a beating? Why?" Matthew could not believe his ears.

"Just listen to what he said: 'It's the royal right to give you privileges, and mine to count your bones, you mongrel. You'd better remember it: in the palace you may be a royal, but at home you are no more than a private. And a father's hand is more reliable than royal favor. Capish?!'"

Matthew decided to be cautious. He had already learned a thing or two: haste makes waste, or more haste, less speed. Now he knew that there was no sense in hurrying. Life and war do have a little in common: in order to win, you must prepare your attack carefully.

Truly there had been no need to rush with Felix's document; instead of thinking it over, he made a silly mistake. He stirred up trouble for himself and a hornets' nest for Felix. Now his royal honor was tarnished, for how could a non-commissioned officer dare to beat the bearer of a royal document issued by the king himself?!

"Listen Felix, we needn't have hurried so much with that document I gave you. Remember? I even wanted to wait a little. Let me explain something to you."

Matthew told Felix how it had been with the chocolate affair.

"Kings cannot do everything they want."

"I see, Your Royal Highness…"

"Listen Felix, I hope we are still on a first name basis. We fought the enemy together, and it was thanks to you that I regained my freedom."

So, the boys decided that while alone, they would use each other's first names, and otherwise Felix would address Matthew formally.

"Sure thing, Goliath."

"Sure thing, Cyclops."

Now it was a breeze for Matthew to recover the questionable document.

"In return, I'll give you a pair of skates, two soccer balls, a stamp album, a magnifying glass and a magnet."

"And the old man will give me another hiding."

"I know, my friend, but do be patient. You have seen for yourself that kings shouldn't be rushed into doing stupid things. Kings must also observe the law."

"What does that mean?"

"The trouble is that for the moment I'm not really sure. It has something to do with learned books or something…"

"I see," said Felix sadly. "Since you're always in conferences with your ministers, you are learning these things step by step. And I…"

"Don't worry, my friend. Everything's going to be fine. If I can give away chocolate to five million children, I can also do good things for you. But it must be done legally. You don't even know how long I have to count sheep to fall asleep at night. I toss and turn, and even when I get tired of counting, I can't stop thinking.

But from now on, it will be much easier, you know.

Now I have one burden off my chest: I don't have to rule over adults. What do I have to offer grownups, anyway? Cigarettes…? Well, that's no good, for they have money and can buy them themselves. If I were to give them vodka, they would get drunk on the spot, and what's the point of being unable to walk straight?"

"I don't know," said Felix shrugging his shoulders. "You've begun to think of everybody else but yourself. I would have a swing built in the park as well as a carousel that would play music…"

"You see, Felix, you are not the king, so you don't understand these problems. OK, let's have a carousel but not just one. At the next Cabinet meeting, I will put forward a motion that swings and carousels should be built at every school."

"And bowling alleys and shooting ranges."

"Now you see…"

As soon as the ministers were released from prison, they went to a local café for coffee and cream cakes. Even though they had regained their freedom, they were none too sure about their future. They knew that with King Matthew the First on the throne, life would not be a walk in the park for them.

"First of all, we need to borrow some money."

"Can't we just print some more?"

"That's out of the question; we printed far too much during the war. We'll have to wait a little bit."

"Easier said than done with the size of the debts hanging over us."

"That's why I say that we must borrow from the foreign kings."

They ate four cream cakes apiece, drank their coffee and went home.

The following day, the Prime Minister had another audience with the king and said that a large sum of money would have to be borrowed from the richer kings. It was not an easy task, for the letter required very clever wording to be effective. To that end it was decided that two assemblies would be held daily.

"While you are meeting around the conference table, I will have my first lesson with my captain," Matthew declared.

Soon the Minister of War arrived, accompanied by the captain in question. Matthew greeted them warmly and even asked if they could promote the captain to major, but it was technically impossible because not so long ago he was still a lieutenant. In other words, he was just too young.

"You will be teaching me every subject except for foreign languages, which I will learn with the foreign tutor."

Matthew threw himself into the task of making up for the time he had lost during the war, and he forgot all about fun and games.

The captain lived far away, so Matthew suggested that he and his family should move into the palace. The captain had a son, Stanley, and a daughter, Helen, who was more or less the same age as the king. So, they usually had their lessons together and afterwards spent their leisure hours together, playing in the royal garden. Felix also attended the lessons occasionally, but he was not a very diligent student.

Now Matthew was rarely present at Cabinet meetings.

"It's a waste of time," he maintained. "Why should I be there if I soon get bored and don't understand anything?"

The royal garden was eagerly frequented by other children, if invited by Matthew, that is.

Felix's father, who had been a carpenter before joining the army, made a seesaw for them. The children also played tag, hide-and-seek, soccer and fire brigade. Sometimes they rowed on the pond, and as a special treat, they fished for carp. The royal gardener was not very pleased with these new practices and filed complaints with the palace administration. A few window panes had already suffered from the children's carelessness, but such small mishaps always went unheeded, for now King Matthew I the Reformer was in the thick of introducing his own new order.

Matthew had already arranged to have a tiled stove fitted in the throne room in autumn, because he had decided that he didn't want to feel cold during audiences anymore.

When it rained, the king's guests played in the royal chambers. The lackeys were a bit cross that the palace floors were trodden by dozens of children's feet, and subsequently needed to be cleaned and polished. But since they did not have to pay so much attention to their appearance anymore—now that there was no punishment for undone buttons—they had more time for keeping the palace clean. Previously a sad and silent place, the palace was now full of laughter and a joyful hustle and bustle in which even the captain and the old doctor occasionally took part. The children sometimes made them dance or skip rope. Great fun was had by all!

Felix's father, apart from the seesaw, made them a cart. It may have had only three wheels, but perhaps thanks to this, it was a universally favorite toy and everybody wanted to ride it; the cart kept falling over, but it was pretty harmless and only made the children laugh.

The distribution of chocolate in the capital took place in such a way that the children from all the schools stood lined up on both sides of the city streets, waiting patiently as trucks filled with soldiers passed by, handing out chocolate bars. When they were finished and the trucks disappeared, King Matthew toured the streets of the capital in an open limousine—everywhere children were eating, laughing and shouting:

"Long live King Matthew!"

Every now and then, Matthew stood up in his royal vehicle, blew them kisses, waved his hat and handkerchief, smiled and moved in ways that left no doubt he was no porcelain doll.

To be sure, everybody knew it was the genuine Matthew. Smaller children were accompanied by their elders: mothers, fathers or grandparents, also glad to have such a benevolent king. The children were now learning more diligently, for they knew that the monarch liked them and was mindful of their needs.

The Minister of Education, wanting to reward the most diligent and polite pupils, had offered them free tickets for a new theater performance. So, that very evening, Matthew, the captain, Felix, Helen and Stanley occupied the royal box in a theater full of children.

When King Matthew entered the royal box, the orchestra struck up the national anthem. Everybody rose, and the monarch stood at attention until they finished playing in accordance with royal etiquette. It was the first time that the children had had the opportunity to see their ruler that evening; they were both pleased and worried. Glad to see him in his military uniform but worried that he was not wearing his crown.

The ministers did not attend the performance, for they were up to their ears with work, striving to draft the diplomatic request for a foreign loan. Only the Minister of Education dropped in for a couple of minutes and commented, visibly satisfied:

"This is how it should be. Here we have assembled those who should enjoy a well-deserved reward."

Matthew thanked him politely, and the minister's visit was a nice ending to a very nice day.

However, the following day was anything but pleasant. Truly, it was hard work.

All the foreign ministers and envoys had already arrived and, with due ceremony, were to be handed the request for the loan.

Matthew had to sit as meek as a lamb and listen to what they had written for the past three months. It was even more difficult for Matthew to keep a straight face now that he had grown unaccustomed to formal meetings, especially after such a pleasant evening.

The document consisted of four parts.

In the first, the ministers wrote in the name of the king how Matthew's great ancestors had often provided assistance to the foreign kings and had lent them money when they were in need. This was the historic part of the document.

It was followed by a very long geographic section, which specified how much land belonged to King Matthew, how many towns, how many forests, how many coalmines, salt mines and oil wells he had, how many people lived in Matthew's kingdom, how many factories, how much grain, potatoes and sugar was produced yearly.

The third part dealt with economics. Here the ministers boasted that their country was very rich, that they had a lot of money, the government received enormous sums from annual taxes so there would be no difficulty in repaying the debt, and therefore in this respect, there was no cause for concern.

According to part four, Matthew wanted to borrow money only because he was concerned with further developing the country's economy. This section enumerated new investments: railroad lines, towns, new houses and new factories.

Listening to all of this might have been interesting but for all those statistics: millions and tens of millions! The bored politicians yawned discreetly and glanced at their watches. Matthew could hardly keep his eyes open but bravely endured until the end.

When the reading of the document was finally over, the foreign envoys said:

"We will forward this letter to our governments. Our kings now wish to live in friendship with King Matthew and are sure to lend him the money."

Now the ministers gave Matthew a gold pen inlaid with precious stones, and he wrote:

Your Royal Highnesses, I defeated you and did not press for any war damages, and now I ask you to lend me money. So, don't be pigs about it, and do lend it to me.
King Matthew I the Reformer

Matt was invited to stay with the foreign kings. In their official invitation, they wrote they would be pleased to see the king, the royal doctor, the captain and his two children, Stanley and Helen.

We can assure Your Royal Highness that you will not regret staying with us. We will do all within our power to make your stay as enjoyable as possible and satisfy your every wish.

Matthew was very pleased to receive such a kind invitation. The only foreign town he knew was the one he had visited in wartime, and now he was about to see three foreign capitals with their palaces and royal gardens. He was curious to know how much they differed from his own capital. One of those capitals was said to have shops with such gorgeous windows that you could gaze at them all year long and never get bored. In the other, a beautiful zoo with animals from all over the world. In the third, there was an incredibly tall building—according to Felix—which seemed almost to reach the sky.

The ministers were deeply offended that they had not been invited, but there was nothing they could do. The Finance Minister beseeched Matthew not to take any money or sign any papers to avoid being cheated.

"Please don't be afraid for me," said Matthew. "I was younger during the war, and I did not let myself be deceived, so there is even less chance I could be fooled now."

"Your Royal Highness, now they will pretend to be your friends, you know—the war is over, but mark my words, they will never stop trying to take advantage of your age."

"You really think that I don't know this?" Matthew retorted, but deep down he was glad to have been warned and made up his mind not to sign any papers while on the visit. It was indeed rather strange that they had not invited any of the ministers.

"I will be extra careful," he added.

Everybody envied Matthew such a long journey. Tailors brought new clothes and shoemakers new shoes, which were then packed into chests. The Grand Master of Ceremonies ran about throughout the palace making sure nothing was left to chance. Helen and Stanley jumped up and down for joy.

At last, two limousines drove up to the palace gates. Matthew and the captain got into one, and the doctor, Helen and Stanley into another. They drove across the capital to the sound of never-ending cheers. When they arrived at the station, the royal train was already waiting for them. Amongst those who had come to say their farewells to the king were all the ministers.

Matthew had already traveled on the royal train while returning from the war, but he was too tired then to pay attention. Now it was quite different. He was traveling for pleasure, so he did not need to think about all of the serious matters plaguing the world at the moment. He fully deserved a rest after such an exhausting war and so much effort on his part. Good-humouredly, he told the co-passengers how he had traveled to the front, hidden under a saddle-cloth from the lieutenant—now a captain and his teacher. He talked about soldier's soup, flea bites, the fleeting eye-contact with the Minister of War when Matthew, standing on a ladder propped against a cowshed, had watched the train he was now traveling on.

"Oh, we once spent a whole day here, and from this station, we were turned back a dozen versts."

The royal train consisted of six coaches. The first was the sleeping car. Everybody had their own compartment, which looked like a regular room with a comfortable bed, washbasin, bedside table and a chair. The second was the restaurant car or rather dining car with a large table in the middle surrounded by a dozen chairs. The floor was covered with a gorgeous carpet and fresh-cut flowers stood in vases. In the third coach, there was a library where apart from books, you could see the most beautiful toys from the royal collection. The fourth had a spacious kitchen in it, the fifth was occupied by the palace servants and the sixth served as a luggage car.

The children either admired the landscape outside the windows or played with the toys in the library. They called at large stations but only to take on water for the locomotive. The wheels of the train rolled so smoothly that there was neither any noise or swinging motion.

They went to sleep in the evening only to wake up abroad the following morning. As soon as Matthew washed and dressed, an envoy from the foreign king arrived to convey his king's greetings. He had boarded the train in the night but did not dare to disturb King Matthew. The envoy had kept a watchful eye on the travelers from the moment he got on the train at the border because Matthew was now under his care.

"What time are we expected at your king's capital?"

"In two hours."

Matthew was very pleased that the royal envoy spoke the language of his guests, because although Matthew understood a couple of foreign tongues, it was always nice to hear your native language, being so far away from home.

It was hard to say at that moment what welcome he would receive. He was coming to the capital of a foreign country not as the conqueror of this fortified city but as the conqueror of the hearts of its entire population. The old and grey-haired king of this country was expecting King Matthew at the station, surrounded by his mature sons and his grandsons. There were so many flowers and so much greenery at the station that it resembled a beautiful garden rather than a train station. Out of the twigs and flowers a sign was woven which said:

Welcome long-awaited, young friend!

Four long welcoming speeches were made, in which King Matthew was referred to as a wise, good-hearted and valiant ruler. It was predicted that he would rule far longer than any other king in history. As a most welcome guest, he was offered bread and salt on a silver tray. Then the highest state distinction of the country was hung around his neck: The Most Noble Order of the Lion. The medal was very valuable for yet another reason: centrally placed on the order was an enormous diamond. The old king kissed him so sincerely that it brought to mind Matthew's late parents and tears rose in his eyes.

The young king was carried triumphantly into a waiting car. In the streets, there were so many people; it was as if they had converged on the capital from all over the world. To mark the occasion, children were given three days off school, and so the streets were also packed with young fans of the heroic ruler. King Matthew had never been given such a red-carpet welcome, even in his own capital.

When they reached the royal palace, a large crowd of people had gathered in the square adjacent to the building and refused to disperse until King Matthew appeared on the balcony.

"We want King Matthew to say something to us!"

It was towards evening when Matthew at last appeared on the royal balcony.

"I am your friend!" shouted the king.

A 21-gun salute was followed by a display of fireworks and Bengal sticks. Overhead in the sky, rockets popped and red, blue and green stars crackled. It was a breathtaking sight.

The entire stay was one big festival of joy and dance: out-of-town trips by day involving picturesque mountain tours and visits to old castles situated in primeval forests, followed by big-game hunting, military parades, gala dinners and theater and opera performances in the evening.

The grandsons and granddaughters of the king took an instant liking to Matthew and were ready to give all their toys to him.

He got two beautiful horses, a small cannon made of pure silver and a wonderful cinematograph with a collection of films.

But the greatest attraction was yet to come. On the eighth day, the whole court made a car trip to the seaside where a mock sea battle was enacted before the eyes of the astounded audience. It was the first time Matthew had sailed aboard an admiral's ship. To commemorate the occasion, the ship was renamed after King Matthew the First.

That was how Matthew was entertained in the first kingdom over the course of the ten days he spent there. Much as he would have liked to stay longer, he had to visit the second king.

This was the very monarch whom Matthew had freed from captivity. This king was poorer, so while the reception was not so grandiose, it was even warmer than the first one. This monarch had many friends among exotic kings, whom he had invited during Matthew's visit. Matthew attended the most spectacular balls during which he met black Africans, Orientals, and Aborigines from Australia, each displaying a different skin color. Some were wearing plaits, others had ornaments made of ivory or seashells in their ears and noses. Matthew befriended those exotic kings, and one of them even offered him four gorgeous parrots which talked; another presented him with a crocodile and a boa constrictor in an enormous glass aquarium. Yet another gave our hero two very funny monkeys, which performed such amusing tricks that Matthew could scarcely keep a straight face.

It was there that the young monarch saw the biggest zoo in the world and in it: giant penguins, white bears, bison, large Indian elephants, lions, tigers, and wolves and foxes, down to the smallest terrestrial and marine creatures. There were myriads of multicolor fish and just as many beautiful, stunningly colored birds as well as at least fifty species of monkeys.

"These are all gifts from my African friends," said Matthew's host proudly.

Matthew made up his mind to invite them to his capital and create a similar zoo. For if he was so fascinated by wildlife, other children must also be fond of animals.

He wished he could stay a bit longer, but he had to visit the third king. It was time to be on the road again. In the capital of this next country, Matthew was hoping to visit the enormous building Felix had told him about.

The reception by the third king proved rather modest, but nonetheless just as friendly as the previous ones. Matthew was slightly surprised and felt a bit disappointed.

Are you a miser or what? thought Matthew, who then decided to grin and bear it.

The palace did not even resemble a royal residence and barely differed from the prettier houses in the center of the capital.

One lackey had slightly soiled gloves, and the tablecloth even had a small hole in it, very tiny but a hole nonetheless. Fortunately, it was neatly patched with silk thread.

There was yet another surprise in store for Matthew on that third visit. The king led him into his treasury vault. There were so many riches there—gold, silver and precious stones—that Matthew could hardly believe his eyes.

"Your Royal Highness is extremely rich," he stammered.

"Oh, no!" protested the king. "If I were to give out the contents of the vault to all my people, each of them would get no more than one small coin."

He said it in such a kind and natural manner that Matthew felt a pleasant warmth in his heart.

This king was the youngest of the three, but also the saddest. If, in the evening, they did not attend the theater , the king played the violin for Matthew, but the tunes he chose were invariably sad.

How different these kings are! thought Matthew and he said:

"I hear that Your Royal Highness has a huge building… A really, really gigantic one."

"Oh yes. I didn't show it to Your Royal Highness because it is the house of parliament. Since in your country there is no democracy, I didn't think it would be interesting."

"But I would very much like to see this…this parliament building."

Matthew did not understand what the king was talking about and thought again:

It's all very strange: they taught me what kings did one hundred, two hundred, a thousand years ago, and they don't teach what they are doing and what they are like now. If I had known them earlier, perhaps we could have avoided war.

The king began to play the violin once again, with Matthew, Helen and Stanley listening.

"Why does Your Royal King play such sad music?"

"Because life is not very happy. And the saddest of all is the life of a king."

"King?" Matthew did not hide his astonishment. "What about the two other kings? They seemed so happy."

"They are as sad as I am, but they pretend to be otherwise in social circles, because that's exactly what court etiquette dictates. How could they be happy when they have just lost the war?"

"Oh, I see, so this is why Your Royal Highness is so worried."

"I'm the least worried of the three. To tell you the truth, I'm even glad."

"Glad?!" asked Matthew still more surprised.

"Yes, because I didn't want war."

"So why did you go to war?"

"I simply had to. I had no choice."

A very peculiar king, thought Matthew. *He does not want to fight and declares war, and is pleased when he loses. Absolutely weird...*

"A victorious war poses a great danger," said the king, as if to himself. "It is easiest then to forget why one is king."

"And why is one king?" asked Matthew naïvely.

"One is not king just to wear a crown, but to give happiness to his people. And how does one give happiness? By introducing various reforms."

Oh, oh! That sounds interesting, thought Matthew.

"But reforms... They are the most difficult side of this business. Yes, the most difficult."

This time the violin played so morosely it seemed to be gently weeping, as if recounting some tragic story.

Long into the night, a host of new thoughts whirled through Matthew's mind. He tossed and turned, unable to sleep, and the sad song kept sounding in his ears.

I'll ask him. He'll give me sound advice. He must be a good man. The trouble is that I'm King Matthew the Reformer and I don't know what reforms are. But he says that this is so difficult...

Matthew thought again:

And what if he's lying? Perhaps they're plotting against me and have arranged for the third king to give me some suspicious document to sign.

Not once was Matthew surprised that so far there had been no word on the loan. In fact, there had been no serious exchange of words on anything. For all he knew, kings visited one another to talk business, politics and other important questions. Yet these three visits were nothing of the kind. He thought they did not want to talk to him because of his age. Why did the third king talk to him like to a grownup then?

Matthew took a liking to the sad king but did not trust him. It is, however, quite natural for kings to learn to be suspicious early in their lives.

Trying to fall asleep, Matthew began to hum sotto voce the saddest of the songs played by the third king when he heard steps in the adjacent room.

Perhaps they want to kill me?

He could not help the thought that flashed through his mind. Matthew had heard about kings being murdered in an ambush. Perhaps such thoughts would not have entered his head if it had not been for those long reflections and the sad songs which irritated him immensely.

Matthew quickly switched on his bedside lamp. Then he put his hand under the pillow for his revolver.

"Aren't you sleeping, Matt?"

It was the king.

"I can't seem to fall asleep."

"So dark thoughts loom large even in the minds of small kings, keeping them awake at night?" said the king, smiling as he sat at the foot of Matthew's bed.

He said nothing else, but sat and watched. Matthew suddenly remembered that his late father used to look at him like that. At the time, Matthew did not like being looked at in this way, but now it filled him with pleasure.

"I know, I know, Matthew, you were very surprised to hear that I had not wanted to fight a war against you, but I did fight it. It's because you still think that kings can do what they please."

"I don't think that at all!" protested Matthew. "I know that a lot of things are dictated to us by etiquette and at least as many by law."

"Clever boy. You know then that we ourselves lay down bad laws, and then have to abide by them."

"Can't we make good laws?"

"We can and we must in the future. You are young. You should learn a lot and then issue good, wise laws."

The king took Matthew's hand in his, and for a while, it was as if he was comparing his big palm with Matthew's smaller one. Then he stroked it tenderly, bent down and kissed it.

Matthew felt very ashamed, and the king began speaking quickly and softly:

"Listen, Matthew: my grandfather gave his people freedom, and it wasn't any good.

He was eventually murdered and the people were still unhappy. My father erected a huge statue of freedom. You'll see it tomorrow: it looks impressive but what good is it, if there are still wars the world over and people are poor and unhappy. I ordered the construction of that gigantic house of parliament. And so what? Nothing changes."

Suddenly, the king seemed to remember something.

"You know what, Matt? We have always made the same mistake. We have carried out reforms for adults. You should begin with children, perhaps you'll succeed… OK, now go to sleep, my dear boy. You have come here to have a good time, and I'm bothering you at so late an hour. Good night!"

When Matthew tried to continue their conversation the next day, the king would not hear of it. Instead he explained to Matthew the exact role of the parliament. It was really an impressive building: gigantic by any standards and very beautiful. Its interior resembled partly a theater and partly a church. On a dais before a table, gentlemen sat just like in his palace in the conference hall. But here there were hundreds of armchairs, in which various gentlemen sat. From time to time, they rose to stand behind what looked like a church pulpit, and they sort of preached a sermon. All around, Cabinet ministers were seated in boxes. To the left, at a separate table, those who wrote for newspapers listened. The audience watched from above in the galleries. Just as they entered, an angry gentleman was making a speech.

"We will not permit it!" he shouted, punching the air and beating the rostrum's top with his clenched fists. "If you don't pay us heed, you'll never again be ministers."

The second speaker said that the ministers were very wise, and there was no need for changes.

Then a lengthy argument ensued, and the deputies and the ministers began to shout all at once. Someone yelled: "Down with the government!", and someone else: "Shame on you!"

When Matthew was leaving the hall, someone shouted: "Down with the king!"
"Why are they quarrelling?"
"Because they don't feel good in this world."
"And what will happen if they really throw away the ministers?"
"They will choose new ones."
"How about the one who yelled 'down with the king!?'"
"He always does this."
"A madman?"

"No. He just does not want me to rule."
"And can they bring bring you down?"
"Of course, they can."
"And what will happen then?"
"They will choose someone else and give him some other title."

It was a very elevating experience. Just like watching those two small monkeys of the African chieftain.

Meanwhile the only topic covered by the newspapers in Matthew's capital was his month-long stay abroad. The press reported details concerning how the foreign monarchs received Matthew, how much they liked and respected him and what beautiful gifts he was given.

Matthew's ministers, taking advantage of the friendly relations between the young monarch and his hosts, wanted to borrow as much money as possible and were hoping for a really gigantic loan. They were, however, against Matthew's quick return to the capital for fear that he might upset the apple cart at the last moment. It was a good thing that the foreign kings did not take exception to Matthew's postscript to the formal request for a loan. Never before had anyone, not even the greatest of kings-reformers, written in an official document:

So, don't be pigs about it…

The ministers resolved that Matthew would stay abroad for another month, claiming that after the toils of war he really did need a good rest.

Not suspecting their true motivations, Matthew was very pleased to hear the news. He asked at once to visit the seaside, whereupon Matthew, the captain, Stanley, Helen and the doctor, went on a journey, but this time in an ordinary train. Matthew even wore normal clothes and instead of a palace, they stayed in a regular hotel. Now Matthew was not referred to as king, but as prince. It was said that the king was staying at the seaside incognito. According to the law, the king could go abroad by invitation only, and if he traveled anywhere at his own initiative, he had to pretend that he was not the king.

It was all the same or even preferable for Matthew because he could play with all the children and be just like everybody else.

It could not have been lovelier at the seaside. They bathed in the sea, collected seashells, made sandcastles, ramparts and fortresses. They sailed in a boat and rode on horseback. In the nearby forest, they gathered mushrooms, which they then dried. They also picked delicious blueberries and hazelnuts.

Time raced, particularly because Matthew had resumed his lessons with the captain. As I have already mentioned, he was an assiduous pupil and liked his new teacher, so these three-hour lessons could in no way spoil his vacation.

Matthew liked Stanley and Helen, and they really got along like a house on fire. They were very well brought up children, and they hardly ever quarreled. Any rare misunderstandings were quickly sorted out.

Once, Matthew squabbled with Helen about a mushroom. It was an enormous penny bun. Matthew and Helen both insisted that each had seen it first. Matthew would have given in, because after all one mushroom was not such a big deal, especially for the king. But on the other hand, Matthew did not like the way Helen boasted about it or how she refused to admit the truth.

"The moment I saw the mushroom, I shouted 'Oh, look over there!' and pointed at it with my finger. It was only then that you ran up to it."

"I picked it."

"Because you were nearer, but I saw it first."

Helen became furious, threw the penny bun to the ground and trampled it underfoot.

„I don't need this silly mushroom!"

Knowing at once that she had acted foolishly, she felt very ashamed and started to cry.

What strange creatures girls are, thought Matthew. She trampled it herself, and now she's crying.

On another occasion, Stanley built a really impressive fortress with a high tower. It is not easy to build such a tower because the sand you use must be very wet, so you have to dig deep. Stanley reinforced the construction of the tower with a stick, but all the same he had to work very hard to get suitable sand. Now he was waiting for a wave strong enough to put the fortress to the test, when Matthew suddenly hit on a different idea and shouted:

"I will capture your fortress!"

With these words, he pounced on it running at full speed, and, of course, the fortress collapsed. Stanley flew into a rage, but as soon as he cooled down, he admitted that it was only natural for a king to try and destroy an enemy stronghold. Stanley sulked even shorter than the incident called for, and the boys were soon friends again.

Sometimes the captain told them how he had fought savage tribes in African deserts. Another time, the doctor transported the children to the world of medicine by explaining how much a disease resembled an enemy that attacks a human being. He believed human blood contained very small white blood cells, which were like soldiers who tried to defeat the attackers and either won, restoring a person to health, or were defeated, causing the sick person to die. In the human body, there were numerous glands very similar to fortresses. There was a maze of corridors, trenches and ambushes there, and when a disease was dragged into such a gland, it got lost in its labyrinth and died from the blows dealt by the white blood cell soldiers.

They soon made friends with the local fishermen, who taught them how to recognize by the look of the sky whether a storm was approaching or not, and whether an impending storm was a heavy squall or a run-of-the-mill downpour.

They really had a great time listening to these mini-lectures or playing, but sometimes Matthew preferred to be alone. He either ventured deep into the forest or strayed from the rest of his company, pretending to pick seashells. When he felt that he was far enough, he sat on a tree stump or a boulder. Folding his hands in his lap, he thought long and hard about what awaited him on his return home, and what reforms he should introduce.

Perhaps he would follow the example of the sad king, who played the violin. Perhaps it would really be better if the whole nation ruled the country and not only the king and his ministers. A king might be too inexperienced to rule and the ministers too ignorant or dishonest. What would he do then? Would he clap his ministers in prison and try to rule unassisted and without knowing how? In a democracy, he could go to the parliament and say:

"Choose new and better ministers!"

Such thoughts crossed Matthew's mind quite frequently, but he needed advice. Once, he asked the doctor:

"Are all children as healthy as me?"

"No, Matthew (the doctor did not call him king, because Matthew was staying at the seaside incognito). There are a lot of children who are weak and ailing. Many live in unhealthy, damp and dark places. They never go on holiday to the countryside, they eat too little and often go hungry and that's why they fall ill."

Matthew had been in dark and stuffy places, and he also knew what hunger was. He remembered that he usually preferred to sleep on the bare ground outdoors rather than in a country cottage. He also remembered peasant children, bowlegged and very pale, coming to their camp to beg for some soup from their kettle and wolfing it down in no time at all. Matthew thought that it was only in wartime that children suffered such hardship, but now he heard even without war, poverty did not spare the youngest.

"Why can't everyone own a nice house with a garden and eat nutritious food?" Matthew asked.

"It is a difficult problem indeed; people have thought about how to accomplish it from time immemorial, but so far unsuccessfully."

"Could I possibly find the answer?"

"It's not out of the question. Of course, you can. The king can do a lot. For example, the last king we visited, the one who played the violin, built many hospitals, orphanages and children's houses. Under his rule, many children are able to visit the countryside in the summer. He issued a law requiring each town to build houses in the country for the sickliest children to stay throughout the summer."

"And how is it in our country?"

"No such law has been issued in our country so far."

"I will issue it!" said Matthew and stamped his foot. "Doctor, you must help me, because the ministers will tell me again how sorry they are, but that something or another won't allow them to implement it, and I for one won't know whether they are telling the truth or are trying to fool me as usual."

"No, Matthew. They will be telling the truth. This isn't easy at all."

"OK, OK, I know. When I wanted to give the children chocolate, they promised to give it out in three weeks. In the end, they did give the children the chocolate but only after more than two months. But they did."

"I see your point, but it is far easier to give chocolate."

"But if it was easy for the king with the violin, why should it be difficult for me?"

"But it wasn't easy for him."

"Well, it might be difficult, but I will do whatever it takes!"

The evening sun was just above the horizon. It was so huge, so red and so beautiful that it set Matthew thinking how to ensure that all the children in his country could see such a gorgeous sunset, swim in the sea, sail boats and pick mushrooms.

"How is it," Matthew wondered, as they were coming back from a walk along the beach, "that the king is so very good, and one deputy still shouted 'Down with the king!'"

"There will always be dissatisfied people. You won't find a king or a minister anywhere around the world that is praised by everyone."

Now Matthew remembered how the soldiers at the front made fun of and gossiped about kings. If Matthew had not been in the war, he might still think that everybody loved and respected him and was ready to throw their hats in the air at the sight of their king.

From that moment on, Matthew applied himself to his lessons even more seriously than before and began looking forward to their return home.

It's about time I started my reforms, he thought. I'm king and I can't be any worse than those who send all the children to the country in the summer.

Matt returned to the capital when preparations for the loan from the foreign kings were complete. All that was needed to finalize the transaction was the king's signature under the conditions of repayment. As soon as Matthew signed the document, the chief state cashier set out by train with dozens of bags and wooden boxes to carry foreign gold and silver.

Matthew waited impatiently for the money he needed to carry out his three great reforms:

1. To build cottages throughout the forests, in the mountains and at the seaside so that poor children could spend summer holidays there.

2. To put up swings and musical carrousels in all the schools.

3. To found a huge zoological garden in the capital, with wild animals kept in cages: lions, bears, elephants, monkeys, snakes and birds.

Matthew waited for the money, but what awaited him instead was little short of a rude awakening. When the money arrived, it turned out that the ministers had not one penny to spare for the king's reforms because it had been worked out in advance how much each minister would take for his expenses.

So much was earmarked for new roads and bridges, so much for railroad lines, so much for new schools and so much to repay debts created by military production.

"Had His Royal Highness told us earlier, we would have borrowed more," the ministers assured Matthew. But in fact, what they really thought was:

It's just as well that the king wasn't at the negotiations. Matthew's reforms would certainly have required so much money that the foreign kings wouldn't have agreed to lend to us.

"Now we'll see who has the last laugh," whispered Matthew to himself. "Since you have cheated me so much, I know what I'll do."

He took his royal pen and wrote a letter to the third king:

I want to introduce the same reforms in my country as Your Royal Highness carried out in yours. I need a lot of money. The ministers borrowed for themselves and now I want to borrow for myself.

Matthew waited and waited for the reply, and when he was beginning to lose hope, he was quite unexpectedly called out of a lesson and told that a foreign emissary had come for an audience with the king. Matthew guessed at once who the newcomer was and invited him to the throne room. Since the mission was confidential, the emissary demanded to talk to the king in private. When they were left alone, the emissary said that his king was ready to lend the money if Matthew changed the constitution, giving his people the right to rule.

"If we lend money only to Your Highness, we can lose it, but if we lend it to the whole nation, that's a completely different story. There is, however, one problem here—the ministers are unlikely to agree," said the emissary.

"They have to agree," said Matthew. "Who do they think they are? If they agreed that I should become King the Reformer, then they'll have to expect reform!"

Quite unexpectedly, the ministers agreed without a murmur. Needless to say, they did it for fear of being imprisoned once again and calculated that:

Should the need arise, we will say that the whole nation wants it and we can't refuse. We simply have to do what the whole nation has told us to. And Matthew won't be able to clap the entire nation in jail.

Prolonged debates began. From hundreds of miles around, from all the big towns and small villages, the nation's wisest men converged on the capital. Days and nights of lengthy discussions turned into stormy disputes and arguments. It proved rather difficult to determine what the entire nation wanted.

The newspapers published so many articles on the debates in the new legislative body known as parliament that there was no room for photos and cartoon strips. But Matthew was now so good at reading that he needed no illustrations to know what was happening.

Separate assemblies were held by bankers who calculated how much money was needed to build houses for children in the country and put up carousels and swings at schools.

Many merchants arrived from all parts of the world to find out what mammals, birds and snakes would be needed for the new zoological garden. Their debates were fascinating and Matthew was always present to witness them.

"I can sell you four beautiful lions," said one.

"And I've got the most ferocious tigers," boasted another.

"I have beautiful parrots," added the third.

"The most fascinating are snakes," assured the fourth. "I've got the most dangerous serpents and crocodiles. My crocodiles are real giants and they live for a long time."

"I have a trained elephant. He performed in the circus when he was young. He rode a bicycle, danced and walked a tightrope. Now he's a bit old, so I can sell him cheaper. And the children will have a lot of fun. They love to ride elephants."

"Don't forget the bears," said a bear expert. "I can sell you four brown and two polar bears."

Among the wild animal merchants—all of whom used to be intrepid hunters—were an authentic Indian and two Africans. Children throughout the capital craned to get a closer look at them while rejoicing that the king was buying so many exotic animals for their enjoyment.

Suddenly the debate was joined by a man, his skin as black as ebony. The Africans the children had seen before were casually dressed and spoke European languages. They lived partly in Africa and partly in Europe. This one did not say a single word that could be understood. He was dressed in seashells, nearly naked in fact, and had so many ornaments in his hair that it was hard to believe that such a burden could be carried on one's head.

In Matthew's country lived one very old professor, who knew some fifty different languages. He was promptly called to translate what this unbelievably dark-skinned African was saying. It seemed like the other Africans could not understand him either, or perhaps they did not want to help and lower their chances of striking a decent bargain.

Indeed, the offer from this African prince—yes, he was a real prince—far overshadowed their own:

"As huge as the baobab tree, as powerful as the sea, as quick as a thunderbolt and as bright as the sun, King Matthew, I have come to extend you the friendship of my monarch. May you live seven thousand years and be blessed with one hundred thousand great-great-grandsons. My king has more fierce beasts in his jungle than there are stars in the sky or ants in an anthill. Our lions eat more people every day than the entire royal court in a month. And ours is no puny court, for it consists of the king and his two hundred wives and one thousand children. May they live five thousand years and not a year less. Awesome King Matthew, don't believe a word those conmen say; they sell toothless lions, clawless tigers, old elephants and dyed-feather birds. My monkeys are more intelligent than they are, and my king's love is greater than their stupidity. They demand money from you. My king does not need gold because there is more than enough gold in his mountains. All he asks is to be invited to your country and be your guest for two weeks, because he's very keen to visit northern countries; the other white kings refuse to entertain him, because they say that he's a savage, and feel it is unseemly for them to befriend the likes of him. If you, King Matthew, would accept his invitation and come to stay in his palace, you would see with your own eyes that what I am saying is true."

The wild animal merchants, sensing that things were not going their way, decided to interrupt:

"Does Your Royal Highness know that this is an envoy from the land of cannibals? We strongly advise His Royal Highness against visiting this ruler or inviting him here."

Matthew asked the professor-interpreter to ask the envoy whether the monarch in question was really a cannibal.

"Oh, King Matthew, as bright as the sun: I've already said that the lions in our jungle devour more people in one day than the entire royal court in a month. Let me tell you one thing, pale King Matthew. My lord would never eat you or any of your subjects. My king is very hospitable, and he would rather eat his two hundred wives and one thousand children…may they live five thousand years and not a year less… than bite off one of your fingers."

"In that case, I'm ready to go!" resolved Matthew firmly.

The wild animal merchants left the kingdom, angry to have missed such a great business opportunity.

The Prime Minister was so angry when he returned home that his wife could not muster up the courage to ask what had happened. The Premier ate his dinner without a word, his children sitting as quiet as mice so as not to suffer his bad temper. The Prime Minister normally drank a shot of vodka before dinner and a glass of wine with his meals. Today he pushed the wine aside and gulped five shots of vodka in short succession.

"My dear husband," she began shyly, so as not to anger him further, "I see that you had another nasty day in the palace. You will ruin your health taking everything to heart."

"This is unbelievable!" exploded the Prime Minister at last. "Do you know what King Matthew is doing?"

The Premier's wife sighed deeply.

"Do you know what he's doing? He's going to visit the king of can-ni-bals. Can you beat that? He's visiting the most savage tribe on the entire African continent. No white monarch has ever been there. Do you understand? He's sure to be eaten. I have no doubt about that. I'm in despair."

"My dear husband, isn't there some way to talk him out of it?"

"Certainly. Dissuade him if you please, but without me. I'm not going to land in prison anymore. He's as obstinate as a mule, and downright reckless."

"I see, but what would happen if he—God forbid—was really eaten?"

"Oh, woman! Do try to understand that we are about to introduce a system by which the entire nation governs; the king has to sign a document called a manifesto, and there must be an inauguration of the parliament. Who will sign the manifesto and who will open the inaugural session of the parliament if Matthew is in the belly of the savage king? They can eat Matthew in a year, but we absolutely cannot do without him until then."

There was one more thing the ministers were concerned about: on one hand, it would be inappropriate, virtually unheard of, to let Matthew set out on such a long journey alone, but on the other, none of the ministers was willing to join him.

Matthew was already preparing for the journey.

The news spread like wildfire that Matthew was about to visit the homeland of the cannibals. The elderly shook their heads in disbelief, but his younger subjects were mostly envious.

"Your Royal Highness," said the doctor, "to be eaten is very unhealthy. They will probably want to roast Your Royal Highness on a spit, and since protein coagulates when subjected to heat…"

"My dear doctor, there was a time when I could have been killed, shot dead or hanged, and it just so happens that I'm still alive. Perhaps the prince is telling the truth—perhaps they are hospitable and won't cook me. I have already made up my mind: I have made a promise and kings have to abide by their word."

The captain was the next adviser who tried to persuade Matthew to back out of his dangerous venture.

"It is extremely hot over there. You will have to ride camels for two weeks. There are many diseases, many of which are fatal: you may catch one of them and die. What is more, you never know where you stand with those savages. They are not to be trusted. I know because I fought them on several occasions. White people would not kill them if they were not so untamed and treacherous."

Matthew nodded his head, never questioning the truth of the words he heard, and continued to pack for his journey.

The capital had to have a zoological garden. For that he needed many lions, tigers, elephants and various species of monkey. If you are the king, you have to fulfill your duties.

The African prince began to press Matthew to leave as he was unable to live without human flesh for longer than a week. He had brought a barrel of salted human meat, eating it stealthily bit by bit, but as his supply was now dramatically low, he was urging Matthew to depart for Africa as soon as possible.

It was finally settled who would accompany Matthew: the old professor who spoke so many languages, the captain, but without his children because their mother would not let them go, and Felix with the doctor, who joined the delegation at the eleventh hour.

The doctor did not know African diseases, so he bought a thick book dealing with that subject and put it into his suitcase along with all the necessary medicines. They did not take too much luggage—first of all because there was no need for warm clothes, and secondly, you cannot have too many trunks and suitcases when you are riding a camel. At the last moment, an English sailor and a French traveler appeared seemingly from nowhere and asked the king to take them along. Permission was granted and they all got on the train. The journey was long but uneventful. When the train arrived at the seaside, our travelers boarded a ship. In the middle of the sea, they were caught in a storm and everybody on board got seasick. It was the first time the doctor had to make use of his medicines.

The doctor was very angry with himself for having joined such a crazy adventure.

"Why did I ever decide to be the royal doctor?" he grumbled to the ship's captain. "If I were an ordinary doctor, I would see patients in a comfortable clinic or work from nine to five in a hospital, but here I'm roaming the world without rhyme or reason. Besides, being eaten at my age would be a very unpleasant experience."

The captain, however, unlike the doctor, was growing increasingly cheerful. The voyage brought to mind the time he ran away from home to join the French Foreign Legion to fight the natives in Africa. At the time, he was a very young and happy-go-lucky boy.

The happiest person aboard was unquestionably Felix:

"When you went to visit those three white kings, you took the captain's brats along instead of me, and now that you are paying a visit to the cannibals, Felix is suddenly good enough for you and those other kids have deserted you."

"Felix, you know how it is. You weren't invited by the foreign rulers," Matthew explained himself, slightly ashamed. "Court etiquette dictates that only those who are invited may come, not those who want to join you. Stanley and Helen did want to come with me, but their mother wouldn't hear of it."

"I'm not angry with you," said Felix.

They sailed into their port of call, disembarked and traveled by train for two days. Now they plunged into the wilderness. Growing on both sides of the track were palm trees, date and fig trees and robust banana trees. Matthew could not help the rapture he felt at the sights outside the window. The prince said nothing but kept smiling, and his teeth glistened like snow, which made everyone uneasy.

"This not a real African jungle; wait until you see the one that awaits."

But instead of jungle they saw desert—nothing but endless sand. The ocean of sand had the same unbelievable vastness as that of the water they had seen when crossing the Mediterranean Sea.

In the last village, there was a small unit of white soldiers and a few shops owned by white settlers. Matthew told them they were travelers on their way to the land of cannibals.

"Go ahead, if you really want to. We've seen many travelers heading in that direction, but we don't remember anybody returning."

"Perhaps we'll be the lucky ones," said Matthew.

"Don't blame us and say that we didn't warn you. The tribesmen you are going to visit are very ferocious people who should always be kept at bay."

The prince bought three camels and departed instantly to make arrangements for their stay with his king. Matthew and his companions were told to wait in the village until he came back.

"Listen," said the officer from the white garrison, "you won't fool me, for I'm too sly for that. You are not regular travelers, and the savage that came here with you must be a very important person, for he has a seashell in his nose that is only worn by members of the royal family."

Seeing that there was no point in pretending, they told the officer the truth. The officer had heard of Matthew because the mail arrived every few months and brought them newspapers.

"Oh, that's a different kettle of fish. In that case, you might pull it off. I have to admit that those cannibals are very hospitable, and for all I know, you have an equal chance of not returning at all, or being presented with armfuls of gifts. They have so much gold and so many diamonds that they don't know what to do with them. But they are willing to pay two handfuls of gold for worthless items like gunpowder or a mirror or pipe."

The spirits of our travelers rose markedly. The old professor lay on the sand in the sun, because the doctor told him it was good for his aching legs. In the evenings, he would visit the shacks of the locals, talk to them and jot down all the new words he heard, all of them unknown to civilization.

Felix gorged himself on so much fruit that the doctor had to give him a spoonful of castor oil from his first-aid kit. The Englishman and the Frenchman occasionally took Matthew hunting. He also learned to ride a camel, and in this way the time flowed quite pleasantly.

Once, in the middle of the night, a black servant burst into their tent shouting that they had been betrayed and were being attacked.

"Oh, poor me, I shouldn't have gone into service with white people. My tribesmen will never forgive me. They will kill me! Oh, poor me! What shall I do now?"

Everybody jumped out of their folding camp beds and took up arms, whatever they had, and waited.

It was pitch-dark outside and the assailants were nowhere to be seen. Suddenly, the distant beat of many hooves reached their ears from the desert. Even stranger, not a single shot was fired from the garrison, nor were there any visible signs of unrest.

The garrison commander knew all too well the customs of the less civilized tribes, so he understood at once that it was not an assault, but still had no idea what was going on, so he sent a scout to find out.

It turned out to be the caravan sent for King Matthew and his companions.

It was led by a royal camel with a beautiful canopy on its back. There were one hundred camels all told, well-groomed and richly adorned, and a lot of black soldiers on foot, forming the flank-guard.

What would have happened if the garrison commander was not so experienced and had opened fire? Better not to think about it. Matthew thanked the commander heartily and gave him a medal for his sensible decision.

The following morning at sunrise, the caravan set forth on its expedition. It soon turned out to be the toughest leg of their journey so far. The heat was unbearable. Of course, their hosts were accustomed to such conditions, but Matthew and his friends were literally gasping for breath.

Matthew, sitting in his canopy, had two black servants fan him with enormous ostrich feathers. The caravan moved slowly with their guide on full alert, watching for the slightest hint of a whirlwind. Unfortunately, whirlwinds were not a rare occurrence at those latitudes, and hot sand blown into the air by monstrous winds was extremely dangerous for travelers. On many occasions, whole caravans were buried in the sand, leaving no survivors.

Nobody talked all day long until late evening when cooler air brought a small measure of relief. The doctor gave Matthew some cooling powder, but it did not help much. Matthew, inured to extreme conditions by war, was no stranger to hardship, but this journey across the desert in tropical heat was by far the worst experience he had ever gone through. He suffered from constant headaches, his lips were cracked and his tongue was always bone dry. He was sunburnt and his skin, covered with red itchy spots, began to flake off. His eyes were red and stinging from the constant glare of white sand. The king could not sleep well at night and had terrible nightmares. He dreamed about being devoured by cannibals, or being burned at the stake. Oh, how pleasant water was in comparison with sand, and how nice it was to travel by ship. But there was nothing to be done; they could not withdraw, or they would immediately become a laughing stock.

Twice on their journey, the group had made camp at an oasis. What a pleasure it was to see green trees and drink cool water rather than the horrid, lukewarm, stinking swill in their leather bags.

They stayed at the first oasis for two days. When they stopped at the second, their stay had to be prolonged to five days, for the camels were so tired that they could barely walk.

"A mere four sunrises and four sunsets spent in the desert, and we will be home," observed the cannibal prince cheerfully.

Over those five days, everybody rested so well that they could not wait to resume the journey. Before their departure, the natives were so full of energy that they lit several bonfires and performed the wildest imaginable war dances.

The final four days, the homestretch of the journey, were not so hard because the desert was about to end. The sand was not so hot anymore, and here and there sun beaten bushes grew, and every now and then, they ran into small clusters of riders.

Matthew wanted to meet them but was strongly discouraged from attempting it as they were desert robbers. Of course, their caravan was safe because it included over two hundred people, and robbers preferred to attack smaller groups.

At last!

Now they could see the jungle from afar, and a damp chill was already blowing towards them. The journey was over, but who could tell what lay in store for them now? They had escaped death in the hot sands of the desert, and chances were that they would now die at the hands of the cannibals.

The first impression, however, was spectacular. The king of cannibals came to meet them with his entire court. At the head of the procession was an orchestra playing not so much music as some unbearable cacophony that seemed dangerous to normal eardrums. Instead of trumpets, they had weird horns, reed pipes, and kettles instead of drums. To say that the noise was deafening was an understatement. The musicians were also trying to sing, but all they produced were ear-piercing screams. After the silence of the desert, it was a hair-raising experience, to say the least.

The reception began with a religious ceremony involving a block of wood adorned with carvings of horrifying animal faces. The shaman also wore a terrifying animal mask. The roar of singing continued, and the interpreter said that it meant they were giving Matthew into their god's care.

When Matthew dismounted his elephant after the ceremony, the king and all his sons began to turn somersaults in the air and jump up and down. This part of the ceremony lasted about half an hour, and then the king addressed Matthew:

"White friend, brighter than the sun, thank you ever so much for coming. I'm the happiest person alive to be able to see you. I beg you, I beseech you, please give me a sign with your hand that you agree, and I will plunge this huge sword into my heart and enjoy the highest privilege of being eaten by my distinguished guest."

Saying this, he pressed the tip of his sword to his breast and waited.

Matthew said through his interpreter that he could not possibly agree to the king's request. He wanted to be friends with the king, talk to him and play, but would never dream of eating him.

At these words, the king, his wife and their children began to weep, walk on all fours and mournfully turn backward somersaults, believing that their noble guest was displeased, considered them unworthy since he did not want to eat them, or perhaps he did not believe they would be tasty.

Matthew found these strange customs very funny, but, suppressing laughter, he chose not to comment.

There is no need for a detailed account here of what Matthew saw and did in the court of the cannibal-king; no need because Matthew's adventures were described by the learned professor in his thick book entitled 'Forty-Nine Days in the Land of Savage Cannibals in the Court of King Bum-Drum—Written by a Member of the Expedition and Interpreter for King Matthew the Reformer'.

Poor King Bum-Drum went out of his way to vary Matthew's stay on his soil and make it more agreeable, but his diversions were rather wild, so Matthew, instead of taking part, just sat and looked on, for quite often these were not sights worth seeing.

There were games Matthew would never approve of, not for all the tea in China.

Bum-Drum had, for instance, an old shotgun which was, with due ceremony, taken out of the treasury vault and handed over to Matthew. He was supposed to fire it at the target, which was none other than the king's eldest daughter. Matthew firmly refused and Bum-Drum took offense.

Yet again, the royal family began to do mournful somersaults. To make things worse, the eldest cannibal shaman was also mortally offended.

"King Matthew pretends to be our friend but does not approve of our ways," he said. "But I know what to do."

In the evening, he stealthily poured poison into the conch out of which Matthew drank wine.

Drinking this type of poison caused the victim to see red, then blue, then green and black and finally death.

Matthew was sitting in the royal tent as if nothing had happened on a gold chair at a gold table and said:

"Why is everything red? The cannibals and everything else looks red…"

The moment the doctor heard this, he jumped up from his chair and began waving his hands in despair, for he knew about the poison from his learned books and that there were cures for all African diseases, but none for this toxin. Needless to say, the doctor had nothing for it in his first-aid kit.

But Matthew, unaware of the danger and still in a very good mood, said:

"Now everything is turning blue… What a nice color."

"Professor," shouted the doctor, "tell those savages that Matthew has been poisoned!"

The professor quickly told Bum-Drum what had happened. The cannibal-king clutched his head, turned a mournful somersault and shot out of the tent like an arrow.

"Have this drink, my friend!" he shouted, breathing hard and proffering Matthew a very bitter liquid in an ivory bowl.

"Yuck, I won't drink this filth. Are you trying to poison me?! Oh my! Now everything is green: the gold table is green and so is the doctor."

Bum-Drum grabbed Matthew around his waist, put him on the table, pried his mouth open with an ivory arrow and forced some of the liquid into Matthew's mouth. The boy struggled in an attempt to spit, but ended up drinking some of the precious medicine.

He was saved.

Although black circles had already begun to dance before his eyes, fortunately there were only six of them, and they soon gave way to green ones. Matthew did not die, but he slept for over three days.

The eldest cannibal shaman felt very ashamed by what he had tried to do, and Matthew forgave him. In return for this, the shaman agreed to show Matthew his most secret and clever magical tricks, which he was allowed to perform in public only three times in his lifetime.

Everybody sat down in front of a tent on the lion skins spread out for this purpose, and the show began. There were a lot of tricks too difficult for Matthew to understand, some of which were explained to him.

For example, the shaman took a tiny creature out of his magical box and put it on his hand. The animal, which resembled a tiny snake, wove itself around his finger and stuck out its small thread-like tongue, gave out a weird hiss and, attaching itself with its jaws to his finger, stood on its head. The shaman yanked the snake's head off his finger, revealing a drop of blood. All at once, the audience enthusiastically applauded the trick. Matthew was puzzled… In his lifetime, he had seen several other tricks that seemed much more difficult, but he soon understood how wrong he had been once they explained to him that the creature was more dangerous than a leopard or hyena. The bite of this small creature caused death within one second.

The shaman walked on fire, and flames went out of his mouth and nose, but he never even winced.

Then forty-nine gigantic snakes danced as he played the reed pipe. After the dance, he started to blow on an enormous palm tree that was over one hundred years old. The palm began to bend slowly and finally broke. Then he drew an invisible line in the air between two trees with his magical wand and walked along it like on a tightrope. Then he threw an ivory ball high in the air, which subsequently fell right on his head. The ball disappeared inside the magician's head, leaving no sign on his skull whatsoever. Then he began to revolve, which he did very quickly and for a long time. When he stopped, the audience saw that he actually had two faces—one that laughed, and another that cried. Then he took a small boy, cut his head off with a sword and put both head and body into a wicker box. He performed a very wild dance around it and when he kicked it, someone inside began to play the reed pipe. The moment the box was opened, the boy, in excellent health, got out of the box as if nothing had happened and began to do push-ups. The next trick was similar. The shaman released a pigeon from a cage, and when the bird was high up in the air, he shot it with his bow. The arrow pierced the pigeon, which came down to earth with a muffled thump. Instead of being dead, the bird pulled out the arrow with its beak, flew over to the shaman and returned the arrow. The pigeon flew away as fit as a fiddle.

Matthew decided that there was nothing wrong in being slightly poisoned if he could see such clever tricks afterwards.

Matthew and his traveling companions spent a lot of time exploring the cannibals' land. They often went for rides on elephants or camels, visiting all the nearby villages in the jungle. Most villagers lived in shacks; there were no brick houses to be seen. Wherever they looked, they found grease and grime. People lived with animals in the same dwellings. Many villagers suffered from various diseases, which was highly regrettable because it would not have taken much to cure most of their ailments. The doctor gave the sick people medicines, for which they were very grateful. In the jungle, they often encountered the remains of those who had fallen prey to wild animals or had been bitten by venomous snakes.

Matthew felt genuinely sorry for all those kind and good people.

Why don't they build a railroad? he thought. *Why don't they build power stations, and why don't they have cinematographs? Why can't they build comfortable houses for themselves? How about buying rifles and shotguns to defend themselves against wild beasts? After all, they have so much gold and so many diamonds that their children play with them, as if they were worthless trinkets.*

Matthew saw all too clearly that the poor black people of Africa were going through real hardship because their white brothers, who feared them, would not hear of helping them. It suddenly occurred to Matthew that on his return home, he would write to the newspapers and try to encourage those who could not find a job to go to Africa and build brick houses and railroads for their black brothers.

Matthew was racking his brains thinking how to help the cannibals, but his thoughts were also on the reforms at home, for which he needed financial backing.

They were just visiting a huge goldmine when it dawned on Matthew to ask Bum-Drum for a loan. Bum-Drum burst into a roar of laughter as he did not need gold at all and could give Matthew any amount he wanted, as much as Matthew's camels could carry.

"Would I lend my friend gold? Never in my life! No, my white friend can have anything he wants for free. Bum-Drum loves his little white friend and will be his servant till the end of time."

When Matthew was getting ready for his return journey, the cannibal-king threw a gigantic party to celebrate their friendship…and that's how it was…

Once a year, all the inhabitants of the kingdom gathered in the capital to choose those who were to be eaten by the royal court in the following year. Those who were chosen felt privileged and were very happy; those passed over were, of course, very sad. The lucky chosen performed a savage dance of joy, and the ones passed over walked on all fours—also a form of dance, but a mournful one; they also sang, but their song was very sad; they pretended to be crying.

Then the king scratched his finger with a sharp seashell, and Matthew followed suit. The king licked the drop of blood off Matthew's finger, and Matthew had to do the same with the king's blood. Matthew was disgusted with himself for taking part in such mumbo jumbo, but he also wanted to avoid offending the king. The young king reminded himself that he had been poisoned for his unwillingness to observe the cannibals' customs, so now he did not shrink away from doing what he was asked. After this 'blood brotherhood ceremony', there was more in store for Matthew: as a next step, he was thrown into a pond replete with venomous snakes and crocodiles, only to be rescued by King Bum-Drum, who jumped in after his guest and rescued him from that hell on earth. Next Matthew's body was smeared with grease, and he had to jump into a bonfire. No sooner had Matthew found himself in the flames than Bum-Drum jumped in as well and quickly dragged him to safety. King Matthew's hair was slightly singed, but otherwise, he did not suffer any harm. Finally, Matthew had to jump off a very high palm tree in order for Bum-Drum to catch him in mid-air. He did it so deftly that Matthew did not even touch the ground.

Later the professor explained to Matthew what all these theatrics were about: exchanging blood, apart from 'blood brotherhood', meant that if Matthew found himself in the desert with no water, his true friend would offer him his own blood so he would not die of thirst. Wherever danger lurked—crocodile-infested waters, raging fire or falling—Bum-Drum would rescue his white friend, even at the expense of his own life.

"We, white people," explained the professor, "want to have everything in black and white, on paper. Since they cannot write, they make contracts in a different way."

Matthew wished he could stay with his new friend longer, but he was impatient to meet the foreign kings and convince them that cannibals might be savage but are good people all the same. He hoped all three kings could be convinced to make friends with them and would not begrudge King Bum-Drum their assistance. But in order to make this dream reality, one reform was essential; namely, that King Bum-Drum and his subjects cease to be cannibals.

"Brother Bum-Drum," said Matthew when they were talking on the eve of his return home, "I kindly ask you—do stop being a cannibal!"

Matthew explained to his host at great length that it was not at all nice to eat other people, that the foreign kings would never forgive him for this bad habit and that King Bum-Drum must introduce a reform to ban eating people.

"You know, my friend, 'Needs must when the devil drives', as they say," observed Matthew. "Once the reform is carried out, a lot of white people will come here to establish a new order, and life will become far more agreeable for the inhabitants of this beautiful country."

Bum-Drum listened sadly to Matthew's words and told him that there had been one king very keen on such a reform, but he had been poisoned, and that the task was far from easy, but he would consider it.

Matthew took a short walk into the jungle to think about his talk with Bum-Drum. The night was quiet and pleasant; the moon shone brightly… But suddenly, he heard a suspicious rustle in the brush. What could it be? Perhaps a snake or a leopard. Matthew went on walking, but he still felt as if he were being watched. Now he heard footsteps behind him. He took out his revolver and waited…

It was Clue-Clue, the little daughter of the cannibal-king. The moon shone so brightly that Matthew recognized her easily, and surprised by her presence, asked in her native tongue:

"What do you want, Clue-Clue?"

"Clue-Clue kiki rec—Clue-Clue kin broom."

Matthew had learned /learnt a few words in her tongue, but that obviously was too little. However, he remembered a couple of separate words:

"Kiki, rec, broom, buzz, kin."

He knew that Clue-Clue was very sad because she was crying bitterly. He felt pity for the girl, but, not knowing what her problem was, he tried offering her his watch, a mirror and a lovely little bottle. Despite all his efforts, Clue-Clue would not stop crying.

"What could the problem be?"

When they got to his tent, Matthew asked the professor to translate the words he remembered. It turned out that Clue-Clue loved Matthew dearly and wanted to go with him to his country.

Matthew asked his interpreter to explain to Clue-Clue that she could not go on her

own, but her father, King Bum-Drum, was sure to be invited to Europe, so she could perhaps accompany him on that trip.

Matthew gave no more thought to little Clue-Clue, particularly because of all the preparations that needed to be made before the journey. Five hundred camels were being loaded with wooden boxes full of gold and precious stones as well as tons of delicious fruit, exotic beverages, various African delicacies and…wines and cigars as presents for the ministers. They agreed that in three months' time Matthew would send metal cages for the wild animals to be sent for his new zoological garden. The cannibal-king was also forewarned that Matthew might want to send various things for him by airplane and that Bum-Drum should not be frightened at the sight of a white man arriving on an enormous iron bird.

The caravan left early in the morning. The road was no easier than the first time, but they all knew what to expect and had somehow grown accustomed to the desert.

Meanwhile, the ministers had drawn up the new constitution and were waiting for the king to return. They waited and waited, but their lord and master was nowhere to be seen. What on earth had become of him? Nobody knew.

Matthew had sailed to the African coast, and then traveled by train up to the last settlement bordering the desert. There the group had stayed in tents, passing time in talks with the garrison commander until a camel caravan, sent by the cannibal-king, had arrived. That was where the trail went cold—Matthew had vanished into thin air.

Then, out of the blue, when all hope seemed lost, a telegram was received announcing that Matthew was alive and well. He had already boarded the ship and was on his way home.

"How does this kid always land on his feet?" wondered the foreign kings, not without some jealousy.

"What a lucky boy he is," commented the ministers, sighing heavily in the realization that if they thought coping with the king after his return from the war was difficult, dealing with him after his visit to the land of cannibals might prove to be impossible.

"When he returned from the war, he clapped us in jail, and now—who knows what he learned there—he might just eat us all."

Matthew was pleased as punch and proud as a peacock. His journey to the kingdom of cannibals, which at first had seemed to be such a risky endeavor, had turned out to be a tremendous success. As befitting someone coming back from the Dark Continent, Matthew was as brown as a berry from the African sun. He had also grown a couple of inches and displayed a healthy appetite. Not knowing what the ministers had been saying to each other, Matthew decided to strike a humorous note.

The moment all the royal Council was summoned he asked:

"Are the rail problems solved?"

"Yes, they are," answered the Transport Minister.

"That's good, or else I would have told the chef to cook you in crocodile sauce. How about you, Mister Minister? Have you built many new factories?"

"A lot," answered the Minister of Heavy Industry.

"Lucky you, otherwise I would make you into a roast stuffed with bananas."

It was plain that the ministers were frightened to death. Matthew could not keep a straight face anymore and burst out laughing.

"Gentlemen, you have no reason to be afraid of me. Not only have I not become a cannibal, but I'm hoping to persuade my friend, Bum-Drum, to give up those barbaric practices of his and be like us."

Matthew began to give the ministers a vivid account of his adventures in Africa, which the ministers would have dismissed as pure fantasy, but for the fact that Matthew had arrived in the capital on a train full of gold, silver and precious stones. The ministers cheered up when Matthew gave them the presents from King Bum-Drum: delicious African wines and fine cigars.

Then a manifesto was read out in which King Matthew the First appointed his people to govern the country. First, the newspapers would make known what the king and his ministers were planning to do, and then everybody would have the right to express their opinions in parliament or write to the press. The whole nation would finally be able to say whether they wanted the ministers to do one thing or not do another.

"So far, so good," said Matthew, "and now please take down what I want to do. Now that I have the necessary funds, I can take care of the children. Each child is to be given two rubber balls for the summer and a pair of skates for the winter. Every day each child will get, after school, one sweet and a cream cake. Girls will be given new dolls on a yearly basis and boys pocket knives. Carousels and swings will be built in the playground of each school. Apart from that, in bookshops all over the country, colorful pictures will be added to each and every book. This is just the beginning, for I'm planning to introduce many other reforms. So please calculate how much it is going to cost and how much time is needed to carry all this out. I will expect an answer in a week."

Can you imagine the joy of the school children at the news of Matthew's reforms? What he had given them so far had been great, but there was more to come. Much more.

Children who knew how to write now wrote to King Matthew to ask for this, that or something else. Whole sacks of letters were received from children by the royal chancellery. The secretary was opening, reading and throwing them away. That's how it had always been in the royal courts. But Matthew did not know this until he saw a lackey carrying a basket with some papers to the royal rubbish bins.

Perhaps there is a rare stamp on one of those letters, thought Matthew because he collected post stamps and had a whole album of them.

"What are those papers and envelopes?" asked Matthew.

"How am I to know?" replied the lackey.

Matthew cast an eye over the papers and saw that all the letters were addressed to him. He ordered that the letters be brought to his study at once and called the secretary.

"What are these papers, Mr. Secretary?"

"Nothing of importance—just letters to His Royal Highness."

"And you ordered the lackey to throw them away?"

"That is how it has always been."

"Then it has been a bad practice!" shouted Matthew impetuously. "If a letter is written to me, I'm the only person in the world who can say if it's important or not. And I don't want anybody to read my letters. Just deliver them to me. I will know what to do with them. Is that clear?"

"Your Royal Highness, people write letters to kings by the thousands. Sometimes they are very peculiar letters. And if their senders knew that kings actually read them, the amount of correspondence would multiply, and nobody would be able to cope with the volume. We already employ ten clerks to read them day in and day out to decide which are important and which are not."

"And which letters are important?"

"Important letters are those that come from the foreign kings, various manufacturers and great writers."

"And which letters are unimportant?"

"A large majority of letters to His Royal Highness come from children. They write whatever comes to mind. And some of them are such messy writers that the messages are impossible to decipher."

"I see. If you find it impossible to read children's letters, I'll be reading them. Give those clerks something else to do. I'm also a child, as you might have failed to notice, and yet I defeated three adult kings and recently made a journey nobody else dared to make."

The court secretary bowed low by way of reply and left while Matthew got started on his correspondence.

King Matthew the First was by nature very thorough and full of enthusiasm; whenever he undertook something, he never gave up. Now he sat in his room and began reading; he was so engrossed in his reading that he forgot to come to dinner. The Grand Master of Ceremonies had already peeped through the keyhole a couple of times, but seeing the king so busy, he did not dare to knock on the door.

This was the first time that Matthew had had no choice but to admit defeat. Some of the letters were really illegible. Matthew soon decided to ignore them. But there were also very interesting letters, beautifully written. One boy wrote to Matthew about what he would do when he got his skates. Another described a dream he had. A third wrote about his pigeons and rabbits and said he wanted to present Matthew with two pigeons and one rabbit, but did not know how to go about it. One girl wrote a short poem about King Matthew and sent it to him along with a lovely drawing. Another girl described her doll, which rejoiced at the news she would soon have a sister. There were a lot of letters with illustrations in them. One boy sent Matthew a whole album entitled 'King Matthew in the Land of Cannibals'; the pictures bore little resemblance but were very pretty, and Matthew examined them with pleasure.

But most letters contained requests. Someone asked for a pony, someone else for a bicycle, the author of the third letter wanted a camera; the fourth asked if he could have a real soccer ball instead of a rubber ball. One girl wrote that her mother was ill, and since they were poor, they could not afford to buy medicine for her. A schoolboy wrote he had no shoes to wear and could not go to school. His school report was enclosed to show that he was a good pupil.

Perhaps instead of dolls and balls, it would be better to send children shoes, thought Matthew, who had come to appreciate comfortable shoes during the war.

The king went on reading for hours when quite suddenly he felt his tummy rumbling. He rang for the lackey and asked to have his supper brought into his study, because he had some important business to attend to.

Matthew pored over the letters until the small hours of the morning. The Grand Master of Ceremonies returned to peep through the keyhole to see why the king was not yet asleep. Although he and all the lackeys were very sleepy, they had to stay awake until the king switched off the light in his bedroom.

Matthew put the letters with urgent requests in a separate pile.

"It's obvious that you can't leave the girl's mother without the medicine she needs so badly. And you can't be deaf to a request for shoes from such a good pupil."

Matthew's eyes were beginning to hurt. He thought about ignoring all the illegible letters. But that wouldn't be right. Not so long ago, Matthew's own writing was pretty sloppy, and yet he still had to sign very important papers.

A child is a child, but even a child may have serious problems that are not difficult for me to solve then and there. The child's handwriting is one thing, but problems...are problems. They need solving, and I should do what I can to help, thought Matthew. *The clerks can rewrite most of the messy letters for me.*

But when another two hours had passed, and some two hundred letters were still lying on the table, Matthew understood that he would not manage.

"I think I'd better call it a day and finish tomorrow," said Matthew to himself and, feeling dejected, he went to his bedroom.

Matthew felt that the situation was getting out of hand. If he had to read so many letters every day, he would not have time for anything else. But he would not throw the letters into the rubbish bin; that would be a rotten thing to do. They were interesting and important letters. But why were there so many of them?

On the following day, Matthew got up very early, drank a glass of milk and directed his royal steps to his study. Since he had no lessons, he read the letters until dinner. He was just as tired as after a long march or his journey across the desert. When his hunger had grown so intense that all he could think about was dinner, the door to his study opened to admit the court secretary followed by four servants.

"Today's royal correspondence, Your Majesty," said the secretary.

It seemed to Matthew that the secretary smiled, and this angered him so much that he stamped his foot and cried:

"What is it? Do you want me to go blind, Mr. Secretary?! For goodness sake, no king can possibly read such a pile of letters. How dare you make fun of the king? I will put you in prison!"

The more Matthew shouted, the better he understood that he was wrong, but at the same time he thought it unseemly to admit it.

"You employ a bunch of freeloaders who can do nothing at all but throw away children's letters or burden me with the duty of reading them."

Fortunately, the Prime Minister arrived precisely at that moment. He told the secretary to take away the sack with the royal correspondence and wait for him in the adjacent room while he had it out with the king over those unfortunate letters.

Matthew calmed down completely at the sight of the four lackeys taking away the huge sack, but he pretended to be annoyed just in case.

"Mister Prime Minister, I cannot abide a situation in which letters addressed to me go unread to the rubbish bin. Why shouldn't I know what the needs of the children in my country are? Why should a clever boy not attend school for want of usable shoes? This is an unbearable injustice, and I just can't understand how the Minister of Justice can turn a blind eye to it. It's true that my friend King Bum-Drum goes about barefoot, but he lives in a hot climate, and he's not yet civilized."

A heated debate ensued and lasted for several hours. Once again the secretary was summoned. He had been dealing with royal correspondence for at least twenty years and had handled letters written to the boy's father and grandfather—his experience was nothing to sneeze at.

"Your Royal Highness, in the days when your great-grandfather ruled, he received no more than one hundred letters daily. These were good times. In the entire kingdom, there were only one hundred thousand inhabitants who could write. Since your grandfather Peter the Erudite built schools in our country, that number has increased to two million. And then the influx of letters written to the king increased from six hundred to one thousand letters daily. It was then that my duties began to weigh heavily on me, and I employed five clerks. And since our gracious King Matthew offered a gigantic doll to the fire brigade captain's daughter, children have begun writing en masse to the palace. And now the daily number of letters varies from five to ten thousand. Most letters come on Mondays, for on Sundays, all schools are closed and children have more free time. They adore their king, so they write letters to him. I was considering asking for five more clerks because the existing clerks are beginning to run out of steam, but…"

"I know," interrupted King Matthew. "But what's the point of reading the letters if they are then consigned to the rubbish dump?"

"The letters must be read because we keep a book where each letter is filed under its own number, and—if it is legible, we make a note who wrote it and what it was about."

Matthew wanted to make sure if the secretary was telling the truth, and asked:

"Could you tell me if among the last batch letters that the lackey was told to throw away, there was one containing a request for shoes?"

"I don't remember, but we can see in a minute."

Two clerks brought in an enormous book, and there, under the number 4700000000 in black and white, was written: Christian name, family name, address, and below—synopsis: request for school shoes.

"I have been a court secretary for over twenty years, and there has always been order in my chancellery."

Justice was not foreign to Matthew's nature. He shook hands with the secretary and said:

"Thank you very much for your help, Mr. Secretary."

Finally they worked out the following scheme: the letters would be read as before by the clerks. The more interesting specimens would be picked out for Matthew, seeing that their number never exceeded one hundred. The letters with requests would be read separately, and two clerks would check whether what was in the letters was true or not.

"The boy writes that he needs shoes. How do we know whether he's lying? Who knows whether, when the king sends him a pair, he may sell them to buy some unnecessary rubbish?"

Matthew had to admit that the remark made sense. He remembered one soldier on the front who sold his shoes and bought booze instead, and then demanded a new pair saying that the old ones had outlived their usefulness.

"It is such a pity that you cannot trust people. But that's life."

"Perhaps it would be a good idea—after the royal clerks have checked the veracity of the letter—if the royal chancellery sent for the child. After an audience with Your Majesty, Your Majesty could give the gift personally."

Oh, that does seem to be a good idea, thought Matthew. *It would be nice to give audiences not only to foreign diplomats and ministers, but also to children.*

"Very well then," declared Matthew.

Now he knew what he had to do, as the king of children. In the morning, he would have lessons until twelve o'clock. At noon, his royal lunch would be served, followed by an hour for receiving deputies and ministers, and then until dinner he would read letters. After dinner he would give audiences to children, then conduct the Cabinet meeting until supper time, and then—retire to his bed.

When his daily schedule was ready, Matthew suddenly grew very sad. It was becoming clear, he would not have a single hour for fun and games. Heigh-ho! After all he was king, and although still very small, he had to take care not only of himself, but of everybody else as well.

Maybe a little later, when he had given the needy their due, he would have more time for himself. Perhaps an hour a day…?

"After all, I've already traveled a lot. In my short life, I have attended many balls and theater plays. I was at the seaside for a month and I was in the cannibal kingdom; so now instead of playing, I can get down to business and set about my royal duties."

Now his daily life was organized like clockwork.

After his morning lessons, Matthew had the letters read to him. The clerk who read them was as quick as a flash, and since, while listening, it was hard for Matthew to stay in one place, he soon took to pacing with his hands behind his back. The doctor advised him, weather permitting, to conduct this letter reading in the garden, which was a very good idea—business and pleasure in one.

The audiences were endless. Both foreign and domestic diplomats were frequent guests. Foreigners asked mainly about the inaugural session of the parliament as everybody was anxious to see how the whole nation would govern. Matthew's own ministers arrived with the manufacturers who were to put up carousels and swings all over the kingdom to ask the monarch how he wanted it done. From the most remote places in the world, various savage people arrived to declare that their rulers wished to strike up a friendship with King Matthew.

If King Matthew could be on friendly terms with Bum-Drum, the king of cannibals, he was unlikely to turn down their offers of friendship, for savage as he and his people were, they had given up eating people a long time ago.

"In my country, they stopped eating people thirty years ago, said one."

"And in mine the last man was consumed forty years ago. And even that was an exceptional case. He was a great loafer and a rascal to boot—absolutely good for nothing, a black character. His only advantage was his great fatness. When he was tried in court for idleness for the fifth time, it was agreed that he should be eaten."

King Matthew was more cautious now; he did not promise anything outright, asked to have what was said in writing and told the foreign envoys to return for his answer in a week's time. He would have to consult the Foreign Minister, and everything would be clear after the Cabinet meeting.

The audience with the children was a pure pleasure. The kids were allowed in the throne room one by one to receive what they had asked for in their letters. Each child was assigned a number that corresponded to the number on the parcel. Nobody was granted an audience until it was determined that the sender of the letter really needed what he or she had asked for in their letter and until the item was bought at the behest of Matthew. Everything proceeded smoothly, and the children were pleased to be given their presents.

One boy got a warm coat. Another was given books that he needed for school and which his parents could not afford. Girls often asked for combs and toothbrushes. Those who drew well received crayons and water paints. One boy very much wanted a violin, for he had been able to play the mouth organ for some time but got tired of it. The boy jumped up and down for joy when he was given the instrument in a beautiful case.

Sometimes, during audiences, children asked for something they had not mentioned in their letter, and Matthew did not like that at all. One girl, who had just been given a lovely dress for her aunt's wedding, asked for a doll reaching for the sky.

"That is stupid," said Matthew dryly, "and if you ask for too much, you will get nothing, not even the dress you wrote to ask for."

All in all, Matthew was now an experienced ruler, and no girl could twist him around her little finger. Not anymore.

Once during the after-dinner audience, the king heard an unusual noise in the hall. He was not surprised at first, because the children became fidgety from waiting their turn and ceased to be as meek as lambs. But the noise did not sound anything like something made by a child. It sounded like a grownup making a fuss about something. Matthew sent a lackey out to see what was going on. The servant returned to report that some gentleman was insisting on seeing the king. Matthew, his curiosity aroused, agreed to see the intruder.

A moment later a young, long-haired gentleman with a briefcase entered the throne room. Without sketching anything remotely like a bow, he started speaking loudly, paying little attention to court etiquette:

"Your Royal Highness, I'm a journalist, which means that I write for a newspaper. I've been trying to have an audience with Your Majesty for a month, and they never let me in. They keep repeating 'tomorrow, tomorrow', and then tell me to come the following day because the king is too tired to see me. Until today!

Today I said I was the father of a certain child in the hope that this would help me get in easier. I was wrong. The lackeys recognized me on the spot and would not allow me in. As it happens, the matter I've come with is very important. To be quite truthful, it's more than one problem, and I'm sure Your Royal Highness will be kind enough to give me a hearing."

"OK," said King Matthew, "but you'll have to wait till I have received all the children because these are their hours. And then, of course, I will be at your disposal."

"And will Your Majesty let me stay in the throne room while the audience lasts? I'll stand here quietly and won't be a nuisance to you at all. And tomorrow, I'll describe a royal audience in the newspapers, which will interest our readers very much."

Matthew ordered that a chair be brought for the journalist, and the latter sat quietly making notes in his notebook.

"Now you can begin your story," said Matthew when the last child left the royal hall.

"My lord," said the journalist, "I won't take much of your valuable time. I'll make it short and sweet."

But in direct opposition to that assurance, the journalist spoke for three hours or so. Matthew listened very carefully, and at last he said:

"I see that the matter is really very serious. So please stay for supper, and when we have eaten, we will go into my study and you can finish your story."

The journalist spoke until eleven p.m., and Matthew paced up and down the study with his hands behind his back, listening as attentively as ever.

It was the first time Matthew had seen a man who wrote for the papers. The king had to admit that the reporter was very clever despite being an adult and that he was unlike any of his ministers.

"You write articles, yes? And do you draw as well?"

"No, in each editorial staff, there are people who write, and those who draw. If Your Royal Highness would do us the honor of visiting our office, we would be extremely happy."

Matthew had not left the palace for a long time, so he decided to take the reporter up on his invitation, and the following morning he went to the editorial office by car.

This impressive building was decorated with national flags and flowers in honor of the royal visit—it was a red-carpet reception in the literal sense of the expression. On the ground floor were huge machines which printed the newspapers. Above the printing office was a depository from which the newspaper was sent to the post office and sold. On the left was the booking office where classified advertisements and payments were received. Still higher was the editorial staff office where gentlemen sat around several tables to write articles which were promptly printed on the ground floor. Matthew got into the thick of things: here telegrams were received from around the world, there the telephone rang; busy boys ran to and fro, carrying articles, notes and photos to the printing office. Here reporters wrote, there cartoonists drew, and over there the rumble of the printing press rumbled just like in the war during close quarter combat.

Matthew was presented the latest edition of the newspaper on a silver tray. On the front page was a photo of the king with some children during one of the audiences, and under the photo were the children's questions and Matthew's answers.

Matthew spent two hours in the newspaper headquarters, and he liked it very much, especially the hustle and bustle of the place and the fact that everybody knew their duties so well. He was no longer surprised that newspapers reported so much information about so many things at once—earthquakes, fires, thefts, car crashes, and the actions of kings and ministers around the world.

The journalist who had an audience with him yesterday was right when he said that the newspapers knew everything. How quickly they reported on his stay with foreign kings, and they wrote so much about the war and knew at once that Matthew was returning from the land of the cannibals!

"So why didn't you know that I had escaped to fight the war and that only a porcelain doll remained in the capital impersonating me?"

"Oh, we knew all too well, but we could not write everything. The newspapers print only those things which are necessary, and information that the public doesn't need to know, we keep to ourselves. The nation has no business knowing certain things. And more importantly, we must remember that the outside world, which is not always friendly to us, will also read our newspapers."

Matthew once again talked to the journalist long into the night, and that is what the king told him:

"All the things that I'm doing are not reforms. I'm not yet a reformer, but I could become one. I want to give my whole nation the power to rule. But the children are also part of the nation, so they must also have power. So there should be two parliaments: one for adults, and the other one for children. Let the children choose their own deputies and let them speak for themselves. They will then say whether they prefer chocolate, dolls, pocket knives or something else. Maybe they will choose sweets, or shoes, or money so that everyone can buy themselves whatever they please. The children should also have a newspaper just like grownups. It should appear daily. And they should write in it what they want the king to do for them, and not what the king thinks fit, because he can't possibly be aware of everything; he can't know everything like the newspapers do. For example, not all the children were given chocolate when I ordered it, because in the countryside the clerks ate it themselves; in many villages, the children didn't even know that they were to be given some chocolate, because they don't have their own newspaper."

All of this seemed so obvious to Matthew that he believed he should have already thought it up all on his own a long time ago. Now that he had spent two long evenings with the journalist, it all clicked into place, and he raised the issue at the Cabinet meeting.

"Ministers," began Matthew, taking a sip of water before starting what was going to be a long speech, "we have taken steps to allow the people to rule and articulate their needs. But you have forgotten, gentlemen, that the nation is not only composed of adults; children are a part of it as well. We have several million children—so they too should govern. Let there be two parliaments: one for our grownups with their ministers and deputies, and the other for our children, with their own ministers and deputies. I'm king of both adults and children, and if the grownups regard me as too small for them, so be it. Let them choose one for themselves, and I will be the children's king only."

Matthew drank water four times, and the ministers soon understood that this was no laughing matter involving chocolate, skates or swings, but a very serious reform indeed.

"I know that it is difficult," concluded Matthew. "There are no easy reforms. But we have to get started. If I don't succeed, my son or my grandson will have to take up my banner and finish my reforms."

The ministers bent their heads. It was the first time King Matthew had given such a clever and lengthy speech. He was absolutely right—the children were also part of the nation, and as such they also had the right to rule. But how to bring it about? Were they really fit to govern or were they too stupid?

The ministers simply could not say that the children were too stupid for the simple reason that Matthew, their lord and master, was a child himself. Well, it could not be helped: they needed to give it a try. A newspaper by children for children could certainly be founded. Matthew had brought in a lot of gold, so they had the money. The question was, however, who would write for such a newspaper?

"I have already a journalist."

"And who's going to be minister?"

"I have a good candidate: Felix."

Matthew still thought highly of Felix and cared for their friendship, because Felix often teased him by saying:

"Great men's favors are uncertain. Felix was good during the war under enemy fire. But Stanley and Helen are better companions at the theater, to attend balls, to pick seashells at the seaside. And again when it comes to visiting the dangerous land of savage cannibals, mommy can't bear to let her children go. But Felix? You can always count him in. I'm an ordinary platoon commander's son, and not a captain's. Perhaps something dangerous will develop soon, and then, who but Felix will prove to be a best friend."

It is very unpleasant when you are accused of being too proud or worse still—ungrateful. This was the perfect occasion to convince Felix that he was not a foul-weather friend needed only for dirty jobs. Moreover, Felix happened to be the perfect candidate because he was forever running the streets, knew about life, the children and their needs.

Poor Matthew. He wanted so much to be a real king, to govern by himself, to understand what it was all about. Now at last, all these wishes were coming true. Little did he know, however, how much work and how many problems and worries would fall on his head.

At home, everything went well. In the woods, they began building houses for the children; builders, bricklayers, carpenters, stove makers, tinsmiths, locksmiths and glaziers were completely snowed under, but were glad to be making money hand over fist. Brickyards, sawmills, glassworks and a special factory producing ice skates worked at full capacity. Four new confectioneries and chocolate factories were opened. Special cages were being made for wild beasts as well as custom-built train cars for animal transport by rail. Such cars were not easy to design, and they cost a small fortune, especially those built to house elephants and camels, to say nothing of the one designed for giraffes because of their extremely long necks. Outside the city, gardeners were now laying out the zoological garden. Two gigantic buildings were under construction: the future houses of parliament—one for the adults, and the other one for the children, where deputies from the whole country would hold debates and introduce new laws, new rules and regulations.

In the children's parliament, everything was like the one for adults with a few exceptions. Door knobs were placed lower so that small deputies could open the doors themselves. The chairs had shorter legs to accommodate the shorter legs of the deputies, and the windows were not as high so that the deputies could look through them, if the debates did not prove to be very gripping.

The locksmiths and workers were glad to be able to earn money. Glad were the manufactures, which now churned out high profits. Glad were the children, for the king cared about them. The children read their newspaper where everybody wrote what they pleased, and those who could not read were now learning at a breakneck pace, because they wanted to know what was happening, and write freely to their paper about their own problems.

The parents and the teachers were also glad that their children were so diligent. Scuffles among schoolchildren, once such a commonplace, were now few and far between, because everybody wanted to be liked and possibly be elected as a deputy.

Now not only the army loved King Matthew, but he was adored by almost everybody.

"Such a small king, and he's been so quick to learn to govern, and so well at that," they said.

Little did the nation know what problems lay ahead of Matthew. The worst of all was that the foreign kings began to envy Matthew's success.

"Who the hell does he think he is?" they repeated through clenched teeth. "We've been reigning for a long time, and Matthew wants to be the first among equals straight away. It's easy to play a guy with a heart of gold with someone else's money. Bum-drum gave him gold, and Matthew is buying love and respect with it. By the way, is it seemly for a white ruler to be on such friendly terms with cannibals?"

Matthew knew about all this from his spies, and the Foreign Minister warned that war was again in the air. War was the last thing Matthew wanted at that moment. He was focused on his reforms and did not want to get distracted. How would that work? Most bricklayers would have to go to the front and leave the children houses unfinished. Matthew wanted the children to go to the countryside during the coming summer and planned inaugural sessions of both parliaments for autumn.

"What can I do to prevent war?" Matthew asked the Foreign Minister, pacing the throne room to and fro with his hands behind his back.

"We have to try and divide the foreign rulers. While they are quarreling with each other, we will renew our friendship only with the strongest of them."

"Oh, that would be an excellent solution. I think that the third king, the sad one who played the violin, could make lasting peace with us. He told me that he had been against the war. As a matter of fact, he did not suffer serious losses because his armies were kept in reserve, and it was he who advised me to carry out reforms for our children."

"What Your Royal Highness has just said is very important," observed the Foreign Minister. "Yes, he can make friends with us, but the remaining two will always be our enemies."

"But why?" asked Matthew frowning.

"The first one does not like it at all that the people will govern in our country."

"But it's none of his business!"

"I'm afraid it is. The moment his people learn what's going on here, they'll want to have the same system in their country. As the king is unlikely to give in, they will likely have a revolution."

"How about the second one?"

"The second? We can probably come to terms with him. He's mostly angry with us, for now the savage kings prefer Your Royal Highness to him. They used to send him presents, but now they have chosen Your Majesty. We could make a deal with him—he can retain all the Oriental kings, while we will be friends with the African ones."

"OK, let's give peace a chance, because I don't want to make war!" said Matthew decidedly.

The same evening, Matthew started writing a letter to the sad king who played the violin.

My spies have reported that the foreign kings envy me my good relations with Bum-Drum who sends me gold, and are likely to attack me once again. So I ask Your Royal Highness kindly to become my friend and save your anger for them.

Matthew also described his reforms to the sad king and asked his advice what to do next. He wrote how busy he was and asked the sad king not to be worried if someone in his parliament shouted 'Down with the king!' out of anger about something which the king had failed to do. The truth was, of course, that there are plenty of fish in the sea, and there were certainly those who were pleased with their ruler.

It was late at night when Matthew put down his pen. Then he went out onto the balcony of the royal palace and gazed at his capital. Streetlights were burning, but all the windows in the vicinity were dark because everybody was already asleep.

"All the children are sleeping so peacefully, and I'm staying up to write letters to prevent the war so that the children's houses can be finished in the countryside and the children can stay there throughout the summer. A child cares only about his or her school and toys, and I do not even have time to study or play because I have to think about all the children in my country."

Matthew returned to his bedroom, where he gazed sadly at his toys. They lay undisturbed, covered with dust, and Matthew did not remember when he had touched them last.

"My marionette," said Matthew to his puppet, "you must be angry with me for not playing with you for such a long time. You are a wooden marionette, and if nobody breaks you in half, you can lie patiently never asking for anything."

With this short monologue, King Matthew turned off the light and was just about to fall asleep when he remembered that he had not written a letter to the second king suggesting that he take presents from the Oriental kings and leave Matthew's African friends alone.

What should he do? The two letters had to be sent together. He could not postpone them. What would happen if they declared war before receiving those letters?

So our brave king got up in spite of the headache he had earned by writing until the wee hours. It was completely light outside by the time a long letter to the second king was ready.

So, after a sleepless night, Matthew worked all day long and the day proved very difficult.

A telegram came from the seaside town that King Bum-Drum had sent a ship full of wild animals and gold, but the transport was denied passage through the territory of one of the foreign kings.

The ambassadors of the foreign kings, who had an audience with King Matthew the following morning, said that their states did not agree that presents from cannibals should be transported through their countries. It was true that they had agreed once to give him free passage, but that did not mean they had to listen to Matthew, who had obviously gone too far. The fact that he had defeated them once did not mean much, now that they had bought new heavy guns and could not wait to test them. In any case, they were not afraid of Matthew anymore.

It was clear from the start that the ambassadors were spoiling for a fight, and one of them even stamped his foot, but the Grand Master of Ceremonies called him to order by reminding him that etiquette did not permit one to stamp one's foot in the presence of the king.

At first Matthew's face grew red with anger as the blood of Henry the Impetuous flowed through his veins, and when they said they were not afraid of Matthew, he was itching to cry out:

"I'm not afraid of you either! Let's fight it out and we'll see who's right!"

But a moment later his face paled, and he began to speak as if he did not understand what was happening:

"Gentlemen, there is no need to get so angry. I have absolutely no intention of frightening your kings. It so happens that last night I wrote two letters offering my friendship to your kings. Please pass these letters on to your masters, and I'll soon write to the first king. If you do not accept the transport of King Bum-Drum's presents through your beautiful countries free of charge, I will be happy to pay whatever they see fit to ask. Pray tell your kings that I did not mean to hurt anybody's feelings."

The ambassadors did not know what was in the letters Matthew had written to their kings, because the envelopes were glued shut and bore the royal seal, so they did not say anything more but left murmuring under their breath.

Matthew had a word in secret with the journalist, then another with Felix and then a meeting with the ministers. These sessions were followed by a string of audiences, and then the king had to sign some documents, and to top it all off, a military parade celebrating the anniversary of the battle won in the days of Paul the Conqueror had been scheduled.

All this after a sleepless night! It was no wonder that Matthew looked a sight in the evening when a worried doctor had a look at him.

"You have to take care of your health," warned the doctor. "Your Royal Highness has been working too hard for too long. Your Majesty eats too little and sleeps far less than required. You will fall ill with consumption and begin spitting blood."

"I already spat blood yesterday," said Matthew.

The doctor became even more frightened, but fortunately the blood turned out to be from a lost baby tooth and not consumption.

"Where is the tooth?" asked the Grand Master of Ceremonies the next morning.

"I threw it in the wastepaper bin."

The Grand Master of Ceremonies said nothing but thought:

Alas, the time has come when royal teeth are being thrown in the garbage. According to court etiquette, royal teeth should be mounted in gold, put in a box inlaid with diamonds and kept in the treasure vault.

It was about time a congress of kings was organized. As Matthew had already paid them a visit, it was his turn to invite them to his capital. Secondly, the inaugural sessions of the two parliaments called for pomp and circumstance, and the presence of the three foreign kings would certainly add to the dignity of the occasion. Furthermore, Matthew needed to show them his new brainchild—the zoo. Most importantly, they had to establish once and for all whether they wished to live in peace or not.

Letter after letter was sent, telegram followed telegram, and ministers came and went. It was a matter of life and death and the choice was simple: friendship between kings and peaceful work towards making the world a better place to live in, a place where everybody had a well-paid job, where everything was cheap and of good quality…or another war.

Cabinet meetings were held day and night. The same flurry of activity was going on in Matthew's palace and the residences of the foreign kings abroad.

Having been granted an audience with King Matthew, one of the ambassadors said upon arrival:

"My king wants to live in peace with Your Majesty."

"Then why is your king forming new army divisions and building new fortresses? If someone wants peace, he does not build new fortifications."

"My king," said the ambassador, "has lost one war, so he has to be on his guard, which does not mean that he wants to attack Your kingdom."

"But my spies have reported that it is the first king who is making the most threats against me."

In point of fact, it was not the king himself who was pressing for war with Matthew, for he was old and tired, but his eldest son, heir to the throne, who could not wait to declare war on King Matthew. Matthew's spies even overheard one conversation between the old king and his son.

"You are old and weak," said the son. "It will be best if you give up the throne, and I will take care of this Matthew once and for all."

"What harm did Matthew do to you? He's very nice and I like him very much."

"Like it or not, he wrote a letter to the sad king asking him to break ranks with us and join forces with him. He wants to give the second king all the Oriental monarchs and keep Bum-Drum and the rest of the black African kings for himself. Who shall we be left with? Who will send us gold and gifts? And as soon as we are alone and they are on friendly terms with Matthew, all three will attack us. We must build two new fortresses and have more troops."

The son of the old king knew all of this because he had a spy network and his agents reported on everything they saw or heard to their paymaster. The old king had to agree to more troops and the construction of additional fortresses, because he was afraid that if another war broke out and he lost again, his son would say:

"Didn't I tell you all along that this was bound to happen? Had you given the throne to me, we wouldn't have lost the war, and we wouldn't have lost face."

That is how it was all autumn long. Nobody knew who would make friends with whom.

The truth was only exposed when Matthew sent out invitations to all of them.

Yes, it will be our pleasure to attend, but on one condition: that Matthew does not invite Bum-Drum. We are white kings, and we do not want to sit at the same table with cannibals. Our royal upbringing and our honor do not allow us to fraternize with savages.

Poor Matthew was deeply offended by this answer, because it suggested that Matthew himself was uncouth and dishonorable. The Foreign Minister advised the king to pretend that he had overlooked or misunderstood the slight, but Matthew would not hear of it.

"I don't want to pretend that I misunderstood it. I, for one, will take 'no' for an answer. They have offended not only me, but my friend as well. Bum-Drum promised me loyalty through thick and thin and is ready to die for me in water, fire and air; and to prove how much he loved me, he even wanted me to eat him. The hard facts are: he was wild, very wild, but he has promised to reform. He's my true friend, he trusts me and I trust him. Our countries don't spy on each other, of that I'm sure. And the white kings are just jealous! I vow to write and explain all of this to them."

The Foreign Minister was terribly frightened at his words.

"Your Royal Highness does not want another war, and such an answer would be tantamount to a declaration of war. Of course, we should answer them, but in a different way."

Matthew had another sleepless night, but this time his answer to the foreign kings was written with his ministers.

What it boiled down to was:

King Matthew made friends with King Bum-Drum so that the latter would give up cannibalism. Bum-Drum promised Matthew that he would not eat people any more. If Bum-Drum did not keep his word, it was because he was afraid of being poisoned by his priests who do not want their people to become civilized. At any rate, Matthew was ready to verify if Bum-Drum had given up cannibalism or not and would soon give the white kings an answer.

In conclusion, Matthew wrote:

Let me assure Your Royal Highnesses that I also hold dear my black friend's honor and my own, and I'm ready to defend my honor at the expense of my blood or even my life.

This, of course, meant that the foreign kings should beware of Matthew's wrath because he would not let anybody offend him, even though he was reluctant to begin a new war.

The foreign kings replied:

Should Bum-Drum truly stop being a cannibal, he will be allowed to take part in our congress.

The foreign kings, and more precisely, the first one, wanted to delay the whole thing because his fortresses were not yet ready.

Before Matthew's reply, the foreign kings reasoned along these lines:

"If Matthew were to write that Bum-Drum was no longer a cannibal, then we will write that the black African kings are lying, treacherous and not to be trusted, so we, the foreign kings, cannot pay Matthew a visit."

But they did not expect Matthew to play such a trick on them, and Matthew, the moment he received their answer, announced:

"I'm going to pay him a visit by airplane to make sure he's not eating human flesh."

Try as the ministers might, they could not talk Matthew out of such a dangerous escapade. The wind could blow the airplane down, they could run out of gas, the pilot could lose his bearings, or something could go wrong with the engine.

Even the manufacturer, who was commissioned to make the airplane, a man who knew his trade inside and out, tried to dissuade Matthew:

"I cannot guarantee you that the airplane won't suffer any damage after five days in the air. Airplanes usually fly in colder zones, and we don't know whether the heat can cause something to go wrong. Besides, even if something as trivial as a loose screw happens, there are no mechanics in the desert that can repair a faulty plane."

To make matters worse, the airplane could only carry Matthew and the pilot. How was Matthew going to communicate with Bum-Drum without the professor who knew fifty languages?

Matthew nodded his head to show that he fully appreciated that the journey was very difficult and dangerous, that he could indeed perish in the sands of the desert, and that having no interpreter would not help him communicate with Bum-Drum, but nevertheless he knew what he was about to do—he would go to Africa and then he would cross the desert by air.

He asked the manufacturer not to spare any expense in hiring the best specialists available and importing the best tools and materials to build the finest airplane he had ever produced—as soon as possible.

The manufacturer put aside all his other orders and hired all of the best mechanics he could find, who worked around the clock in three shifts. The chief engineer in the factory pored over his calculations so thoroughly and so often that he finally went mad and had to spend two months in a sanatorium. Matthew visited the factory day in and day out, spending a few hours each time inspecting each nut and bolt carefully.

What impression the news of Matthew's plans created at home and abroad is not difficult to imagine. The newspapers left hardly any room for articles other than those concerning the royal journey. In the press, Matthew was referred to as 'King of the Air', 'King of the Desert', 'Matthew the Great' and 'Matthew the Insane'.

"This will be the end of him," repeated those who envied Matthew his luck.

So, contrary to the saying that 'Good things always come in threes', they predicted his third trip would have an unlucky outcome.

Matthew took a long time to find a pilot. Only two volunteers came forward. One was a little bit past his 'best-by' date—over sixty, legless and with only one eye. The second was none other than Felix.

The pilot without legs happened to be the senior mechanic in the factory, which was assembling Matthew's airplane. He was already flying at a time when airplanes were still very unreliable and often crashed. He himself had survived seven crashes and was badly injured four times, losing his eye, crushing both legs, breaking two ribs and suffering such a serious concussion that he spent over a year in hospital, even losing his speech temporarily. His last accident had grounded him for a while, but his love for airplanes was so great that he soon returned to work assembling flying machines.

Now, despite his obvious disabilities, he declared his readiness to fly Matthew to Africa; his hands were strong, and his one good eye was as valuable as two.

It did not take much to convince Felix that he had no chance to compete with such an experienced pilot. Felix decided to withdraw his name as a candidate, believing as everyone else did, that it was a flight of no return.

But 'Matthew the Insane' and his legless pilot thought otherwise. They departed without a shred of fear between them.

Smoking his pipe, the commander of the white garrison was sitting in the radiotelegraph cubicle engaged in small talk.

"What a nuisance to be sitting in this African village on the edge of the desert and far from the civilized world. Since King Matthew visited the area, traffic has increased considerably. Hundreds of wagons have traveled through the village with wild beasts and sacks full of gold from King Bum-Drum to Matthew, and this has made things even worse. These animals will be living in Matthew's capital, in a beautiful town inhabited by white people, but I have to sit in this desert till the end of time. In the old good days, at least the Africans were unruly, and you had to fight them so there was at least something to do. Now that they're friends with King Matthew, they're as meek as mice and never attack us, which makes me wonder what we're doing here. Another year or two and we will forget how to shoot."

The telegraph operator wanted to say something by way of an answer when the telegraph rang.

"Oh, there is news!"

The apparatus gave off a series of clicks, producing a sequence of black letters on the white strip of paper.

"Oh, quite interesting news!"

"What is it?"

"Well, I don't know yet. Just a second…"

Tomorrow at 4 p.m., King Matthew will arrive by train. He plans to fly across the desert by airplane to visit Bum-Drum. The airplane will be transported on the same train. Top Secret: whoever is charged with unloading the plane must damage it so that Matthew cannot fly.

"I see," said the commander. "It looks as if our kings do not like it at all that Matthew is on such good terms with King Bum-Drum. This is a despicable order. They didn't want to make friends with the cannibals themselves but are ready to stab Matthew in the back for doing so. How wicked of them! But it can't be helped, I'm an officer and orders have to be carried out."

The commander called for a trusted soldier and told him to dress up as a railroad porter, explaining:

"Railroad porters here are generally black, so when Matthew sees one who's white, he'll certainly hire him to keep an eye on the savages so they don't damage the flying apparatus. Your task is to unscrew some part or find another way to immobilize the airplane."

"Yes, sir!" said the soldier, walking away to disguised himself.

Sure enough, the train soon arrived and Matthew and his pilot got off. Black porters crowded around Matthew, and he began gesticulating with his hands to show the porters how to remove the machine from the platform car without damaging it. Matthew was not sure if they understood him. Fortunately, the arrival of a white man appeased his fears. Matthew, pleased as punch, said:

"I'll pay you well, but please explain everything to the porters and see that they don't damage my plane."

Meanwhile the commander ran up to Matthew, pretending that he had just learned about the king's arrival.

"What? By airplane? Well, well, a wonderful journey, isn't it? Why tomorrow? Why so quickly? Why don't you stay with us for a couple of days? Your Royal Highness could at least rest a bit. Oh, do come around to my place for supper."

Matthew accepted gladly, but the pilot declined the invitation, insisting on remaining with his airplane.

"I prefer to oversee everything with my one good eye, in case the porters should tamper with one thing or another."

"Oh, don't you worry, I will keep an eye on them," said the soldier disguised as a porter.

But the legless pilot stood his ground. He would not move until they had assembled the airplane and taken off.

There was nothing to do but respect the pilot's decision. First, the porters unloaded the wings separately, then the fuselage with the engine and the propeller. Then they began the assembly of the entire airplane. The disguised porter tried time and again to get rid of the pilot, but in vain. At last, he offered him a 'sleeping cigar'. The pilot took a few puffs and soon fell asleep.

"Let this white man sleep. He's very tired from the journey, and you're obviously tired from all this work," said the white porter to the black ones. "Here's your money; you can go to the canteen and order yourselves some drinks."

With the black porters gone and the pilot sleeping, the soldier was free to do what he pleased. Without further ado, he unscrewed the most important flywheel and dug it deep in the sand under a palm tree. With that part removed, the airplane would definitely not fly!

The pilot woke up after an hour or so, feeling both guilty and ashamed that he had fallen asleep instead of keeping an eye on the black porters. Still a bit dizzy, he finished assembling the airplane and then called the porters over to roll the flying machine across the station platform and up to the camp.

"How did it go?" the commander asked the false porter with a sly smile.

"Everything's all right, everything's fine. The flywheel's been unscrewed and buried under a palm tree nearby. Shall I fetch it?"

"No, what's the point? Let it rest in peace."

An hour before sunrise, Matthew began getting ready for the flight. He took a four-day water supply, just a little food and two revolvers. They tanked the airplane up and took some oil and grease for the engine, and that was it—the airplane was to be as light as possible.

"Everything is ready. Let's fly!"

But what was wrong? The engine was not working. What could it be? The pilot had packed and assembled it himself.

"The flywheel is missing!" exclaimed the pilot suddenly. "Who on earth could have unscrewed it?"

"What wheel?" asked the garrison officer, pretending astonishment.

"It was here, secured to this shaft. We can't fly without it."

"Haven't you brought a spare wheel?"

"Am I going crazy? I brought the things that could be broken or stop working on the way, but the flywheel could neither break nor stop working."

"Perhaps you forgot to install it."

"That's not possible! I bolted it on myself in the factory. I saw it yesterday when the engine was being removed from its case. Someone must have removed it on purpose."

"If the wheel was made of shining metal, then the black porters might have taken it," said the garrison officer. "After all, they are very fond of shiny objects."

Matthew, deeply worried by such a grave setback, stood brooding beside the airplane when all of a sudden, a shiny object in the sand nearby caught his eye.

"And what's over there, shining like a mirror? Go and have a look, gents!"

No words could have described their surprise when they saw that the shiny object was the very wheel they were looking for.

"What a devilish country!" exclaimed the pilot. "Very strange things are happening here! All my life, I have never fallen asleep at work—until yesterday. Various things have broken down or ceased to function in my airplanes, but never have I seen a flywheel come off; it is always screwed on as tightly as possible. And how could it have gotten there?"

"Let's not hurry to take off," said Matthew. "In fact, we've already lost an hour."

The garrison officer and the soldier, who was now standing nearby in his battledress, were even more surprised.

This must be some cheap trick of those black devils! thought the soldier, and he was absolutely right. In fact, when the porters went to the canteen, they began to talk about the strange machine they had been unloading from the train.

"Just like a bird, but much bigger. They say the white king is to fly in it to the cannibal-king, King Bum-Drum."

"Think of something and those whites are sure to invent it!" remarked the black porters, shaking their heads in utter amazement.

"For me," said one old African, "that 'living' white man is far stranger than the 'dead' bird. I've been working for the whites over thirty years, and I have never once seen a white guy taking pity on a black worker and giving him money before the work was finished."

"Where did he come from? Did he arrive with the king?"

"I'll bet you a glass of rum that he's one of the locals from the garrison, disguised as a porter—he knows our language far too well."

"And did you notice that the legless pilot fell asleep after the white man gave him a cigar. It must have been a sleeping cigar."

"There must be something to it," they agreed.

When their work was done and with the white porter gone, they sat not far from the palm under which the wheel had been buried. Suddenly, a young boy shouted:

"Look, someone's been digging here: the sand's still wet!"

It dawned on them that when they had initially come to unload the iron bird, the sand had been undisturbed.

They began to dig and, finding the wheel, their suspicions were confirmed.

What were they to do? The whites were trying to pull a trick on Matthew, a tiny king so loved by the black people. They had been making a pretty penny since they began unloading the heavy cages, wooden boxes and sacks from Bum-Drum's camels, and then loading them onto the cars of that fire-belching dragon which the whites called a train.

Something had to be done. But what? If they went straight to Matthew to return the wheel, they risked being severely punished by the garrison commander. Finally, they decided to sneak into the camp at night and put the wheel somewhere near the iron bird.

And that's what they did. So, thanks to the help of these kind-hearted Africans, Matthew was able to take off as planned and embark on the final leg of his journey.

They were lost!

Anyone who has not had a similar experience will never understand how much terror these words convey.

If you get lost in the woods, at least there are trees to use as landmarks, or the odd secluded gamekeeper's hut. There are berries galore for picking and crystal clear streams for fresh water, not to mention the possibility of enjoying a lovely nap under any tree you wish. If a ship loses her bearings, there are usually other people aboard to talk to and cheer you up, there is a stockpile of food, and you might even see some islands. But to get lost, with only one other person, in the air over the desert, is probably the most dreadful thing that can befall you. No policeman to ask the way, no traffic signs showing the right direction, no option of falling asleep to regain your strength.

You are sitting in this awesome iron bird, and you know that it is speeding like an arrow, but you do not know where. One thing you do know is that it will speed onwards just as long as it has gas and oil for its engine—yet it will drop out of the sky the moment it runs out of fuel. With the demise of the gigantic bird, there is no hope, only the specter of death in the hot sands of the desert.

Two days before, they had flown over the first oasis, yesterday over the second, and this morning at seven they should have flown over the third, putting them in Bum-Drum's kingdom by 4 p.m. The itinerary had been calculated by no fewer than twenty eminent professors. They made allowances for the wind. They had taken into account just one direction because in the air there are no obstacles to steer clear of.

So, what had happened?

At seven this morning, they should have flown over the third and final oasis, and now it was seven forty, and the oasis was nowhere to be seen—just sand and more sand.

"How long can we remain in the air?"

"Six hours at the most. We have gas for a longer flight, but this beast drinks enormous quantities of oil, and that is unavoidable. It's so hot that it's no wonder she's so thirsty."

They understood quite well what thirst was because they were running out of water themselves.

"Why doesn't Your Royal Highness drink some water; I don't need so much liquid since my missing legs don't need anything to drink. After I die, I'll have a devil of a slog on all fours to get home and look for my poor legs."

He was trying to make light of their situation, but Matthew knew the courageous pilot had tears in his eyes.

"Seven forty-five!"

"Seven fifty!"

"Eight o'clock."

Alas, there was no sign of the third oasis.

Perhaps if the conditions were harsher, say, a storm or a whirlwind, it might be easier to die… Everything had been going so well. They had passed the first oasis ten seconds too early and the second, four seconds later than scheduled. They had continued to fly at a steady speed, and a five-minute delay would have been acceptable, but not a whole hour.

They were nearly on target; their dangerous venture was scheduled to end that day. So much was at stake, so much depended on that journey. So now what should they do?

"Perhaps we should change direction?" wondered Matthew aloud.

"This would be no problem. The machine is very obedient and will change course on a whim. It is flying in a straight line. Even if we have flown off course, which is not at all certain, it is not the airplane's fault. But change direction? Why? And in which direction? I think we should go on. Perhaps it's another trick, just like with the flywheel. How did it get lost and why did it turn up so quickly?"

Turning to his flying machine, the pilot added:

"The engine wants another drink. Here you are. Have a tumbler of oil, but remember that heavy drinking is always a recipe for disaster, and yours will be a particularly dastardly end."

"OASIS!" shouted Matthew, who had his eyes glued to his binoculars and almost fell off the plane for joy.

"That suits me fine," said the pilot, cool as a cucumber and with the same steady disposition through thick and thin. "It could be better, for we are an hour and five minutes late. But it's not a tragedy. We've got fuel for three hours, more than enough, and a favorable wind. So let's drink to our well-being."

The pilot poured a mug of water and clinked it against the oilcan.

"Cheers!"

Having lubricated the machine generously, he gulped down the whole mug of water.

"Could Your Royal Highness let me have the binoculars for a while so that I may have a one-eyed look at this wonder?"

"Well, well, what lovely trees Bum-Drum has. But is Your Royal Highness sure that he's no longer a cannibal? To be eaten may not be the worst business if you know that they will praise you for being tasty. But I'm as tough as old boots…even without my legs. To make things worse, human broth isn't typically very nourishing if the ribs are broken."

Matthew was amazed at how this silent man, who until now had scarcely uttered a word, all of a sudden became so talkative and joyful.

"But is Your Majesty sure that this is the right oasis, because I would hate to fly across those damn sands again. Maybe it would be better to land here."

Matthew was not one hundred percent sure, because he had never had a bird's-eye view of the place before. To make things worse, landing in the wrong place was a dangerous proposition because of desert robbers or wild animals.

"Perhaps it would help if we descended just enough to get a closer look?"

"OK, that's a good idea," said Matthew.

They had been flying very high because the heat was intolerable and they had to save oil. But now that only a few hours stood between them and their destination, there was nothing to be afraid of.

The airplane growled, jerked and began to descend.

"What's this?" exclaimed Matthew, suddenly frozen in place.

"Up! Up! There's no time to lose."

The right wing of the plane was bristling with arrows.

"Are you hurt?" Matthew asked the pilot anxiously.

"Not in the least," answered the pilot. "Wonderful reception by those black bazoos," he added.

A few more arrows whooshed past but none of them hit the airplane / aeroplane, and they soon reached a safe height.

"Now I'm sure it's the same oasis. Those desert robbers do not venture too far, because there's nothing out there. They hang around Bum-Drum's jungle and camp in the nearest oasis."

"So, Your Royal Highness is sure that we will be returning on camels and not in our airplane?"

"It goes without saying that Bum-Drum will send us on our return journey the same way as the first time. Anyway, even if we could get oil in his country, we certainly won't find gas."

"If this is so," said the pilot, "we can take a risk. When a train driver is late, he puts so much coal into the locomotive that more often than not, he makes up for the lost time. I'll do the same with our flying arrow. We'll fly at maximum speed to reach our destination on schedule. Sink or swim, this could well be my last flight."

The airplane shot forward, leaving the oasis and the robbers behind.

"And these arrows, won't they make any difference?" asked Matthew uneasily.

"Let them dangle in the wind. They don't matter in the least."

They were flying at top speed, devouring mile after mile. The well-lubricated engine played a tune that was very pleasing to a pilot's ear. Once again, bushes and then small trees were beginning to appear on the ground below.

"Well, well, I see that my horse is beginning to smell the stable," joked the pilot.

They drank up their water and finished their food rations so as not to touch down on empty stomachs; it was not clear how long any welcoming celebrations would last before they were fed. Anyway, it wouldn't do to arrive as hungry as a wolf, making their hosts think they had only come to be fed.

Very carefully, they began to descend, slowing down considerably, because Matthew recognized from afar the edge of Bum-Drum's jungle.

"Everything's fine," said the pilot, "but is there any clearing where we can touch down, because we can't land on tree tops. As a matter of fact, I once landed in the forest, and it was not so much a landing as a fall. It was then that I lost my eye. I was very young at the time, and so were airplanes, young and very unruly."

It so happened that in front of the royal palace, or rather the royal tent of Bum-Drum, there was a spacious clearing. Now they began circling quite low, looking for it.

"A bit to the right!" cried Matthew looking through the binoculars. "That's too far! Go back!"

The airplane made a full circle in the air and...again the clearing was nowhere to be found.

"To the left and make a smaller circle."

"I see, I see, a clearing, all right. But what is it?"

"Up, Up!" shouted Matthew, panic-stricken.

Again they climbed, and this time a chorus of loud cries reached their ears. It sounded as if the whole jungle was yelling. The clearing before King Bum-Drum's tent was full of people—a sea of heads.

"Something must have happened. Either Bum-Drum has died or there is some kind of celebration underway."

"OK, well, we can't land on their heads," said the pilot.

"All we have to do now is ascend and descend till they understand that they have to disperse."

The pilot and Matthew had to go up and down seven times before the savages understood that the huge bird was trying to alight in the clearing. The crowd reluctantly withdrew into the trees and the airplane landed safely.

No sooner had Matthew gotten his feet on the ground than a strange shaggy creature ran up to him, grabbing him around the neck with incredible force.

When Matthew regained his balance, his head stopped spinning and red and black specks stopped flickering before his eyes, he saw the curly head of a black child, and when the child raised its head and looked into his eyes, he instantly recognized the royal daughter—sweet little Clue-Clue.

Matt did not understand what was going on. It all happened so quickly that he thought he was watching a film in the cinema.

The first thing King Matthew noticed was King Bum-Drum, bound with rope and lying on a pyre surrounded by shamans. They all looked terrible, but one was far more ominous than the rest; his body was adorned with two wings, two heads, four arms and two legs. In one hand, he held a plank on which something was written or drawn with human blood, and in the other hand was a burning torch. Matthew surmised that they were going to burn Bum-Drum alive. Standing next to the pyre and bound to one another were the king's one hundred wives, each holding a poisoned arrow whose tip was directed towards their hearts. Bum-Drum's children were crying bitterly, walking on all fours or doing mournful somersaults. Little Clue-Clue pulled Matthew by the hand towards her father, repeating something under her breath that Matthew could not understand. Matthew drew his revolver and fired twice in the air.

At the same moment, he heard a muffled cry behind his back. It was the pilot. Hands fluttering in the air, somehow he managed to jump upward with his legless trunk before his face grew livid and he fell heavily to the ground, dead on the spot.

As if at an agreed signal, all the savages made such a terrific racket that Matthew thought they had gone mad. While they howled, yelled and screamed, the two-headed shaman cut Bum-Drum's bonds and began to perform the wildest dance imaginable, and soon he himself mounted the pyre where Bum-Drum had just been lying. The shaman touched the kindle wood with his burning torch. The wood must have been impregnated with some inflammable liquid because all at once it burst into flames so high that Matthew and Clue-Clue barely managed to jump aside in time. A split second later and they would have perished in the flames just like the elder shaman.

The airplane had landed near the pyre, and now one of its wings caught fire. Soon there was a dazzling flash followed by a loud boom as the gas in the fuel tank exploded. Matthew was seized by Bum-Drum's wives and placed on the gold throne, and then Bum-Drum and all the lesser kings and princes laid their heads on the steps leading to the throne, kicking themselves in the neck with their right feet and uttering magical curses, the meaning of which Matthew did not understand.

They wrapped the body of the dead pilot in a shroud scented so heavily with fragrant oils that it made Matthew's head spin as he kneeled in prayer for the departed soul.

"What was that all about?" Matthew asked himself.

Something unusual had happened, but what? It looked as if Matthew had saved Bum-Drum and his one hundred wives. Matthew also seemed to be quite safe. But could you ever be absolutely sure of anything in the land of these strange people?

Where had all these people come from? What were they going to do? Now they were dancing, playing and singing around several thousand bonfires in the jungle. Each group played different music, and each tribe sang a different song.

That they were not Bum-Drum's subjects was plain from their attire. Some must have come from the jungle, for they were dressed in green and wore many feathers; some of the newcomers had huge turtle shells on their backs, and others wore ape skins. There were also naked tribespeople with ornaments in their ears and noses.

Even though Matthew did not scare easily and had never looked death in the face, he was suddenly frightened to find himself all alone among savage people and thousands of miles from home. This was a bit too much even for Matthew's brave heart. When he remembered his faithful companion, the fearless pilot, who died so mysteriously, he felt so overwhelmed by grief that he burst out crying.

Housed in a separate tent made of lion and leopard skins, Matthew thought he could weep freely in private—but he was wrong; little Clue-Clue was watching him. When he finally noticed her, she seemed to glow like an enormous diamond. Little Clue-Clue was also weeping. She put her tiny hand on his forehead as the tears flowed down her face.

Oh, how Matthew wished he knew their language. Clue-Clue would, no doubt, have explained everything, but although she talked and talked to him, he didn't catch a single word. Then she started to speak very slowly, repeating the same words and phrases several times, hoping he would understand. She also used sign language. Matthew guessed two things: Clue-Clue was his most faithful friend in the world, and he was perfectly safe. No immediate danger would threaten him now and in the future.

Despite terrible fatigue, Matthew could not sleep a wink. Only in the small hours of the night when all the tumult died down, did Matthew get some sleep. But it was not long before they woke him up, sat him on the throne and each group of delegates brought him their gifts. Matthew smiled and thanked them, but he knew all too well that there were not enough camels to carry all those treasures across the desert. Besides, the foreign kings had stated categorically shortly before Matthew's departure that only cages with wild animals would be granted passage through their countries and nothing more, no matter how much money he offered.

Oh, what a pity, thought Matthew, that my country has neither its own port nor its fleet of ships. But in all honesty, were a new war to break out, and I were to win it once again, then the foreign kings would have to hand over one seaport so I would never need to ask them for any favors.

Matthew would gladly have stayed a week or so to rest, but he could not. What would happen if another war broke out in his absence? How would he later cope with reading the letters? Had he not agreed to read one hundred letters a day and give one hundred children the things they had asked for?

"It's time for me to return home," said Matthew to Bum-Drum, pointing to a camel and waving his hand towards the north.

Bum-Drum understood.

Then he mimed that he would like to take the body of the brave pilot home.

Bum-Drum also understood.

When they unwrapped the scented shroud, Matthew saw that his dead friend was as pale as snow and as hard as marble. Bum-Drum's servants put the pilot into an ebony trunk and gave Matthew to understand that he could take the body with him.

The servants started to put the remnants of the plane in the second trunk, but Matthew politely declined, gesturing in sign language that he was not going to take it. It came as a complete surprise to Matthew how overjoyed Bum-Drum was to receive a burned-out hunk of rubbish as if it was a precious treasure.

But Matthew still did not know what he had come to find out, namely whether Bum-Drum was still a cannibal or not. There was nothing else to do but take Bum-Drum with him. The caravan headed by Bum-Drum and Matthew set off for home across the desert.

Matthew only understood all the strange things he had witnessed in the land of the cannibals once he was back home in the royal palace. The professor who knew fifty languages explained them to Matthew as follows:

When one of Bum-Drum's ancestors decided to give up cannibalism, he was poisoned by the shamans, and the eldest priest of the savages made this prophecy:

"The time will come when all cannibals change their ways. Towards evening, an enormous bird with an iron heart will appear. From its right wing ten poisoned arrows will dangle. This bird will circle the royal clearing seven times before coming to rest. This bird will have gigantic wings, four hands, two heads, three eyes and two legs. One head and two hands will be poisoned by one of the ten arrows and die. Two loud claps of thunder will follow. At that point, the eldest priest will be burned on the pyre, the iron stomach of the huge bird will break, and all that will remain of the bird will be a chunk of marble and a handful of ashes…and a white man who will become king of all the black kings. Then, black people will cease to be cannibals and begin to learn from the craft and wisdom of their white brethren. Until the bird appears, nothing can be changed, and any king who attempts to change our ways will die by poison or fire."

Bum-Drum had chosen death by fire, and when the ceremonial burning of the king and poisoning of his one hundred wives was about to take place, the airplane had arrived with two travelers. Matthew fired two shots and the pilot—the two hands and one eye of the bird—died, having carelessly injured himself with one of the ten poisoned arrows shot by the desert robbers. The elder priest burned himself of his own free will, the huge bird burned to cinder, and Matthew became king of not only all the cannibals, but all the black kings as well. From then on, cannibals would never eat humans again. They now wanted to learn to read and write and wear clothes like civilized men and would no longer put seashells and bones in their noses and ears.

"That's splendid!" exclaimed Matthew. "We must tell Bum-Drum to send us one hundred of his subjects. Our tailors will teach them to make clothes, our shoemakers will teach them to make shoes, and our builders and bricklayers will teach them to build houses. We will send them gramophones, so they will learn our music; but before that, we'll send trumpets, drums, flutes, violins and pianos. We will teach them our national dances and send them toothbrushes and soap. When they get used to soap, maybe they'll whiten up a bit. Though, to tell you the truth, it doesn't matter at all that they look so different from us."

"I know what I'll do," exclaimed King Matthew quite suddenly. "I'll have a wireless telegraph installed in Bum-Drum's kingdom! It will make our contacts so much easier, instead of traveling such a distance to do business."

Then Matthew asked to see the royal craftsmen and told them to make twenty suits for Bum-Drum, twenty coats, twenty pairs of shoes and twenty hats. The barber cut his hair. Bum-Drum accepted all of these ministrations very good-humouredly. The black king, however, felt a bit uncomfortable after eating a tin of shoe polish and a bar of scented soap which he was supposed to have used in his bath. From that moment on, four lackeys kept a watchful eye on Bum-Drum so that he would not do something silly by mistake.

The morning after Matthew's return, the Prime Minister called a Cabinet meeting, but the king asked him to postpone it until a later date. The previous night, a beautiful, white and fluffy snow had fallen, and about twenty boys had already gathered in the royal park, among them Felix and Stanley. Matthew was desperate to join them.

"Mister Prime Minister," said Matthew, "I just returned from a tiring and dangerous journey yesterday. All in all it was a rather fruitful venture. Even though I'm king, I think I should have at least one day off. I'm still a small boy who likes to play from time to time. If there's nothing particularly urgent, how about putting off the debate till tomorrow? Today, I'd rather spend my time with the boys in the park. The snow's so lovely, and it might the last snowfall of the year."

The Prime Minister felt sorry for the boy, and although Matthew was not actually asking his permission but just wanted to work out a compromise on the question of the Cabinet meeting, it all sounded like a special request, which pleased the Prime Minister very much.

"Oh, all right. We can wait one day," said the Premier.

Matthew actually jumped for joy. He put on a short royal parka, so that he could run about unencumbered, and a moment later was making snowballs, having joined in a snowball fight. The boys at first shrank from throwing snow at the king, unsure if it was permitted. But Matthew soon put them at ease shouting:

"Hey, boys! This is ridiculous. We can't play like that. I'm throwing snowballs at you, and you're hitting each other. It's unsportsmanlike conduct. Don't be afraid for me—I can defend myself. Snowballs are nothing compared to poisoned arrows."

Circumstances being what they were, the boys divided into two teams: the attackers and the defenders. The racket was so loud that some lackeys ran out of the palace to see what was going on; however, the moment they saw King Matthew, they were a little astonished but said nothing and went away.

Nobody would have recognized the king if they did not know him. He was as wet and snow-covered as any of the other boys, having fallen a few times, and had been hit in the back, the back of the head and the ear. But he fought like a wounded tiger.

"Listen! New rules!" he shouted suddenly. "Let's make believe that whoever is hit by a snowball is dead and must pull out of the game. Then, we will be able to crown a winner."

This was not a good idea because everybody was killed too quickly. So they changed the rules: players were eliminated once they were hit three times. Some fighters were hit

more than that, but cheated and continued to fight. However, the new rules made the game a bit quieter. The boys now made better snowballs and took aim more carefully. Then the rules were changed again: you were 'killed' if you happened to fall down.

They all had a wonderful time.

Then the boys made an enormous snowman and gave him a broom to hold. He was given coal for eyes and a carrot nose. Matthew had run into the royal kitchen in search of the right materials:

"Mr. Cook, I need some charcoal and a carrot for my snowman."

The cook was angry because pretty soon all the boys followed suit, and since it was hot in the kitchen, the snow they tracked in on their shoes melted and the floor got dirty.

"I have been the royal cook for twenty-eight years, but I cannot remember such a pigsty in my kitchen," murmured the chef under his breath, hurrying the kitchen hands in cleaning it up.

"It's a pity it never snows in Bum-Drum's kingdom," regretted Matthew. "I would teach the black children to make snowmen."

When the snowman was ready, Felix suggested some sleighing for a change. There were four small sleighs for royal children as well as four ponies. In no time, they harnessed the ponies to the sleighs.

"We will drive ourselves," shouted Matthew to the grooms. "Let's race around the park. Whoever circles the park five times wins."

"Deal!" agreed the boys.

Matthew was just about to get into the sleigh when he saw the Prime Minister hurrying towards him.

"Who else could he be after if not me?" said Matthew to himself, sadly.

The king could not have been more right.

"I'm sorry, Your Royal Highness. Please accept my humblest apologies, but I really had no choice but to interrupt your leisure activities."

"What rotten luck! Have a good time without me lads," shouted Matthew to his playmates. "So, what has happened?"

"Our top foreign spy has returned from his secret mission abroad," whispered the Prime Minister. "He has brought news that could not possibly have been written down for fear that the letter might get intercepted at any step along the way. We have to summon an assembly right away, for will arrive in three hours."

At that moment, the first sleigh overturned. It had been a long time since the pony had been harnessed, and it threw quite a temper tantrum for such a small horse. Already following the Premier, Matthew looked back and saw two boys getting to their feet to put the sleigh back on its runners after the mishap.

What else could he do? He was back in the world of grownups. On the other hand, Matthew had to admit that he could not wait to see a real spy, because so far he had only known this cloak and dagger world from hearsay.

Matthew thought he might see a barefooted boy or an old beggar carrying a sack over his shoulder, but the man standing in front of him was a well-dressed gentleman. (Initially, he thought the top spy was the Minister of Agriculture, whom he did not know too well, because the minister spent most of his time in the country and made rare appearances at Cabinet meetings.)

"I'm the chief spy in the capital of the first foreign king," announced the elegant gentleman, introducing himself. "I have come to warn His Royal Highness that the son of the first king has just completed a powerful fortress. But this is not the worst news: last year he built a top secret ammunition factory in the forest and is in full combat readiness. He has six times the amount of gunpowder we have."

"What a scoundrel!" exclaimed Matthew, clenching his boyish fists. "I have been building children houses in the forests so that they can spend their summer holidays having fun, and he has been making cannon balls and heavy guns to attack my country and destroy what I've built!"

"Just a second, Your Royal Highness; that's not all. Knowing that Your Majesty is about to send out invitations to the foreign kings to attend the inauguration ceremony for our parliaments, he bribed our court secretary who, instead of invitations, will be sending out false declarations of war."

"Oh, no! I knew all along that he was a wicked rascal and that he hated me."

"I haven't finished yet," the eminent spy interjected. "He's as cunning as a fox; I mean the son of the old king. Should the court secretary fail to replace the contents of the letters, two identical documents with Your Majesty's forged signature are ready to be sent by the son of the first king to the sad king and to the second one, the friend of the Asian kings. Now, Your Royal Highness will please excuse me, for I feel I have to stand up for the king's son."

"But how could you possibly defend such a perfidious scoundrel?"

"The point is that he's trying to safeguard the interests of his own country just as we're taking care of ours. We want to have the upper hand, and so do they. There's no need to take offense; we just have to be on guard and always be quick to act."

"So, what am I supposed to do?"

"Your Royal Highness will sign the invitations for the foreign kings, and I'll take them secretly. Tomorrow after the Cabinet meeting, you'll be debating how and when to invite the foreign kings. You must pretend that the letters haven't yet been sent. The court secretary should be allowed to open the letters and replace them. We will arrest him at the last moment."

"So far, so good. But what about the fortress and the ammunition factory?"

"Oh, that's nothing to write home about," smiled the chief spy. "Both the fortress and the factory should be blown up. I've come here to obtain Your Majesty's permission."

Matthew's face turned ashen and pale.

"I don't understand… We're not at war: It's not quite the same to blow up the enemy's powder magazines during war as in a time of peace. We're inviting our neighbor to visit our country while we pretend not to know what he's doing and plan to inflict so much harm."

"I understand, Your Majesty," said the chief spy. "Your Royal Highness thinks it unfair. Of course, if Your Royal Highness doesn't give me permission, I won't blow them up. But I wouldn't recommend it: he has six times the gunpowder we have."

Matthew paced up and down the study, more nervous than ever before.

"And how will you pull it off, if I may ask?" said Matthew.

"The assistant of the chief engineer in the factory is in the pay of our intelligence services. He knows exactly where everything is located. There's a small outbuilding where planks are stored and many saw shavings. When they catch fire, it will create a major blaze in only a matter of seconds. Nobody will even guess what happened."

"So, they will extinguish it."

"They will not!" smiled the head of spies, his eyes creasing. "Because, by sheer coincidence, at that very moment the water main will break, leaving not a single drop of water in the entire factory. Your Royal Highness can rest assured of that."

"What about the workers? Won't someone get hurt?"

"Fires usually break out at night, so it's highly unlikely that there'll be many casualties. And remember that if war was declared, there would be hundreds or thousands more victims."

"I know, I know," answered Matthew resignedly.

"Your Royal Highness, we really have to do it," chimed in the Prime Minister meekly.

"I know that we must do it. So why are you asking my permission?" retorted Matthew angrily.

"Because we must" answered the Prime Minister.

"We have to, we can't. So, please burn the factory, but do not touch the fortress for the time being."

Matthew quickly signed the invitations for the three kings to attend the inauguration of the two parliaments and left for his study. He sat at the window watching Stanley, Felix and the remaining boys sleighing around the park. Propping his head up with his hands, he thought:

Now I understand why the sad king plays the violin so morosely, and why he did not want to, but was forced to declare war on me.

When the last Cabinet meeting was to start, the one at which the invitations signed by Matthew would be put into envelopes and stamped with the royal seal, Matthew waited impatiently to see the court secretary replace the invitations for the inaugural parliament session with false declarations of war. Matthew could barely hide his surprise when the court secretary's assistant showed up instead of his superior.

"So, the children's houses will be ready?" asked Matthew.

"They certainly will."

"Great."

The celebrations were planned as follows:

The first day: a church service, military parade, gala dinner and gala performance at the theater.

The second day: the inaugural session of the parliament for grownups.

The third day: the inaugural session of the parliament for children.

The fourth day: the official opening of the zoological garden.

The fifth day: a great procession featuring the children who would be spending the summer in the country houses built for them by King Matthew the First.

The sixth day: a great farewell ball for the foreign kings.

The seventh day: farewell to the children leaving for the countryside.

Matthew expanded the program by adding the unveiling of the statue of the brave pilot who died during their last journey and a ball for the black African kings on 'day four'. All the balls were to be attended by the deputies of both parliaments. Minister Felix would sit to the left of King Matthew, and the Prime Minister to his right. This meant one thing: the Prime Minister for adults and the Prime Minister for children were equal before the king, and Felix was to be addressed as Prime Minister just as the head of the government for grownups.

When everything was resolved and the pros and cons weighed, Matthew signed the invitations for the foreign kings: on white paper for white kings, on yellow paper for the Oriental kings, and on black paper for the black African kings.

The invitations for the white kings were written in black ink, for the Oriental kings in red ink and for the black African kings in gold ink. The invitations for the black African kings were to be delivered by Bum-Drum and to the Oriental kings by their friend, the second king. But the three foreign white kings had established beforehand that the second king would never deliver the invitations and the Oriental kings would take offence at Matthew and would renew their friendship with him.

The Grand Master of Ceremonies brought the box with the royal seal. The invitations were put one by one into the envelopes and the court secretary's assistant sealed them with red and green sealing wax.

Matthew did not let the assistant out of his sight. Until now the ceremony of sealing royal correspondence had always made Matthew laugh, for he had regarded it as a waste of time.

All the letters had already been sealed, apart from the last three. The ministers got bored with the ceremony, so they lit their cigars and talked in whispers, even though the regulations did not permit any conversations when diplomatic correspondence was being sealed. But they did not know what was going to happen. There were only three persons who knew: King Matthew, the Prime Minister and the Minister of Justice. Afterwards, the Foreign Minister took umbrage at them for having kept such important information from him.

The court secretary's assistant paled visibly, but his steady hands betrayed no emotion, and just as he was about to put the invitations into the envelopes, he was suddenly overcome by a severe burst of coughing. He frantically began to search for a handkerchief, turning his pockets inside out, and though it looked like madness, there was method in it. Together with the handkerchief, he deftly removed identical sheets of paper and hid the original letters. All this lasted no more than five seconds and would only have been noticed by someone in the know.

"Excuse me, Your Royal Highness," he said meekly, "but there is a broken window in my study, and I caught a rather nasty cold."

"Oh, that's all right," replied Matthew. "It so happens that I broke the window when we were having a snowball fight."

The court secretary's assistant was feeling pretty proud of himself, sure that he could not have made the exchange any smoothly, when suddenly the Minister of Justice said:

"Gentlemen Ministers, could I have your attention please. Put away your cigars."

All at once, they knew that something important had happened. The Minister of Justice put on his spectacles and turned to the court secretary's assistant:

"I hereby arrest you as a spy and traitor. You will be hanged in accordance with paragraph 174."

The wrongdoer stood there goggle-eyed and began to wipe the sweat from his forehead with the very same handkerchief, feigning ignorance.

"Sir, I don't understand what you are talking about. I have a cold because of a broken window in my study. All I need to do is go home to bed."

"Easy there, laddie, you won't escape justice this time. They will cure you of your cold in prison."

At that very moment, five prison warders entered the conference hall, cuffing the spy's hands in front and shackling his legs.

"But what happened?" asked the ministers in shock.

"You will soon see for yourselves. Will Your Royal Highness please break the seals on those letters?"

Matthew opened the envelopes and showed them the forged letters.

Each of them read:

Now that all the savage kings are my friends, I do not care a fig about you. I have defeated you once, and I will defeat you again. And then you will be obedient to me.

I hereby declare war against you.

The fifth warder took three crumpled invitations for the three white kings together with his handkerchief out of the assistant's pocket.

The court secretary's assistant, still handcuffed and shackled, was made to sign a deposition of confession. Then the court secretary was summoned by phone. He came as quickly as he could, very frightened.

"What a rascal!" he shouted. "I wanted to come in person, but he begged me to let him replace me. He even bought me a ticket to the circus, saying that the performance was unforgettable. I didn't suspect anything…like a fool."

When the accused was tried for treason, five generals cross-examined him in court.

"The defense can only help if the accused decides to tell the truth, but woe to him who lies."

"I will tell the truth."

"How long has the accused been a spy?"

"For three months."

"Why did the accused become a spy?"

"I lost a lot of money at cards and I had nothing to pay my debts, which needed to be repaid within twenty-four hours… So, I took government money."

"You stole it."

"I thought I would be able to return it the moment I won my money back."

"And?"

"And I played poker again, but instead of winning, I lost even more."

"When was this?"

"About six months ago."

"And what came next?"

"Then I lived in constant fear that they would find out that the money was missing. So, I went to the foreign king and became his spy."

"How much did he pay you?"

"That depends. For important information, I was paid a lot and only a little for unimportant news. For this botched task, I was to earn a small fortune."

"Generals-judges," said the Minister of Justice, "this man is guilty of three crimes: The first is stealing government money. The second is being a spy, and the third involves his attempt to cause a new war to break out, a war in which so many people would have died. I demand the death penalty for the accused in accordance with paragraph 174. The accused is not a serviceman, so he won't be executed by firing squad, but will be hanged. As far as the court secretary is concerned, he's also responsible for his assistant. I like going to the circus myself, but he should have attended such an important meeting in person, instead of sending his assistant. This is grave misconduct, punishable by half a year in prison."

The generals retired to deliberate, and Matthew approached the Prime Minister and asked:

"Why did the master spy tell us that the deception was to be carried out by the court secretary personally, and not by his assistant?"

"The information a spy uncovers is not always one hundred percent accurate. Spies cannot be too inquisitive and ask too many questions because it would raise suspicion. A spy must be very cautious and keep his wits about him."

"And how clever of him to wait with the arrest until the last moment, until the Cabinet meeting," Matthew was filled with admiration for the spy's self-control. "I would have been tempted to arrest him at once."

"Oh no, that wouldn't do. The best way is to pretend that you know absolutely nothing and catch the rogue red-handed so he can't possibly get out of it."

The Grand Master of Ceremonies tapped his silver mace against the floor three times, the generals entered the courtroom, and soon the judge pronounced sentence:

"The court secretary is sentenced to one month of imprisonment, while his assistant will be hanged."

The accused began to weep so loudly that Matthew took great pity on him.

All at once the king remembered being court-martialed himself. Matthew owed his life to the fact that the judges had not been able to decide whether he should be shot or hanged.

"It lies within Your Royal Highness's power to pardon the sentenced offender. You can commute the death penalty in favor of life imprisonment."

Matthew wrote on the death sentence:

"I hereby commute the death penalty in favor of life imprisonment."

Now try and guess what time it was when Matthew went to bed.

Three in the morning.

Matt was still having breakfast when the journalist arrived.

"I wanted to be the first to bring Your Royal Highness's newspaper. I think that Your Royal Highness will be satisfied."

"And what's the news?"

"Have a look Your Majesty"

On the front page was a picture of King Matthew, sitting on the throne surrounded by thousands of kneeling children with bouquets of flowers. Under the picture, there was a poem praising King Matthew the First, referring to him as the greatest king since Creation and the greatest reformer of all time. The poem also called him the son of the sun and the brother of the moon.

Matthew did not like either the picture or the poem, but seeing how proud the journalist was, he decided not to voice his opinion.

On page two was a photograph of Felix and an article entitled:

'The First Minister-Child in the World'

Felix was also praised for being so wise and brave. According to the author, Felix was a person who, just like Matthew, had helped to defeat the adult kings and would get the upper hand over the adult ministers.

Adults cannot rule, wrote the author of the article, because they neither can nor want to fly in an airplane. They are too old and their bones ache.

The text was a page long.

But again, it was not at all to Matthew's liking. There was no point in boasting when you did not even know what the future would bring. It was quite unfair to bad-mouth your elders. Since Matthew truly began to rule, he had gotten along with his ministers very well, willingly listened to their advice and as a result had learned many practical things.

The article was followed by the news of the day: 'Royal Forest Blaze'

"The largest forest of the foreign king is on fire," said the journalist. Matthew nodded his head to show that he had noticed and began reading the article very carefully. Workers who were felling trees had reportedly discarded a cigarette butt, which immediately started a fire.

"It is very strange," said the journalist. "I understand that after a long period of sunny weather when the forest is bone-dry, trees can catch fire easily, but only a few days ago the ground was covered with snow. Rumor has it there was a loud explosion. When there is a forest fire, you don't hear explosions, do you?"

Matthew was busy eating and did not answer.

"What does Your Royal Highness think about all this?" asked the journalist. "I find this forest fire to be most suspicious."

The journalist said the last sentence in a soft and friendly tone but Matthew, without knowing why, thought:

I must be careful here.

The journalist lit a cigarette and changed the subject:

"I hear that the court secretary was sentenced to one-month imprisonment yesterday. I did not pass that news on to our newspaper because the children pay little attention to adult affairs. If there was something wrong in their ministry, it would be a different kettle of fish.

Your Royal Highness doesn't even know what a lucky choice Felix was for the post of minister. The army is very proud that a platoon commander's son became minister. News agents know Felix because he occasionally sold newspapers before the war. All the children are very happy about the current situation, and by the way, why did that poor court secretary go to prison?"

"For the mess he made in his chancellery," answered Matthew evasively, because it suddenly occurred to him that the journalist might be a spy.

When he was gone at last, Matthew could not help thinking about spies:

"I must be seeing things. A lack of sleep combined with too many recent cloak and dagger stories…and I'm ready to suspect everyone."

It was not long before he forgot about spies, though, because he had a lot of work to do.

Now was the time for regular and unending consultations with the Grand Master of Ceremonies. In all haste, they renovated the summer palace in the park for the black African kings, not far from which a less sizable mansion was erected in record time, just in case more Oriental kings should arrive. The white kings were to stay in the royal palace.

Cages with wild animals began to arrive, and it was about time, otherwise the zoo would not be ready in time for the festivities.

The children's houses and the two buildings housing the parliaments were still under construction.

A general election to select deputies of both parliaments began. For the small parliament, as it came to be known, it was decided that deputies should be no younger than ten years of age and no older than fifteen. Younger pupils in each school chose one younger deputy, and pupils from older classes also chose one deputy around fifteen years of age. Unfortunately, it turned into a bit of a mess because there were more schools than initially expected and the chamber would not hold all the elected deputies. Many letters came, keeping Matthew busy for long hours in his study. The letters raised important questions:

'Can girls be elected as deputies?'

'Can deputies who cannot write too well yet be elected?'

'Where will deputies from the countryside and towns outside the capital stay?'

'Will there be a school for teenage deputies so that they do not fall behind in their lessons while they attend parliamentary sessions in the capital?'

The court secretary was released from prison and put under house arrest, which meant that he had to stay at home and was not even allowed to go out for a walk for a month; instead, he was transported in one of the royal cars to the palace because Matthew simply could not do without his assistance.

The Grand Master of Ceremonies was drawing up the ceremonial schedule and worked out many other vital details such as the number and location of triumphal arches to be built for the foreign kings, on which streets orchestras should play and what flowers to import. Hundreds of crockery and cutlery sets had to be ordered. More cars had to be bought. Protocol issues had to be resolved, such as seating arrangements for meals and at the theatre. More important kings needed better seating. It was also crucial not to sit unfriendly monarchs next to each other. Wine, fruit, and flowers were imported from warm countries. Dilapidated facades of buildings were repainted. Faulty flagstones were replaced in the streets and sidewalks. Matthew did not sleep or eat but worked practically around the clock.

"Your Royal Highness, the general builder requests an audience."

"Your Royal Highness, the gardener begs your advice."

"Your Royal Highness, the Foreign Minister has come."

"Your Royal Highness, the ambassador of the Oriental king has arrived."

"There are two gentlemen who desire to see Your Majesty."

"What two gentlemen?" asked Matthew impatiently as this was the third time his dinner had been interrupted.

"They want to talk about fireworks."

Angry and hungry, Matthew went into his study, for now he was receiving very few petitioners in the throne room. There was no time for ceremony, so he asked the petitioners to get to the point:

"What do you want, gents? Please be brief, for there's no time to waste."

"We've heard that some savage kings are coming soon, so we should show them something they'll really enjoy. The zoo won't cut ice with them, for in their country, wild animals are a dime a dozen. And the theater, well, it's not their cup of tea."

"OK, OK," guessed Matthew, "so you want to make a fireworks display for them?"

"That's right."

The plan was to set up firework launchers on all the roofs of government buildings. They would build a tall tower in the royal garden. Further on, a firework windmill and a sort of waterfall, and in the evening, all of these structures would shine with multicolor lights. From the upper part of the tower, firework rockets would be launched, sending red sparkles in all directions, and green and blue balls in halos of red and yellow sparks would fall. The display would also include magnificent multicolor peony flowers blooming. The waterfalls would flow with fiery rain.

"Here are the drawings to illustrate what it will all look like. Will Your Royal Highness have a look?"

There were one hundred and twenty drawings all told. Matthew looked through them with growing interest, but his dinner steadily cooled in the meantime and was soon inedible.

"And how much will it cost?" asked Matthew warily.

At the last Cabinet meeting, the Finance Minister had spoken of the necessity for a new loan.

"Why?" asked Matthew, who could hardly believe his ears. "We had so much gold?!"

"That's true, but the reforms carried out by His Royal Highness cost an arm and a leg."

Now followed a long litany of how much the houses for children, the two gigantic parliament buildings, the zoo, monthly rations of chocolate, dolls and skates cost.

"We may consider ourselves lucky if we have enough money for the reception of the foreign guests."

"And could we run out of funds?" asked Matthew, seriously frightened.

"Yes, but there's a solution. We can always pass new taxes. Now that everybody is earning well, our citizens can pay back some of their money to the government."

"Oh, if only we had our own seaport and our own fleet, then King Bum-Drum would send us as much gold as we wished!"

"Where there's a will, there's a way," observed the Minister of War with a cunning smile. "If we didn't stint money on cannons, rifles and on fortresses, then we could have our own seaport. Yes, big guns are more important than chocolate and dolls."

Matthew's face grew red. Yes, that's true. They could do with a few more fortresses. The War Minister always repeated at Cabinet meetings that the army should get some of Bum-Drum's gold. But Matthew was too concentrated on his own plans to pay attention and kept telling the minister to be patient.

Matthew agreed to the fireworks display with a heavy heart and said:

"Hard luck… We'll scrimp and save later on. But we have to prepare something really special for our guests."

Late at night when Matthew tossed and turned, unable to fall asleep, his thoughts turned to military matters:

Perhaps I made a mistake not telling the master spy to blow up the enemy fortress. His defenses would be weaker. But if he wants war, let there be war.

This time, however, Matthew would not be so merciful and would say:

"I have defeated you, and you must give me one port and ten warships."

Matt had already paid a visit to the foreign kings, so he knew what it was like to entertain guests. They had been very hospitable and had given him the red carpet treatment, but what Matthew prepared for his guests was absolutely extraordinary; all the kings acknowledged the fact without even being asked. A lot of things had been arranged in advance, but Matthew had thought up almost as many surprises during their visit. Each day offered something completely different; if not a big game hunt, then out-of-town excursions or an evening in the circus watching strongmen competitions or performing animals.

The first to arrive were the black African kings. There was no end of trouble with them at the summer palace where they were lodged. If not for kind-hearted Bum-Drum, who undertook to see that order was maintained, nobody would have managed to keep them in check.

The worst thing was that they were always spoiling for a fight. And some fighting it was. Normal fights pale in comparison. They bit and spat, scratched and tore at one another. They clinched each other so tight that it was impossible to pull them apart. Another time, they gorged themselves on the delicacies the royal chef had cooked for them and then complained of stomach aches, and when the doctor told them to fast for a day, they kicked up hell, damaged furniture and broke window panes. In addition, they were easily scared. King Lum-Bo got such a fright when he saw himself in the mirror that he had to be given one and a half teaspoonfuls of medicine to calm down. King Du-Nko, instead of coming down the stairs, slid down the banister, fell down and broke his leg. King Mup bit off a lackey's finger out of spite. The number of bumps and bruises were impossible to count. King Pu-Bu-Ro brought twenty wives, none of whom had been invited. King Dul-Ko-Cin brought a sausage made of four Africans. Another blazing row broke out when the sausage was taken away. The king climbed a pear tree and wouldn't come down for five hours. When the royal guards attempted to get him down, he spat, kicked and bit. The fire-brigade had to be called, and proceeded to shoot him with such a powerful stream of water that he fell directly into a special safety net spread out below.

Bum-Drum was ashamed of his compatriots and was afraid they would ruin the entire festivities. Never mind the skirmishes in the palace where they stayed, but what if they had the urge to let loose during a gala performance or gala dinner?

Bum-Drum insisted that nothing short of whipping or prison would make them see sense and start behaving properly.

King Matthew held out against drastic measures, but he realized the sense of Bum-Drum's words pretty soon—Bum-Drum could not cope with the black kings using peaceful strategies. One of the royal halls was transformed into a museum to display various torture instruments with which Henry the Impetuous punished his subjects. The collection included a breaking wheel, the awl for gouging out eyes, forceps for pulling out fingernails or toenails, horrible saws for cutting off arms and legs, various iron instruments for breaking limbs, cat-o'-nine-tails, whips, truncheons and maces. The sight of those devices was enough to make your hair stand on end. Matthew abhorred the museum and never even poked his nose into the 'chamber of horrors'. Down the garden, there was a deep well devoid of any water. Those sentenced to death by hunger were formerly thrown into it.

Bum-Drum decided to take advantage of the museum. On the eve of the white kings' arrival, he led the savage kings first to the well and then to the atrocious museum of torture instruments and made a long speech to them.

Matthew had no idea what he actually said to his compatriots, but he must have threatened them, because after the demonstration, they behaved quite decently both in the streets and during the festivities.

Only on two occasions did King Bum-Drum punish his compatriots. One got ten whips for biting off the finger of the white lackey, and the other one spent a whole day in an iron cage for roughhousing at night.

This is how it happened. The offender had begun to play on a reed fife on a whim. Someone pointed out that it was well past midnight and everybody was tired and wanted to sleep. The 'musician' could not care less and continued to play. When they tried to snatch the instrument from him, he jumped on top of a wardrobe and began bombarding the assailants with whatever he had at hand: flower vases, various knick-knacks and even plaster busts of Matthew's ancestors. To make things worse, he jumped out of the window and rushed into the park. Then, on the terrace of the winter palace, he raised some war cries in his native tongue that woke up all the white kings, who immediately complained to Matthew.

"As if it were not enough that we have to share a table with those savages and put up with their table manners, which includes eating with their fingers instead of knives and forks, ignoring napkins and handkerchiefs, burping and what not. We have already lost our appetites, and now they won't let us sleep at night."

Matthew bent over backwards to explain to the foreign kings that they would improve their ways and that it had taken Bum-Drum, who had also been uncivilized, two months to learn to wash with scented soap and even use toothpicks.

There was a real danger that the white kings would leave, and it took some doing to make them eat in another dining room on their own or with the least savage African kings.

Among the black African kings were three quite decent and educated monarchs who wore trousers and white shirts and could wind up the gramophone.

Perhaps the white kings would not have given in so easily, had there not been some attractions planned; some of them were waiting for a big game hunt, the others for strongmen competitions, and all of the monarchs, without exception, were looking forward to the fireworks display.

Of the Oriental kings, only two were in attendance. King Kito-Sivo looked for all the world like a Caucasian, wore glasses and spoke European tongues. Tsin-Dan, although he did not resemble the white kings, was no savage and knew etiquette. But there was another problem with him. His behavior was a bit peculiar when it came to greetings and farewells. There was nothing precisely wrong about how he did it, but the way he performed those rituals was truly a sight to see. First, he made fourteen preliminary bows, then twelve routine ones, which were followed by ten etiquette bows; then came eight ceremonial, six solemn, four additional and two final bows, and only then could the person the bows were addressed to consider himself greeted.

So, there were $14 + 12 + 10 + 8 + 6 + 4 + 2$ bows altogether, which lasted a total of forty-nine minutes each time, because the preliminary bows lasted half a minute each, while each of the remaining forty-two took exactly one minute.

"My ancestors have been doing this for five thousand years, so I don't see why I should give up the tradition."

"I see your point, Your Majesty. But even if you can greet one or two monarchs in this way, how can you manage with such a swarm of kings?"

Life is quite strange, thought Matthew. Some people are lacking courtesy rather badly, whereas others are far too polite. How can one reconcile it?

King Tsin-Dan had come with two learned scholars, who somehow managed to convince him that it was pointless to greet the black African kings, which made quite a difference since they were the most numerous. As for the white rulers, he did not have to bow to them personally; it was enough to perform all those bows before their portraits. Thus photos were taken of all the white kings, which were then enlarged and hung in king Tsin-Dan's chamber where he could bow to them twice a day, in the morning and in the evening. When he had finished with one, the lackeys set up the photo of the next king, and so on. King Tsin-Dan never once arrived on time for breakfast, even though he got up two hours earlier and went to bed two hours later than anybody else.

As far as the black African monarchs were concerned, they also had their peculiar ways of greeting other kings. Some of them, by way of greeting, stuck out their tongue twice, others four times, still others put the little finger of their right hand into the left nostril; there were also those who kicked themselves in the back with their heels, jumping up three or six times.

Matthew was very surprised to hear from Bum-Drum that in the previous century, a terrible war over a greeting incident had been fought for over fifteen years. One king had stuck the little finger of his right hand into his left nostril, while the other king did the opposite. Both nations were in an uproar. Other kings and high priests got involved. Opinions were split, and a fierce fight began to decide who was right. They burned each other's tents and then even whole villages. They killed women and children, took prisoners and threw them to the lions. On top of that, there was an outbreak of plague which was followed by such a famine that they could fight no more, yet both sides stuck to their guns…or should I say noses. Now these two kings did not greet one another at all and ignored one another at table.

Even getting them to the table was no easy task. It took some doing on the part of Bum-Drum to make the black kings understand that chairs are made for sitting and not for breaking heads.

But it was by far the children who had the most fun in Matthew's capital. Schools were closed because no one was attending lessons.

The savage kings did not like cars, and instead of being driven, they preferred going everywhere on foot. Each was followed by hordes of boys. It was a very trying time for the police forces as well. After the congress, the Police Prefect complained that he had lost fifteen pounds.

"Just think, gentlemen. Hundreds of wombats and weirdoes scattered all over the capital, and we had to watch out that no ruffians threw a stone at them, that no vehicle ran them over, and last but not least, that they did not eat anybody, for even this was not out of the question."

Matthew was to award him a medal. On the whole Matthew gave out many different medals in recognition of various merits. Some of the black kings hung their medals on their noses, while the white kings wore theirs traditionally on their chests. Everybody was pleased that there was no cause for complaints.

But there was one unpleasant surprise awaiting Matthew. The black kings did not think much of what was heralded as big game hunting, for it was far removed from their expectation. The 'game' was no bigger than hares or deer, whereas they were used to elephants, lions and crocodiles. The white kings may not have liked everything very much but were better brought up and pretended that everything was first class, for they saw that Matthew was bending over backwards to please his guests. But the savage kings were badly brought up and perhaps even thought that Matthew was making fun of them. They made such an unearthly racket and began to shake their bows and spears in the most threatening manner that the white kings got back into their limousines and were ready to leave, while poor Bum-Drum ran about like a madman fluttering his hands in the air in an attempt to calm troubled waters, a feat that he finally accomplished.

No particularly dramatic events occurred during the hunt. The white kings shot two boars and one bear, hoping that the black monarchs would understand at last that there were dangerous beasts in Europe. The one who shot the bear stayed with the black kings until the end of the hunt, trying to pal around with them and boasting in sign language what a good hunter he was. He looked at their bows and spears with fake admiration and even asked them to let him sleep in the summer palace. On the following morning, he said at breakfast that the black kings were very friendly and that one could learn a lot from them. He even began to wonder if food might taste better when eaten with one's fingers, instead of those cold, sharp forks.

Believe it or not, but an extraordinary thing happened. It turned out that a stowaway was discovered in the monkey cage. The very brave, little daughter of King Bum-Drum had hidden in one of the metal cages and traveled all the way to Matthew's kingdom.

And here is how it happened:

The zoological garden was, for all intents and purposes, ready. All the animals had already been placed into their cages. On Wednesday the ceremonial opening of the new zoo was planned, which meant it would be open for visitors on Thursday; however, the zoo's management was still expecting the delivery of one last wooden crate with three rare species of monkey, which none of the white kings had ever had in his collection.

During the opening ceremony, the duly delivered crate was to be emptied. It was placed as close as possible to the cage entrance to ensure safe transfer of the monkeys. Everybody stood and watched. The moment the crate was opened, first one, and then another monkey ran into the cage. But the third animal could not be found! The crate was pushed aside from the cage door, and, lo and behold, what did the onlookers see but little Clue-Clue, who jumped out of the box and threw herself at her father's feet! She was saying something in their native tongue, but nobody knew what it was.

Bum-Drum was very angry, and although he was less savage and more civilized, he still wanted to punish her, but Matthew was quick to stand up in her defense.

Clue-Clue knew it was wrong to run away from home. It was wrong that she had opened the crate to set one monkey free and then had taken its place. But justice had already been done, for she had traveled with two monkeys, the equivalent of six weeks imprisonment. It was very unpleasant, even more so because she was not an ordinary African girl but a royal daughter accustomed to a comfortable life. In the crate, she had not even enjoyed the same comforts as her inmates, for she could not come near the crate window through which they were given food, for fear of being discovered.

"King Bum-Drum, my friend Bum-Drum," said Matthew deeply moved. "You can be proud of your daughter. No white girl…or boy would ever muster up the courage to do anything like that."

"I might as well turn this unruly, disobedient girl over to you since you defend her so eagerly," said Bum-Drum, angered beyond belief.

"Good," agreed Matthew without hesitation, "I've already thought about it; she'll stay in the palace and learn the necessary knowledge to become queen. Once she is the ruler, she'll become a reformer among her black brothers and sisters as I am among white people."

One strange thing is worth noting: only an hour after the row, Clue-Clue was already behaving as if she had been in Matthew's court for a long time.

When the old professor who knew fifty languages spoke to her in her native tongue and explained what Matthew was planning to do with her, Clue-Clue answered at once:

"That's exactly why I came. My golden professor, wise as an owl and strong as a buffalo, you must start teaching me your language at once, or else I won't be able to tell Matthew what I think and what I plan to do. I don't like to wait and my plans can't be delayed either."

It was soon apparent that Clue-Clue already knew one hundred and twelve European words, which she had learned during Matthew's stay in Africa.

"It is unbelievable how capable this tiny cannibal is," the professor remarked in amazement. "What a superb memory!"

What was still more unusual was that Clue-Clue remembered not only words, but where she heard them as well as those who said them. It also turned out that while traveling in the cage, she had picked up a lot of words from the sailors who fed the monkeys.

"Shame on you, Clue-Clue!" said the professor. "Where did you learn all those bad words? They are absolutely unrepeatable. I hope you don't understand what they mean."

Clue-Clue explained:

"Those three words were used by the porter as he was putting the crate on his back. Those four words, he said when he tripped over the threshold and almost fell down. That's what the attendant said when he was feeding us. These were the yells of the sailors when they got drunk."

"It's regrettable that those were among the first words white people exposed you to," commented the professor. "You must make every effort to forget them. We white people do not use such offensive words in everyday conversations. I'll be very pleased to teach you to speak our language, brave Clue-Clue."

Until the end of the festivities, Clue-Clue was always in the foreground. In all the exhibitions and displays, photos of the girl were featured prominently. The boys tossed up their caps and cheered when they saw Clue-Clue in the royal limousine.

When, during the ceremonial opening of the Children's Parliament, she gave a speech in a European language ("On behalf of my compatriots, black children from Africa welcome this first Children's Parliament worldwide!"), the audience burst into such stormy applause that even Felix, capable as he was in moments of crisis, could not restore order. The standing ovation soon degenerated into total chaos. Felix, angrier than ever before, threatened to knock out one of the deputy's teeth if he did not shut up.

"Listen, pal, if you don't shut your mouth, I will have no choice but to knock out your teeth!"

These were the exact words Felix used.

While his angry words made a bad impression on the foreign kings, they did not bat an eyelid.

I would be delighted to describe in detail all the festivities and diversions, but then there would be no room for more important things; after all, this book tells the story of the king-reformer and not the king-entertainer. Readers should bear in mind that Matthew invited all those guests not just for fun, but for more important political considerations.

The guests included the old king and his son—Matthew's arch enemy—as well as the king who was friendly with the Oriental monarchs. Of course, the sad king, who played the violin and with whom Matthew had had a few long conversations, had made the trip.

"Dear Matthew," confided the sad king, "I must admit that not only have you begun your reforms very bravely, but the reforms are both very interesting and important. So far you have been very successful. But remember that reforms have their price, and this price usually involves blood, sweat and tears. This, of course, does not spell the end of your reforms; it's perhaps the end of the beginning of your steep road to success. Don't labor under the delusion that it will always be like that, and do not be too self-confident."

"Oh, I know how difficult it is," answered Matthew.

He told him how long he had to work, how many sleepless nights he had had, how many times he ate his dinner cold.

"The worst of all is that I don't have a port of my own," complained Matthew, "and this causes problems for me when I want to import gold."

The sad king became thoughtful and said:

"You know what, Matt; I think that the old king might give you one of his ports."

"Out of the question. His son would never agree."

"But I think he'll agree."

"But he hates me—no two ways about it. He envies me and suspects the worst. He feels deeply offended and…"

"Yes, what you've just said is absolutely true. But he'll still agree."

"Why?"

"Because he's afraid of you, and he cannot count on my friendship," smiled the sad king. "As for the second king, he's content with the Oriental rulers."

"It's obvious that I can't have everything for myself," remarked Matthew, shrugging his shoulders.

"It's very wise of you, Your Royal Highness, not to want to rule the whole world. But there were, are and always will be those who will never stop trying. Maybe you yourself will try one day."

"Never!"

"Never say never. People change and nothing corrupts as well as success."

"But not me."

At that moment, the old king entered with his son.

"And what are Your Royal Highnesses talking about, if I may ask?"

"You may. Matthew has just been complaining that he does not have a port of his own. Matthew has mountains, woods, towns and fields, but he has neither a port nor ships. And now that he has made friends with the black African kings, he needs a seaport."

"And I quite agree," answered the old king. "But where there's a will, there's a way. In the last war, Matthew beat us and imposed peace without demanding reparations. It was most noble of him. So, now it's our turn to prove that we know what gratitude means. Don't you think, my son, that with no detriment to our own interests, we could give up part of our coast and one of our ports to King Matthew?"

"But he will pay us for the ships, won't he?" added the son. "After all, he's got so many rich friends."

"Absolutely. I'll be only too happy to oblige," said Matthew, beaming with joy.

The Foreign Minister and the court secretary were summoned at once and the necessary document was drawn up on the spot and submitted for all the kings present to sign. The Grand Master of Ceremonies brought the box bearing the royal seal, and

Matthew, hands shaking nervously, applied the seal to the document. The timing was impeccable because the moment had come for the fireworks display.

It was a sight worth seeing. The whole capital had taken to the streets. The royal park was occupied by the deputies, the army and the government administration. There was a separate press sector for journalists from all around the world, who converged on the capital to report on all the wonders they were witnessing. On the balconies, in the windows and on the terrace of the royal palace, all the kings had gathered. Some of the savage kings climbed onto the roof for a better view. The tower built in the garden was shining like a beacon. Bengal fireworks, firework rockets sending red sparkles in all directions, and green and red balls were soaring into the sky. The multicolor fire serpents and fire windmills were also very impressive, but a collective gasp of delight was heard from the spectators when the firework waterfall was lit, which produced myriads of variegated sparks, all this accompanied by gun reports and loud cracks of shells breaking up in the air.

"We want more!" chanted the black African kings, astounded and enraptured by the display, calling Matthew 'King of Multicolor Skies' or 'Fire Conqueror'.

But the guests had to go to sleep early because their departure was scheduled for the next morning.

One hundred orchestras played in the streets when the royal vehicles drove the guests to the railroad station, where ten royal trains waited to take them home. Thus, all the monarchs left behind the hospitality of Matthew's capital.

"We have won a great diplomatic victory!" beamed the Prime Minister with delight, rubbing his hands on the way back from the station.

"What does that mean?" asked King Matthew.

"Here is a genius!" exclaimed the Prime Minister. "His Royal Highness, even without realizing it, has accomplished a great thing. Victories can also be secured in times of peace. You don't have to fire a gun to defeat an enemy and demand reparations. To win a diplomatic victory, without war, means to trick someone into doing what is good for you. We have a seaport and this is what matters most."

Matt had to get up at six o'clock in the morning, otherwise he would constantly fall behind schedule. His new timetable ensured him two hours a day for his studies, even though he had to attend parliamentary sessions and read two newspapers each day to keep up with the times: one for grown-ups and the other for children.

So, when one day, at eight in the morning, no sound was heard from Matt's bedroom, the palace personnel was seriously worried.

"Matt must have fallen ill."

"I think that it was to be expected."

"No adult king works as much as him."

"He has been very pale recently."

"And has been eating far too little."

"And you can hardly say anything to him because he's become so short-tempered."

"Yes, true enough, he's been very impatient recently."

"I think the doctor should be sent for."

The doctor came as fast as he possibly could, and in an unheard of departure from court formalities, even without as much as taking off his coat or knocking, he barged into the royal bedroom.

Matt woke up, rubbed his eyes and asked anxiously:

"Has something happened? What's the time?"

The doctor, without any further ado, began speaking very quickly fearing that Matt would interrupt him:

"My dear, beloved Matt, my laddie, I have known you since you were born. I am very old. I don't give a damn about my own life. Order to have me hanged, beheaded or clapped in prison; it makes no difference to me. Your dying father entrusted you to my care. I will not allow you to get up and that's final! I'll tell the lackeys that whoever comes to bother you must be thrown down the stairs. Matt, you want to do in a year what other kings do in twenty years. It simply won't do. Look at yourself in the mirror! You look like a piece of uneaten hard tack. Not like a king but a beggar's child. If the prefect of the police lost seven kilos, that's all the better for him, for he's such a fatso. But you have lost weight and you are still growing. You take care of all the children in the country. Tomorrow twenty thousand children are going into the country to rest in the houses you built for them. Why should you be losing your health so recklessly? I'm so ashamed…a ham-fisted, old fool…"

The doctor passed a mirror to Matt:

"Look Matt, look."

The old doctor could not help but start weeping.

Matt took the mirror. The doctor was right. He was as white as paper, his lips were pale; he had bags under his sad eyes, and a long, thin neck.

"You will fall ill and die," said the doctor stifling tears, "and will not finish your life works. You are ill already."

Matt put down the mirror and squinted his eyes. He felt good, for the doctor did not address him as 'His Royal Highness' but as Matt, did not allow him to get up, and threatened to throw anybody who tried to bother the little king down the stairs.

It's a good thing to be ill, he mused, then stretched and yawned lazily.

Matt thought he was only tired. That is why he did not want to eat even though he was hungry. That is why he had difficulty in falling asleep and often had nightmares when he did go to sleep. Once he dreamt that the black kings pounced on little children and ate them, another time that rain of fire was falling on his head, on still another occasion that he had both legs cut off and one eye plucked out. Last night he had a nightmare that he sat in the well sentenced to death by hunger. He often suffered from such severe headaches that he was sitting in his lessons, understanding very little or next to nothing and he felt thoroughly ashamed of himself, especially because his classmates, Stanley and Helen, had no such problems. As for Clue-Clue, she excelled and after three weeks could read a newspaper, wrote dictations and had no difficulty drawing the route from Matt's capital to King Bum-Drum's country on a map.

"And what happens if the king is ill? Who rules instead of him?" ask Matt in a weak voice.

"Anyway in the summer, parliaments have vacations. There is plenty of money; it's only a matter of transporting it. We have a seaport and ships. The children houses have been built. The rest is in the hands of the ministers and the lower-level administration. And Matt, you'll have a regular two-month summer holiday."

"Why, aren't I going to take possession of the port and ships?"

"Because I am your doctor and I will not permit it. You will be represented by the Prime Minister and the Commerce Minister."

"I was supposed to attend the military manoeuvres."

"The Minister of War will no doubt be the right person in the right place and at the right time."

"What about the letters from the children?"

"Felix will stand in for you."

Matt sighed. It was not easy to delegating when you had grown accustomed to seeing to everything personally. But Matt had indeed run out of steam.

Matt had his breakfast in bed, and then little Clue-Clue told him beautiful African fairy tales. Then he played with his favourite marionette and looked through the beautiful illustrations in some of his books. Then it was time for lunch: three scrambled eggs, a roll with fresh butter and a glass of milk. Only then was he allowed to get dressed and sit in a comfortable armchair on the balcony.

Matt sat there free from all the cares in the world. For once did not have to ponder the most important affairs of state or worry that something might go wrong. No petitioner waited for an audience, nor any minister or journalist. All he did was relax and listen to the birds singing in the royal garden. This was indeed a very pleasant occupation that lulled him to sleep. Matt slept peacefully until dinner.

"And now it is dinnertime," said the doctor smiling. "After dinner you can take a short ride in the coach through the park. Then a nap till supper. After supper a bath, and around ten o'clock a good night's sleep."

Matt slept, slept and slept, making up for his recent string of restless nights. He rarely had nightmares now, and he ate far more. In three days, he put on over three pounds.

"This is what I like to see" declared the doctor, elated. "In a week, if all goes well, I will address Matt as 'His Royal Highness', because now he is not a king but a bag of bones, an underfed orphan. He wants to look after the whole world, but there is no one to take care of him, because he does not have his mother."

After a week, the doctor passed Matt a mirror.

"Almost a king now or not?"

"Not yet," answered Matt who liked very much this tender tone the doctor had adopted. Apparently, he missed being treated like a child and was a bit fed up with being called 'Royal Highness'.

Matt had been given a new lease on life and was again the same lively and cheerful boy, and again it was difficult to send him to bed for a few hours.

"And what does the newspaper say? What's the news?"

"It says in today's newspaper that Matt is ill and that, just like all other children in the state, he is leaving tomorrow for the whole summer on holiday in the country."

"Tomorrow?!" Matt was overwhelmed with joy.

"Yes, at noon."

"And who is coming with me?"

"It so happens that I, the captain with his children, and perhaps Clue-Clue, because she would have nobody to stay with."

"Well, it goes without saying that she must join us."

Matt signed but two papers before his departure—one declaring that the Prime Minister would stand in for him in all matters concerning adults, and Felix in all children's matters.

For two weeks, Matt did absolutely nothing but rest. In Matt's group all the games were worked out by Clue-Clue. There were numerous war games, so Matt, who had already fought a real war, could now take part in make-believe ones. The children went hunting every animal they could think of—needless to say that they were all bloodless hunts. Clue-Clue taught everybody to build shacks out of fallen tree branches, which if necessary, protected hunters, the fishermen or the soldiers from rain. Some of the games were played on the ground and some high up in the trees. Clue-Clue climbed trees just as well as her travelling companions, but at first she could not get used to wearing sandals.

"What a strange custom to wear clothes on your feet," she complained.

She was not very happy about wearing dresses or skirts either.

"Why do boys and girls dress differently here? It's an absolutely silly idea. This is why your girls are so clumsy. You can't climb trees in a dress or jump over a fence. No matter how hard you try, the dress always gets caught."

"Hey, Clue-Clue, you climb trees far better than our village boys, to say nothing of Matt and Stanley."

"Some trees they are?" Clue-Clue burst out laughing. "These are sticks for two-year old kids and not for a grown-up girl like me."

One day, as the children admired a squirrel jumping deftly from one branch to another, Clue-Clue remarked:

"I can also jump like that."

Before you could say Jack Robinson, she threw off her dress and sandals and began chasing the squirrel. The small rodent jumped from branch to branch, but Clue-Clue kept close behind it. No matter how long and high the animal jumped, it could not shake off its pursuer. What is more, after a five minute chase, the girl began to gain on the squirrel. The animal decided to take its chances on the ground. Clue-Clue jumped after the squirrel, and when Helen, Stanley and Matt thought she would break her neck, the girl landed safely and soon caught the exhausted critter. Clue-Clue held the squirrel by the neck, so that it could not bite her.

"Is this a very poisonous animal, this little monkey of yours?" asked Clue-Clue.

"Not at all," answered the children. "Only adders are poisonous here."

Clue-Clue asked for a detailed description of the adder, had a close look at one in a picture and went into the forest, soon disappearing amongst the trees. For the whole day, the girl was nowhere to be seen. She returned towards evening rather bedraggled and hungry, but held three live adders in a glass jar.

"How did you catch them?!" asked Matt astounded.

"In the same way as other poisonous snakes are caught," said Clue-Clue shrugging her shoulders.

All the village children were at first rather scared of Clue-Clue, but they soon got to like her and even developed a healthy respect for the small hunter.

"Despite being a girl, she is the first amongst boys. Oh, My! Can you imagine what their boys must be like?"

"Just the same as girls—neither better nor worse," explained Clue-Clue. "It is only amongst white people that girls wear long hair and dresses that stop them from doing anything."

But Clue-Clue was not only the best at throwing stones, shooting a bow, gathering mushrooms and picking nuts. She had a head for botany, zoology, geography and physics. One look at a plant or an insect in a photo or drawing was enough to commit it to memory, and she would never mistake it for something else in the meadow or forest. Once Clue-Clue learned that, say, the sundew grew in swamps, she was off asking the village boys where to find the nearest swamp.

"Oh, quite a long way away… Expect a good two miles."

A long way away perhaps, but not for Clue-Clue. On such occasions she would sneak into the larder, break off a chunk of bread and pocket a piece of cheese before setting out.

Nobody even bothered to try to find her.

"It looks as if Clue-Clue has been in the larder again. Another expedition must be underway."

Night had fallen…and there was still no sign of little Clue-Clue.

Having spent the night in the forest, Clue-Clue arrived in the morning, carrying a bouquet of sundew flowers triumphantly, and as if that were not enough, scores of frogs, newts, lizards and leeches.

Her herbarium was the richest, her collection of insects, butterflies and stones the biggest. Her aquarium was home to the most species of fish and the most fertile snails.

Clue-Clue, always so cheerful with sharp, white teeth perpetually bared in a grin, could also be earnest and caring.

"Oh, Matthew, when I saw those beautiful fireworks and the waterfall, I thought what a wonderful world this would be if black children could see all these marvels of yours. I have a great, great favor to ask you, Matthew."

"What is it?"

"I wonder if you could invite one hundred black children to your country so that they, like me, can learn all those things, and then return to Africa and teach them to all the other black children."

Matthew did not respond to Clue-Clue's request right away because he had decided to surprise her. That same evening, he sent a letter to his capital:

Dear Felix, when I was leaving, they were installing a wireless telegraph on the palace roof. The work was to be finished on the first of August. The wireless telegraph is to serve one purpose: to communicate with Bum-Drum. In our first telegram to Africa, please ask Bum-Drum to send one hundred children to be enrolled in a special school I plan to open in the capital.

Please do not forget my request.

Matthew

He licked the envelope and was just about to seal it when all of a sudden, the door to his room opened.

"Felix, how good it is that you have come! I was about to send a letter to you."

"I have come on serious official business," said Felix earnestly.

He took out a gold cigarette case and offered a cigar to Matthew.

"Would Your Royal Highness like a puff? Excellent stuff. First class cigars, really worthy of your royal nostrils."

"I don't smoke, my friend," said Matthew.

"And that's the point," observed Felix. "That's too bad. The king has to have self-respect. And that's why I'm here to ratify one of my own projects. Here's my ultimatum: first of all, I'm no longer Felix, but Baron Felix von Rauch. My parliament will no longer be known as the Children's Parliament but Progress Parliament— Pro-Par for short. Furthermore, it's high time for us to get rid of this Matthew business. Your Royal Highness is already twelve years old and should be ceremoniously crowned as Caesar Matthew the First; otherwise, all these reforms will come to nothing."

"I had a different project," Matthew retorted. "I wanted the adults to elect a king for themselves, and I would be the children's king."

"Perhaps Your Royal Highness's conception might be codified in its crude form," said Felix. "I would not dare to impose my moratorium on Your Royal Person; however, as regards to my official person, I wish to be Baron von Rauch, Minister of Pro-Par."

Matthew consented.

But this was not the end of his ambitions. Felix also demanded a separate chancellery, two cars and a salary twice as high as that of the Prime Minister.

Matthew consented.

Felix further demanded the title of count for the journalist of Pro-Pap—the children's newspaper, which was to be called Progress Newspaper, or Pro-Pap for short.

Matthew consented.

Felix had already drawn up the documents in the capital, ready to be signed, and Matthew complied.

Matthew found the whole conversation with Felix very, very disagreeable. Matthew was ready to agree to anything to get it over and done with. He had felt so good in the country that he had nearly forgotten the debates and Cabinet meetings. The days when he had worked so hard had been so far out of his mind. Now he was afraid to think what awaited him when the holidays were over. Felix was a painful reminder of his royal duties, and all he wanted was for Felix (or Baron von Rauch) to leave.

Once again, it was the doctor who came to Matthew's aid. Having learned of Felix's arrival, he came storming into Matthew's room.

"Felix, I told you that His Royal highness should not be bothered."

"Dear doctor, please watch your tone and be kind enough to call me by my real name."

"And what *is* your real name?" asked the doctor in utter amazement.

"I am Baron von Rauch."

"Since when?"

"Since His Royal Highness was so kind as to confer the title on me with this official act."

Felix pointed to a paper lying on the table where King Matthew's signature was still wet.

The doctor's long service in the court had taught him respect for royal documents. He changed his tone immediately and he said quietly but firmly:

"Baron von Rauch, His Royal Highness is here on sick leave recuperating and I'm personally responsible for his well-being; on my authority as court physician, I demand that Baron von Rauch get the hell out of here!"

"You will answer for this one day!" threatened Felix, who took his papers and left with his tail between his legs.

Matthew was genuinely grateful to the doctor, particularly because Clue-Clue had thought up a new game: catching horses with a lasso. All you needed was a long and strong rope with a piece of lead tied at one end. The children hid behind the trees, playing hunters. The groom released ten ponies from the royal stable; the children caught them with their lassos, and then mounted and broke them.

Clue-Clue did not know how to ride a horse, for in her country people rode camels or elephants. But she was quick to learn, although she did not like to ride side-saddle or in a saddle of any kind.

"Saddles are fine for grannies and granddaddies who enjoy comfort. And when I ride a horse, I want to sit on a horse, not a pillow. A pillow is for sleeping in bed, not for playing."

So, even the village children had a lot of fun that summer because the children played almost all their games together. Not only did Clue-Clue teach them new games, fairy tales and songs, how to make bows and arrows, how to build shelters, weave baskets and hats, new ways of gathering and drying mushrooms, but this African girl, who could not even speak their language two months before, began to teach the shepherd boys and girls to read.

She compared each new letter in the alphabet to an insect or worm.

"You know various flies, bees, wasps, worms and herbs; you know hundreds of animals, and you can't learn thirty letters by heart? Believe me, you can. It only seems difficult at first. It's the same as sitting on a horse for the first time or skating. It really boils down to believing that it is easy, and so it should be."

The shepherds started to tell themselves that reading was easy to learn, and indeed they soon began reading. Their mothers clapped their hands in amazement.

"That black child is amazing!" they repeated. "The teacher shouted himself hoarse all year long, broke dozens of rulers on the children's fingers and pulled their ears and hair in vain, and she said that letters were like flies and, lo and behold, they're reading."

"And how she milked that cow! Unbelievable!"

"And when my calf was sick," said one village woman, "she only glanced at it and said that the calf would die in three days. I knew as much without being told because I have seen many calves die before. And she told me: 'If such and such herb grows near here, then I can save her!' I went with her out of curiosity. She looked here and there, smelling and tasting whatever she found, then said 'No, I can't find that herb, but let's try this one. It has a similar bitterness to the one we use in Africa.' She picked a little more, added some hot ashes, mixed everything as expertly as a chemist, added it to milk and gave it to the calf. The sick animal drank as if it understood that this was for its own good. It drank the medicine, bitter as it was, mooing and licking its lips. And would you believe it, the calf recovered? Isn't that amazing?"

When the summer was over, women, men and children wished Matthew could stay with them longer; after all, he was king. They regretted having to part with the captain's children, for they were always kind and polite. The villagers were sorry the doctor was leaving, since he treated them for free, but it was Clue-Clue's departure that saddened everyone the most.

"What a clever, cheerful and kind-hearted girl. It's a pity she's so black," said some.

"Well, once you get used to her skin color, she's actually quite nice to look at," added the others.

Matt returned to the capital with a heavy heart. It was not a very pleasant welcome at all. At the railroad station, Matthew noticed that there was something in the air. The station was surrounded by troops. There were fewer flags and flowers. The Prime Minister's face betrayed his embarrassment. The Police Prefect, who had never come to welcome the king, was also present. They got into their limousines and drove off. They took side streets, and it was plain to Matthew they were trying to whisk him to the palace unnoticed.

"Why are we not driving along the main streets?"

"Because of the workers' processions."

"Workers?" asked Matthew, remembering the joyful, multicolor procession of children going on holiday to the houses he built for them in the woods.

"Where are they going?"

"They are not going anywhere. Quite the contrary; they have just come back. These are the bricklayers, carpenters, glaziers, roofers and so on who have been building houses for the children. Now that the work is finished, they have nothing to do so they are taking to the streets."

Suddenly, Matthew saw the protesters. There were workers marching with red flags and singing.

"Why do they have those red flags? Our national colors are not red."

"In every country, workers carry identical red flags. They say that the red flag is a symbol for all the workers in the world."

Matthew became pensive:

Perhaps children the world over—white black and yellow—should also have a common flag, but what color would it be?

They were driving down a sad, narrow and dark street while Matthew recalled the green woods and meadows in the country and said aloud:

"Could the children of the world carry a green flag?"

"Possibly," replied the Prime Minister, wincing as if he had swallowed vinegar.

In the palace, Matthew moped. Even Clue-Clue seemed affected, for she was not the same cheerful, energetic girl everyone knew and loved in the country.

"It's time to get down to work," repeated Matthew to himself, but he really did not feel like doing it at all.

"Baron von Rauch," announced the lackey.

Felix entered and said:

"The first Pro-Par post-holiday session will be held tomorrow. Surely, Your Royal Highness will want to take the floor."

"But what shall I say to them?"

"Usually kings tell the assembly they are glad that the nation will have their say and wish their people success."

"OK, I will attend the session," agreed Matthew.

But he was not a willing participant. He was already imagining all the noise, so many children and everybody staring at him.

When Matthew saw that children from all over the country had come to debate how to make the country a better and merrier place to live in, when he recognized the children he had known and played with in the country, he felt a renewed upsurge of energy and made a very nice speech:

"You are the deputies," he began. "So far I have been alone. I wanted to rule with your well-being in mind. But it is so hard to know other people's needs. It is much easier for many deputies to recognize the needs of their peers than for one king. Some of you know the needs of the city children, and others, what is needed in the country. The younger deputies are better informed about the affairs of small children, and the others know what older children want. I think the day will come when children from all over the world will have their own congress just like in our capital. All children, irrespective of their skin color, will voice their needs. For instance, skates are unnecessary for black children because there are no skating rinks in Africa. The workers," said Matthew, "already have their red flag. Perhaps children will choose a green one, because they love the woods, and the woods are green…"

Matthew spoke for quite some time, and the deputies listened eagerly to his speech. He was very pleased indeed.

Then the journalist took the floor and announced that there was a daily newspaper for the children to read interesting news, and if anyone wanted to, they could write whatever they deemed worth publishing. At the end of his speech, he asked if the children had enjoyed the country.

At that point all hell broke loose. The deputies began shouting all at once and it was impossible to know who was saying what. Felix called for the parliamentary guard to calm frayed tempers. When order was more or less restored, Felix threatened to throw out anyone who dared to be disruptive and asked the deputies to speak one at a time.

The first to speak was a barefooted boy in a worn-out jacket.

"I'm a deputy, and I want to say that we did not have a good time there. There were no games to play, the food was terrible, and when it rained, the ceilings leaked because the roofs had holes in them."

"And we didn't have a change of underwear," shouted someone.

"They served us pigswill for dinner!"

"We were fed like pigs!"

"All the houses were messy, very untidy!"

"We were beaten regularly!"

"And locked up in a cell for no reason at all!"

It got so noisy that a ten-minute break was declared.

Four deputies, who were regular troublemakers, were chucked out, and the journalist explained to the most feverish deputies that it had been very hard to prepare everything, but that the next time, it would be really great. Then, he opened the floor to the deputies again.

Again, the noise became unbearable.

"I want to keep pigeons!" shouted someone.

"And I want a dog!"

"Each child should have a watch!"

"All children should be allowed to use telephones."

"We don't want to be kissed."

"We want to be told fairy tales."

"Sausages."

"Pork brawn."

"We want to stay up late at night."

"Each child should have a bicycle."

"Each child should have a wardrobe."

"And more pockets. My father has thirteen pockets and I have only two. I have nowhere to carry my things. When I lose a hankie, I'm scolded."

"Every child should have a trumpet."

"…and a revolver."

"We want to go to school by car."

"Let there be no girls or babies."

"I want to be a magician."

"Let everybody have their own boat."
"We want to go to the circus every day."
"Let it be Easter Monday every day!"
"And All Fools Day…and Shrove Tuesday, too."
"Every child should have his or her own room."
"We want to be given scented soap."
"And perfume."
"Let each child be allowed to break one window a month."
"And smoke cigarettes."
"Let there be no more blind maps."
"Nor dictations."
"Once a month, adults should be forbidden to leave home so that children can go everywhere."
"Let children be kings everywhere."
"Let grownups go to school."
"Instead of so much chocolate, we want oranges."
"And shoes."
"Let people be angels."
"Let each child have a car."
"A ship."
"A house."
"A train."
"Let the children have money to buy things."
„Every baby should have a milk cow at their disposal."
„Every child should have a horse to ride."
"And let everybody have 10 acres of land."

It lasted over an hour and the journalist kept smiling and taking notes. At first the children from the country were too shy to speak, but once they regained their courage, the list of wants was endless.

Matthew had had enough of the parliamentary session.

"OK, everything has been taken down, now what do we do?"

"We have to teach them good manners," said the journalist. "I'll write a detailed report tomorrow and explain what the deputies can and cannot do in the session hall."

Just at that moment, a boy stood up and expressed his wish that there be no girls.

"Mr. Deputy," asked the journalist, "why do you think the world would be a better place without girls?"

"In our backyard, there's one girl who's nothing but trouble! She's always spoiling for a fight, and when you do something to her, not even hit, but barely touch her, she starts to scream and tells on you. And she always does it, and to everybody. So, we have decided to have nothing to do with her, once and for all."

The journalist stopped another deputy.

"Why, my dear Deputy, don't you like to be kissed?"

"If you had as many aunts as I do, you wouldn't even ask this question. Yesterday was my birthday. They smeared me with so much spit that it made me sick. If grownups enjoy it, let them kiss each other, but I, for one, hate being kissed."

"The journalist took that down."

"Just a word with you, Mr. Deputy. Does your father really have so many pockets?"

"Let's count then. Two side pockets in his trousers and one on the back. Four small pockets on his vest and one in the lining. In his jacket, two in the lining, two side pockets and a breast pocket. My father has a separate pocket for toothpicks, and I don't even have a pocket for my gilli[3]. Moreover, adults always have drawers, desks, sideboards and shelves, and then they boast that they never lose anything and keep their things in good order."

The journalist took that down.

Next were the two deputies who must have suffered because of a younger sibling.

"Who do you think is responsible for pampering and rocking the baby?"

"And you always have to give your baby brother his way."

"And they tell you to set a good example. If a tiny kid does something wrong, they don't tell him off but say: 'He learned that from you.' But did I ever tell him to imitate me?"

The journalist took that down, too.

---

3   Gilli—a piece of equipment in the game of 'Gilli Danda', which is played with two pieces—a 'danda', being a long wooden stick (about 3 feet), and a 'gilli', a small (4–6 in) oval-shaped piece of wood.

The journalist wrote in the newspaper that no parliament in the world could possibly decide that people should become either angels or magicians. He also stressed the impossibility of having Shrove Tuesday every day or going to the circus every evening. No parliament could vote to remove girls or boys from the world, and there had to be room for both younger and older children.

The article was tactfully worded so as not to offend the deputies. The author avoided such expressions as 'rubbish', 'makes no sense' or 'pulls their ears'. The newspaper wrote only what was realistic and what was not.

More pockets? Well that could be done. Tailors would be told to make garments with more pockets.

And so on.

After reading the article, Clue-Clue did not even try to hide that she was angry.

"My dear Matthew, let me be present at the next session, and I'll tell them what I think of the fact that there are no girls in your parliament."

"There are girls, but they don't say anything."

"So, I will say what they should be saying but are afraid to. I'll tell them what I think about the idea that there should be no girls at all just because of one nasty girl in someone's backyard! How many unbearable boys are there in this world? Should they disappear from the face of the earth? I don't understand how white people, who have invented so many wonderful things, could still be so stupid and savage?"

So, Matthew agreed to take little Clue-Clue to the children's parliament. On the way, her heart pounded like a jackhammer. Not because the girl was afraid, but because she was trying to collect her thoughts and not to forget the most important points. Everybody was watching her curiously as she sat in the royal box next to King Matthew, now perfectly composed.

Felix, or should I say Baron von Rauch, opened the session. He rang the bell and said:

"Ladies and gentlemen, the session is opened. Today's agenda: Point One—Each child should have a watch! The next item on the agenda: Point Two—Children should not be kissed. Point Three—Children should have more pockets. Point Four—Let there be no girls."

Regarding Point One—Each child should have a watch—fifteen deputies signed up for the debate.

One deputy maintained that the children needed watches so they could get to school on time and not arrive late for their lessons. The first speaker to take the floor said that adults could sooner do without watches because they could count faster and had a better sense of time.

"If my father and mother's timepieces are slow, why should I suffer for it?" argued the second speaker. "Once I have my own watch, I'll make sure it's accurate and shows the right time."

"A watch isn't necessary only for school," said the third deputy. "If we're late for dinner or supper, we always get reprimanded. And are we to blame if we don't know what time it is, having no watches?"

"You can't do without a watch in some games," reasoned the fourth speaker. "When we race each other or want to know who can stand longer on one leg, a watch is also a useful thing."

"And when we hire a boat by the hour, we're often cheated. We're told that an hour has passed, which is a lie, but we still have to pay for sixty minutes."

Felix rang his bell once again.

"And now we'll take a show of hands—are you for or against the motion? I think the bill will be passed unanimously."

But nine deputies, quite contrary to reason, voted against.

The journalist rushed to them immediately to be first to know their motives.

"Because watches are expensive, and once we begin to wind them, we may very well damage them beyond repair. Because a watch can easily be lost. Because when you want to walk on your hands, it's sure to fall out of your pocket and break. Because, since not all adults have watches, they'll surely become jealous and take ours. Because watches are a needless luxury. Because a father could pinch a child's watch or sell it and drink the money away."

Felix rang the bell once again.

"The bill was passed with 491 votes for and 9 against."

The next bill against children being kissed by whoever felt like it, against children being stroked, being forced to sit on anyone's lap, patted and caressed, was passed unanimously. An exception could be made in the case of parents, but certainly not aunts. A commission was created to draw up the bill once again and include all the possible cases, and only then would it be put to a final vote.

Regarding Point Three on the agenda, it was decided that girls should have two pockets and boys six.

Clue-Clue was outraged. Why should boys have three times as many pockets as girls? But she remained silent and listened.

Felix gave another ring: the question of girls.

And so it began.

Girls are cry-babies. Girls are busybodies and chatterboxes. Girls are tattletales. Girls are born pretenders. Delicate. Butterfingers. Dumb blondes. Girls are secretive. Girls are proud. Girls are touchy. Girls will scratch you.

The poor girls-deputies sat there, their eyes full of tears, unable to defend themselves. From the royal box, Clue-Clue called out:

"I request permission to speak."

Instantly, such a silence fell that you could hear a pin drop.

"In my country, boys and girls are just as agile; girls run as fast as boys, are as good at climbing trees and turning somersaults. I'm at a loss for words. I can't understand. Boys are forever quarrelling with girls; they are regular killjoys. Instead of joining in, they're always trying to spoil the fun for others. You don't have to look closely to see that there are more rowdies and bullies among boys than girls."

"Boo, Boo!" was heard from the rows occupied by boys-deputies.

Felix rang the bell and repeated:

"Order, order!"

"Boys are bullies and are always fighting, their hands are dirty and they wear out their clothes in no time. Boys cheat and tell lies."

"Boo, Boo, Boo!"

"Boys tear pages out of their exercise books and vandalize books. They don't want to study and are too noisy. They break window panes. They bully girls, taking advantage of the fact that girls are weaker because they wear dresses and long hair…"

"Why don't they cut their hair?"

"And put on trousers."

Baron von Rauch used his bell again.

"…girls are weaker, so boys hurt them. And then they put on an innocent air."

Suddenly, all hell broke loose in the session hall. Some stamped their feet, whistled with their fingers and yelled all at the same time.

"Look at her. Some teacher she is!"

"You have white hands!"

"To the monkey cage with her!"

"The king's fiancée!"

"Matthew's wife!"

"Matthew, Matt! Meow, meow! Go catch mice!"

"Canary! Perch yourself on a branch and sing!"

The loudest deputy was from the capital. He jumped on his armchair and yelled so hard that his face became red from exertion. Felix knew him well. Tony, a regular prowler, a pickpocket…

"Tony, I swear!" yelled Felix, "I will knock out all your teeth!"

"Try it, tough guy. Look at him, the Minister, Baron von Rauch, Felix the Great. Do you remember the days when you stole apples from fishwives' baskets? Because I do, Foolix!"

Felix threw an inkwell at Tony and then his bell. The deputies divided into three groups. The first scrambled out of the session hall at full speed while the remaining factions waged a fierce battle.

King Matthew, speechless and white as chalk, watched dumbfounded.

The journalist took notes.

"Baron von Rauch, please calm down. There's nothing wrong going on. This is how political parties come into being," he said to Felix.

Felix really calmed down when he saw that the deputies had forgotten all about him in the chaos.

Oh, how Clue-Clue was tempted to join the battle. All she would need to do was slide down the cornice from the royal box, catch hold of one of the armchairs and show those jackanapes how African girls could fight. Clue-Clue knew all too well that true though her words were, if she had not spoken them, the battle would not have broken out. The girl felt genuinely sorry for Matthew, but she did not regret saying what she had said. That little tongue-lashing really did hurt the boys, but they completely deserved it. And what had they said in return? That she was black? No, really!? And that she had been in the cage with those unfortunate monkeys, but so what? Let that bunch of sissies try to spend an hour in such a cage. Matthew's fiancée? Why not? If only Matthew would agree to marry her. Too bad that that stupid European etiquette did not allow her to take part in the fight!

Oh boy, they cannot fight! thought Clue-Clue. *Some boys they are! Klutzes, baboons, lubbers! They've been fighting for ten minutes and neither side has won. They jump forth and back like little red roosters punching the air. And that Baron von what's his name, he can't aim. If I had thrown something at the scoundrel, be it inkwell or bell, Tony would not be standing so triumphantly on the table right now...*

Clue-Clue couldn't stand it anymore. She grabbed the banister with one hand and an iron bar with another and, like a bird perched on the cornice, took a leap. Bracing her fall by taking hold of the lamp bracket, she jumped over the foreign correspondents table and, pushing aside five attackers, stood face-to-face with Tony.

"You wanna fight?" he asked with a swagger.

Tony took a wide swing to hit Clue-Clue, but regretted it on the spot. In a fraction of a second, she had already landed four blows, head-butting him on the nose, punching him with both fists and planting her boot in him for good measure. Before he knew what was happening, Tony lay on the floor with a broken nose, a numb neck, a limp right hand and missing three front teeth.

Poor white people, what weak teeth they have, thought Clue-Clue.

In no time, she found herself at the Prime Minister's table, where she dipped her hankie in a glass of water and applied it to Tony's nose.

"Don't worry," she said in an attempt to comfort him. "Your hand isn't broken. In my country, people stay in bed for a day after such a mishap, but you're so delicate, and you might take at least a week to fully recover. As for your teeth, I'm really sorry. Our teeth are stronger."

Matt returned to the palace completely offended. Never again would he set his foot in the children's parliament!

All they wanted was to be made magicians and given dolls as tall as a house. Fools, egregious asses! Matthew smiled—he liked strong language.

What ingratitude! Some payment for his hard work and devotion. His honest intentions. For the dangerous expeditions during which he risked life and limb for them. For his heroic defense of the country. He began to wish he had not even tried to make them happy. The roofs were leaking, the food was terrible, no fun and games. In what country did children have such a zoological garden? What about the fireworks display and military orchestras? Who edited and published the newspaper for them. Was it worthwhile? No, it was not! The same newspaper would make it known to all and sundry that King Matthew had been called a cat and a canary. No, it was not worthwhile.

Matthew announced that he would no longer be reading letters from the children, there would be no more after-dinner audiences, and that he did not want to give out any more presents. Enough was enough!

Matthew telephoned the Prime Minister to tell him he was urgently needed in the palace. Matthew felt he could not do without his advice.

"Please put me through to the private residence of the Prime Minister."

"And who is speaking?"

"The king."

"But the Prime Minister is out," said the Prime Minister, not realizing that Matthew would recognize his voice.

"But you are speaking to me now on the phone," said Matthew.

"Oh, it's Your Royal Highness. Oh, I'm so sorry, but I can't come as I have fallen ill and have to stay in bed. That's why I said I was not at home."

Matthew put down the receiver.

"He's lying!" Matthew hissed, pacing up and down his study. "He doesn't want to come, because he already knows. Nobody will respect me now. Everybody will laugh at me and talk about me behind my back."

Then the lackey announced a visit by Felix and the journalist.

"Tell them to come in!" ordered King Matthew.

"I've come to ask Your Royal Highness what I should write in the paper about today's Pro-Par's session. We can leave the incident unmentioned, but this will breed gossip. So, perhaps we could write that the debate was pretty stormy, and that Baron von Rauch handed in his resignation—which means that he got offended and no longer wished to be minister—but the king did not accept it. As it is, Baron von Rauch will remain in office and the king will award him a medal."

"And what will you write about me?" said Matthew.

"Nothing at all. Really! One doesn't write such things about the king. But the worst thing is Tony. After all, he's a deputy, and therefore he cannot be whipped. The deputies can beat one another, but the government cannot do anything to them, for they have parliamentary immunity. In any case, he took an epic beating from Clue-Clue, which serves him right, and perhaps that has taken him down a peg or two."

Matthew was very glad that the newspaper would say nothing of Tony making fun of the king, and he was ready to forgive and forget.

"Tomorrow the session begins at twelve."

"I couldn't care less," said Matthew. "I'm not going to attend."

"That's too bad," replied the journalist. "They might think that Your Royal Highness is a scaredy-cat."

"So, what should I do? I'm not scared, but offended," said Matthew tearfully.

"In that case, a delegation of deputies will come to apologize to Your Royal Highness."

"Good," agreed Matthew.

The journalist left because he had to prepare the article for tomorrow's newspaper. But Felix remained.

"Didn't I tell you to stop calling yourself Matthew?"

"So what?" Matthew interrupted him sharply. "You called yourself Baron Felix von Rauch and they called you Foolix! This is far worse than the names they called me. There's nothing wrong with a cat…"

"I get your point, but wait a minute. I'm a mere minister, while you're a king. It's certainly worse for a king to be called a cat than a minister to be called Foolix."

Clue-Clue did not go to the session, but Matthew had no choice. At first, it was no picnic. But at least everybody was very quiet, and then the speeches became more and more interesting. Matthew soon forgot the bitterness of the previous session.

The deputies raised the issue of red ink and appealed to adults not to laugh at their children.

"The problem is that whenever the teachers mark the children's exercise books they always use red ink. If this color is prettier, then we also want to write with red pens."

"Yes," agreed a girl-deputy, "and they should cover our exercise books with paper because they always get dirty. They could also give us some stickers or flowers to decorate them so that they look prettier."

When the girl finished her speech, there was a round of applause. The boys-deputies wanted to show that they were no longer cross with the girls and that yesterday's row was the fault of only a handful of troublemakers. If out of five hundred deputies only a dozen were rascals, that really wasn't too many.

A lot of speakers raised the problem of grownups laughing at their children.

"If you ask them something or do something wrong, then they either get mad and yell at you, or—which is no better—laugh at you. That's not how it should be! Grownups think that they know everything, but it certainly isn't true. My father, for example, could not name all the promontories in Australia and all the rivers in America; he did not know where the source of the Nile is."

"The Nile is in Africa not America," called one of the deputies from his seat.

"I know that. I just used that example. Grownups know absolutely nothing about post stamps and cannot whistle with their fingers, and that's why they say that it's bad to whistle."

"My uncle can whistle."

"But not with his fingers!"

"Maybe not with his fingers. But how do you know?"

"You're as thick as a brick."

Perhaps another fray would have broken out, but just then Felix rang his bell and said that deputies must not call one another thick for any reason. For such an offense, the deputies would be excluded from the proceedings.

"And what does 'excluded from the proceedings' mean?"

"This is a parliamentary expression, at school we say to throw somebody out."

Slowly but surely the deputies were learning parliamentary etiquette.

Towards the end of the session, a deputy arrived.

"I'm sorry for coming so late, but my mother didn't want me go to the session because yesterday someone scratched my nose and I have a bump on my forehead."

"This is unheard of; a deputy is untouchable, and nobody–mother or otherwise–can forbid him or her to attend a parliamentary session. How would that look? Once one has been chosen as a deputy, one has to serve the country. Someone could scratch your nose at school and your parents wouldn't forbid you to go."

That is how the generational dispute started out, but it was only the beginning.

What neither Matthew nor the deputies knew was that foreign newspapers had already begun to write about the children's parliament, and children abroad began to talk about it both at school and at home. When they got a bad mark at school undeservedly or the teachers were mad at them, they said:

"If only we had our own deputies, such things would be unthinkable."

In a small kingdom ruled by Queen Campanella in southern Europe, the children got angry about something or another and went on strike. Someone had heard that children wanted to have their own flag just like workers, and the flag should be green. So, they held a green-flag procession.

Their elders grew very angry.

"What a fine kettle of fish. We can't cope with our workers and their red flag, and now our children take to the streets. That's all we need!"

The news made Matthew very happy, and the children's newspaper published an editorial entitled:

THE MOVEMENT BEGINS!

The article read that in a small kingdom ruled by Queen Campanella in southern Europe, the climate was warm and the children were hot-tempered. That is why it was the first place where children began to demand their rights.

It will not be long before the green flag is hailed by all the children in the world as theirs. And then they will understand that they should not fight with one another, and there will be love, peace and order. There will no longer be any wars. For if they don't learn how not to fight as small children, they won't know how to avoid fighting as grownups.

It was King Matthew who first said that children should have a green flag. The authors then went on to say that since Matthew came up with this idea, he might become king not only of his own country but of the whole world.

Princess Clue-Clue will return to Africa and explain everything to her black brothers and sisters. Things will change for the better. Children will have the same rights as their elders and will become citizens.

Children will be obedient not out of fear but because they desire peace and order.

There was a lot to read in the paper, and Matthew began to wonder why the sad king had once told him that it was very difficult to be a reformer and that reformers usually came to a wretched end. He claimed it was only after their death that people fully appreciated what a reformer had brought about.

"As far as I'm concerned, I'm doing quite well and no danger threatens me. It's true that I have had some worries and problems, but these are things every ruler must be prepared to cope with."

Quite unexpectedly before the Houses of Parliament, a crowd of youths had gathered. All of them were over fifteen years of age. One of them climbed a lamppost and started shouting:

"They have completely forgotten about us! We also want our own deputies. The adults have their parliament; the children have theirs…and what about us? Are we worth less, or even less than the most worthless citizens? We will never let these puppies run the show. If they are given chocolate, we must be given cigarettes. We want justice!"

The deputies were on their way to the session hall, and the demonstrators would not let them pass.

"Some deputies they are. They don't know their multiplication table and can't tell a 'boom' from a 'bum.'"

"And some of them can't write at all."

"How can they rule?"

"Down with the government of sissies!"

The Police Prefect telephoned to ask Matthew to stay in the palace, for another row had broken out. In the meantime, he ordered the mounted police to disperse the rioters. The latter would not budge an inch and soon began to attack the police with whatever ammunition they had: mostly books and lunch boxes. Some of the more aggressive among them began to pry flagstones up from the sidewalks and hurl them at the policemen.

At that moment, the Police Prefect appeared on the balcony and cried:

"If you don't go, I'll call out the troops! And if you throw stones at the soldiers, they'll first fire a warning shot in the air, and if that doesn't help, they'll shoot to kill."

The prefect's warning did not help. The rioters became even more furious. They broke down the door and barged into the session hall.

"We refuse to leave until we receive the same rights as the children."

Everyone panicked and no one knew what to do. All of a sudden, Matthew entered the royal box. Paying no mind to the prefect's warning, he had come to find out what the problem was.

"We want to have our own parliament, too. We want to have our own deputies. We want to have the same rights."

At first, they shouted and yelled at full volume, so nobody knew who was saying what.

Matthew stood and waited. Some demonstrators, seeing that all that racket cut no ice with the king, began trying to hush their comrades-in-arms:

"OK, OK, now stop that noise!"

At long last, someone shouted:

"The king wants to speak!"

Silence fell and Matthew addressed everyone assembled, both legally and illegally. He gave a long and wise speech and admitted that the protesters were right.

"Citizens," he said. "Yes, you deserve your rights. But before long, you'll be adults yourselves, and some of you will become part of the adult parliament. I began with the children because I'm small myself, and I know their needs better. Rome wasn't built in a day. You can't do everything at once. Anyway, I have always had a lot of work. When I grow up and I'm fifteen like you and have sorted out the problems of smaller children, I'll take care of you."

"But by then we'll be in the adult parliament and we won't need your favors."

Matthew realized that he had made a mistake and tried again on a different tack:

"Why are you picking on me? You've already got moustaches and smoke cigarettes, so go to the second parliament, they're sure to give you a hearing there."

The eldest protester, who really did wear a thin moustache, thought:

He's right; we don't need any kiddy parliament when we could be in a real parliament!

The younger rioters, ashamed to admit that they did not smoke cigarettes, also said: "Point taken."

The crowd set off for the adult parliament, but the soldiers would not let them in. They stood guard, bayonets at the ready, and ordered the protesters to halt. The boys turned only to find that they were being followed by a few hundred troops. So, they split up into smaller groups and dispersed in different directions. But the military followed them into the side streets. They continued splitting into smaller and smaller groups, easy prey for the police, who arrested them one by one.

When Matthew learned about the sad end to the youth protests, he became very angry with the Police Prefect, for now it looked as if the king had cheated the demonstrators, who had trusted him. But the prefect explained that he had had no choice. So, Matthew had notices placed on every street corner, instructing the youths to choose the three cleverest protesters to be their delegates, and he would give them an audience to discuss the matter thoroughly.

In the evening, the king was invited to the Cabinet meeting.

"Things are going from bad to worse," said the Minister of Education. "The children don't want to work hard. If the teachers give them homework to do, they pay no attention and laugh the whole thing off: 'Try and do something to us and we will tell on you to the king. Or, we'll inform our deputies.' And the teachers are helpless. And the older pupils won't listen to the teachers either: 'Those kids do as they please and we have to keep slogging away? No way! If we don't have our deputies, we might as well have no schools.' Previously small children fought with each other and now older children pick on them, teasing: 'Go and tell on me to your deputy.' They grab the poor kids by the ears, and beat them. The teachers say they'll wait another two weeks, and if nothing improves, they don't want to be teachers any longer. A few have already left. One already has a soda water vending machine and another is opening a button factory."

"On the whole, the adults are very dissatisfied," said the Minister of the Interior. "Yesterday a gentleman in a coffee shop said that all the reforms had gone to the children's heads; they think they can do what they please, and the noise they make is slowly driving him mad. They jump on the couches, play soccer in the living room and stay out after dark without permission. On top of that, they keep wearing out their clothes in record time. They'll soon be dressed like people living in the wilderness. The gentleman said many more things, most of which don't bear repeating. I had him arrested and now he faces trial for lèse-majesté, or defaming the king."

"I know what I must do!" exclaimed Matthew. "Let all those who go to school be considered office workers. They also write, count, work and go to school just like office workers go to their offices. So, their work should also be paid. From now on, we will pay them. We will decide whether to pay them with chocolate, skates, dolls or money. But the children will know that they have to do their job properly, or else they won't be paid."

"Well, it's certainly worth a try," agreed the ministers.

Matthew had completely forgotten that he was no longer ruling and such decisions now lay with the parliament, so he had suitable notices written and placed on every street corner.

First thing in the morning, the journalist dropped by, and paying little attention to etiquette, he snapped angrily:

"If Your Royal Highness is going to have all the important news put up in public, then what is my newspaper for?"

Then Felix dropped by:

"If Your Royal Highness is going to introduce new laws, then what's my parliament for?"

"Yes, indeed," admitted the journalist. "Baron von Rauch is absolutely right. The king can only say what he wishes to do, and then the deputies must say whether they agree or not. And who knows? They may come up with a better idea."

It was a bitter pill to swallow, but Matthew admitted he had made a snap decision. What was he to do now?

"Your Royal Highness had better order that, for the time being, chocolate should be given out like before or else we may face a revolution. There's no time to lose, and the matter will be discussed in today's session."

Matthew had grave misgivings—surely something really bad had happened. At first, the deputies decided to refer the matter to the parliamentary committee. But the king would not agree to it:

"It takes time for a committee to reach a decision. And we have to be quick. The teachers threatened they would only wait for two weeks, and if nothing changes, they will resign from teaching. End of story."

The journalist approached Felix and whispered something in his ear. The latter grinned broadly, and when Matthew finished his address, he asked for permission to speak.

"Ladies and gentlemen," said Felix. "I used to go to school, and I know all too well what goes on there. Within one year, I was unfairly punished on hundreds of occasions: I had to stand in the corner one hundred and fifty times, I was kept after school one hundred and twelve times, I was ordered to bring a parent to school seventy times, and I lost count of how many times my knuckles were rapped with a ruler. And it wasn't just one school! I went to six different schools and everywhere it was the same story. Our elders do not go to school, so they can't know what hotbeds of injustice our schools are. I think that if the teachers don't want to teach the children, then we could introduce a law ordering them to teach adults. Once the adults see what a pleasure it is, they will stop forcing us to toil, and the teachers will see that it's even tougher with grownups. When they can't cut it, the teachers will have to stop running us down."

Felix had opened a can of worms. An endless stream of complaints about schools and teachers followed. This deputy had been wrongly forced to repeat the school year; another had made just two mistakes on a test and only scored a 'D'. Another boy had arrived late because of pain in his leg and was forced to stand in the corner. A girl-deputy could not memorize a poem because her younger brother had torn out and destroyed the page, but the teacher did not believe her and claimed that she had invented the excuse.

When the deputies got tired and hungry, Felix put the bill to the vote:

"The committee will decide what to do to make school more just and whether pupils are to be paid for their work just as office workers are paid. And in the meantime, the grownups will go to school. Those in favor, please raise your hands."

A few deputies wanted to say something, but the majority raised their hands and Baron Felix von Rauch announced:

"The law has been passed."

No words can describe what went on in King Matthew's country when the people learned about the law the children's parliament had introduced.

"We will never agree to such a new order!" protested some people. "We don't take orders from snot-nosed kids! We've got our own parliament and the children have theirs. Their parliament decides for them and ours for us. Otherwise, it doesn't make any sense."

"Let's imagine we go to school. Who will work?" said the others.

"Let the children implement their plan. They'll see it's not as easy as they think."

"We'll see," remarked the less hot-headed. "Perhaps it's a blessing in disguise. The moment the children see that they can't manage without their parents, they'll start to respect us."

The unemployed rubbed their hands:

This Matthew is a wise king. We were about to revolt, but he knew better. Digging and carrying bricks is a hard occupation, and now we'll be sitting comfortably at our desks and learning interesting things.

"And how much will we be paid?"

"The new law says that we'll be paid the same as for normal work. Studying is also work. Now according to this law, the grownups have to go to school, and the children will take care of the rest."

This reorganization was creating a lot of chaos because all the boys wanted to be drivers and fire-fighters, while the girls were choosing to be shop assistants in toy and sweet shops. Some, as always on such occasions, talked nonsense: one boy wanted to be an executioner, another an Apache Indian, and still another a loony.

"But not everybody can do the same thing."

"Let somebody else do it. Why should I take a job that nobody else wants?"

Squabbles broke out in many families as children 'passed on' their books and exercise books to their parents.

"You've dog-eared the books and stained the exercise books; we'll look like slobs," said one mother.

"You've lost your pencil and now I have nothing to draw with; the teacher will be cross with me," said one father.

"Breakfast wasn't on time, so now write me an excuse. I'm sure to be late for the first lesson," said one granny.

The teachers were very glad that they could rest a bit, for the adults were much quieter than their children:

"We'll set a good example for the children," said their mothers.

There were also those who had a good laugh, who could enjoy the humor of the situation:

"After all, it won't last too long," they said.

It was a rather strange sight as children left for their offices, factories and shops while the adults went to school with their satchels full of books. Some were very sad and embarrassed, but there were those who could not care less:

"So what? Isn't it nice to be a child again? What's wrong with being a child?"

They looked back on the good old days, met long forgotten friends in the classroom with whom they used to share a desk decades ago. They remembered their old teachers, various practical jokes played on them and old friends:

"Do you remember our old Latin teacher?" an engineer asked his classmate.

"Do you remember how we once had a fight? What was it about?"

"Oh yes, I know. I had bought a pocket knife, and you said it was not stainless steel, but iron."

"And we ended up in detention, as far as I remember."

A certain doctor and lawyer relived those memories so much so that they forgot they were no longer teenagers and began to push one another until their biology teacher reminded them they were in the street and should behave themselves.

But there were people who did not enjoy the masquerade at all. One very fat lady, a restaurant owner, was on her way to school with her books, as mad as a bear with a headache, when suddenly she was recognized by a car mechanic:

"Look at that piglet. Isn't she the one who is always cheating us: she always waters down our drinks and charges for a piece of herring as if it were a whole fish. I don't know about you, but I'm going to trip her. Boys will be boys, won't they?"

He did trip her, and the fat lady nearly fell down, dropping her exercise books in the process.

"You scoundrels!" she yelled, collecting her scattered books.

"It was an accident."

"Wait till I tell the headmistress that you're going around bullying innocent schoolgirls."

Stranger still, the children were very quiet and took their duties very seriously. At nine o'clock sharp, all the offices and shops were open.

At this hour, the grownups were just taking their seats. Grannies and granddaddies sat at the back of the classroom close to the oven, hoping to be able to nap during the lesson.

Everything went as it should; the pupils did what they were told: to read, write and do math problems. The teachers checked how much they remembered. Once or twice, the teacher was a little irked that they did not pay attention, but it was not easy to concentrate because everybody was thinking about what might be going on at home, in the factories and shops, and how the children were doing.

The girls wanted to show that they were born housewives and knew how to keep house. They wanted their first dinner to be the most delicious ever. But the task was tougher than most of them had thought at first.

"You know what? Perhaps it would be better to serve jam instead of soup."

Then they went shopping.

"What a pricey place to do my shopping. I'll go somewhere else."

Some children haggled to show their mothers how cheaply they could buy. But the shop assistants, also children, wanted to show that they could make money hand over fist. Trade was in full swing:

"And a dozen oranges."

"And a pound of raisins."

"And some Swiss cheese. But it better not be too ripe or I'll bring it back."

"My cheeses are always the best quality, and my oranges have the thinnest skin in town."

"That's good. How much?"

The shop assistant, making an unsuccessful attempt at counting, asked:

"How much money do you have."

"One hundred."

"That's not enough. So many different things should cost more."

"Fine. I'll bring some more later."

"OK."

"Can I have my change?"

"Are you crazy? You aren't paying the full bill and you want change back? You'd better have your head tested!"

Undoubtedly, the service provided by the children left much to be desired both in the shops and offices, and at every turn you could overhear:

"Crazy! Stupid! Clear off! Big deal! The door is over there! Get stuffed! Thick as a brick! Get lost!" and so on, and so forth.

Also overheard was:

"Just wait till my mother comes back from school!" or "You're gonna get what's coming to you when my daddy's back from school!"

The worst 'pain in the neck' were the hooligans who barged into shops and helped themselves from the shelves without paying.

There were policemen, but the boys stood on the street corners, not really knowing what to do.

"Some policeman you are! A bunch of lager louts burst in the shop, grabbed a crate of beer and three packets of California dried plums, and ran away."

"And where did they go?"

"How should I know?"

"If you don't know, how can I possibly help you?"

"If you're a policeman, you should have your wits about you."

"Well, you've got one shop, and you can't take good care of it, while I've got fifty shops to keep an eye on."

"You are a fool."

"Maybe I am. Next time don't ask me for help."

The policeman left with a sword dangling by his side; it was far too big for a boy his size.

"Not a single good word, just constant nagging for something that's not your fault. What a lousy life! Stand like a pillar of salt and keep an eye on everything. And those skinflints won't even give you an apple or a sweet. I'll tell them: I don't want to be a policeman and that's final. Let them do what they please. I can even come back to school, but I won't be a policeman."

Then parents came back from school, and the children asked by way of greeting:

"Hi, mom! Did you pay attention in class?"

"Hi, dad! Did you do your homework correctly?"

"Did granny get any good marks today?"

"Granddaddy, who are you sitting next to in class?"

On their way home from the office, the children dropped by school to pick up their mothers or fathers.

"What were you doing at the office today, sonny?" asks father.

"Oh, nothing much. I was sitting at the desk, and then I was looking out of the window and saw a funeral procession. Then I tried to smoke a cigarette, but it was really bitter. On the desk were some papers, so I wrote my name on each of them. Then three gentlemen arrived, but they spoke a foreign language, probably French or German, so I said I did not understand. Then there was a tea break, but without tea, so I ate all the sugar from the sugar bowl. And then I telephoned my friends to know what they were doing, but I only got through to one who told me he was working at the post office and that there were a lot letters with foreign post stamps there."

Dinners in some homes were quite good, but in some others, everything was either burnt or the children had trouble lighting the fire, so the cooking had to be done quickly.

"I've got no time to lose," said one mom, "because I have a huge pile of homework to do for tomorrow. Our headmistress said that the adults should be given more to learn. That doesn't seem fair. My friends in other schools don't have as much to do."

"Have any of you been kept after school or made to stand in the corner?"

The mother, slightly ashamed, admitted that some had.

"For what?"

"Two ladies in row 'D' used to know each other. They once shared a flat or something. Anyway, they talked throughout the lesson. The teacher asked them twice to stop before finally telling them to stand in the corner."

"Did they cry?"

"One was impudent enough to laugh, but the other had tears in her eyes."

"And the boys…don't they chat you up?"

"Oh, they do. A little."

"That's exactly like in our school," laughed the children.

Matt was sitting in his study and reading the newspaper in which that very first day was described in detail. The paper admitted that there were some hiccups; telephones were barely working, there were some problems with letters and postcards at the post office, and yesterday one train had derailed. Nobody knew the number of injured passengers because telegraphs were not working properly. But it was just one of those things. Rome wasn't built in a day. Each reform takes time, and no reform takes place without a shock or even a number of shocks in the economic life of a country.

But there was no cause for concern as a special parliamentary committee was working hard to draft a law on education so that teachers, children and parents—in a word everyone—would be satisfied.

Suddenly, the door to the king's study burst opened, and Clue-Clue burst in. Visibly pleased, she clapped her hands, jumping up and down and singing a song of the jungle.

"Guess what has happened?"

"I've no idea, but do tell me. I'm dying to know."

"One thousand black children have arrived."

Matthew had forgotten that at one time, he had asked Felix to wire King Bum-Drum to invite one hundred children to visit the kingdom, but on the way a zero had somehow been added to the message; King Matthew was hosting not one hundred, but one thousand children!

Matthew felt a little embarrassed, but Clue-Clue was delighted.

"It's even better. The more children are trained in Europe, the easier it will be to put things right in Africa."

Clue-Clue put on a pair of shoes and socks, a habit she had previously scorned, and started to train the children. She led them into the park. She chose the most able children as leaders for each group of one hundred. Each of those larger groups was divided into ten children and led by one of their own. Each child responsible for ten compatriots was called a 'tenner' and given a room in the summer palace, while the 'centurions' stayed in the winter palace. Clue-Clue told the centurions at once what was acceptable in Europe and what was considered bad behavior. The centurions passed this on to the tenners, and they, in turn, to the children under their command.

Matthew still had doubts.

"What will such a big crowd do?"

"The same as the one hundred you meant to invite."

"Where will they sleep?"

"For the time being, they can sleep on the floor. They are still wild and it will make no difference to them."

"What will they eat?" asked Matthew. "You know that all the cooks are going to school now."

"For the time being, they can eat raw meat. They are still wild and it will make no difference to them."

Clue-Clue had never liked wasting time, so she taught the first lesson right after dinner. She was such a gifted teacher that after only four hours, the centurions knew enough to begin teaching the tenners.

Things were beginning to look up, but all of sudden a mounted messenger arrived with the news that some children had unwittingly opened the cages of the wolves in the zoo.

"All the wolves have escaped. The people are so frightened that they won't leave their houses. Even my horse refused to move until I used an iron riding crop on him," said the messenger.

"Why did they let the wolves out?"

"It wasn't their fault. The zookeepers went to school and didn't tell the children who were replacing them that the cages had automatic bolt releases. Since the children did not know, they accidentally opened the cages."

"How many wolves have escaped?"

"Twelve, one of which is a real beast. I have absolutely no idea how to catch him."

"Where are the wolves now?"

"God only knows. They are running wild. People have reported seeing them in the town center, running up and down the city streets. But there's no use giving credit to what frightened people say because they see a wolf in every stray dog. Rumors are already circulating that all the animals have escaped from their cages. One woman swore that she had been chased by a tiger, a hippopotamus and two cobras."

When the news reached Clue-Clue, she took an immediate interest in the wolves because there were no such animals in Africa.

"Do they roar when they are about to attack? Can they jump well? Do they catch with their teeth or claws? Do they always attack people or only when they are hungry? Are they courageous or cowardly? Do they have good hearing, smell, sight?"

Matthew was ashamed to know so little, but what little he knew, he did his best to explain.

"I think," said Clue-Clue, "that they have probably hidden in the garden itself. I'll take the centurions and we'll make short work of it. Oh, what a pity that the lions and the tigers haven't escaped. The hunt would be far more exciting."

So, Matthew accompanied Clue-Clue and ten of her friends on their way to the zoo. People stood in their windows, peering out at the deserted city streets. The city was virtually empty. The shops were closed as if the entire capital was abandoned. Matthew was ashamed of his fellow countrymen. He had not suspected they were so cowardly.

Soon they reached the garden and began to beat their drums and blow their reed fifes. The noise was deafening—as if an entire army was marching. They reached a place where the woody shrubs formed a dense impenetrable thicket.

"Halt!" commanded Clue-Clue. "Get your bows ready!"

Something stirred in the bushes. Clue-Clue dashed forward and jumped on a tree. The moment she caught hold of the branch, a monstrous wolf rushed at her out of the thicket. He braced his forepaws against the trunk, scratching and howling, while the rest of the pack chimed in from afar.

"This is the leader!" cried Clue-Clue. "Now we can drive the remaining eleven into the cage. Round the bushes from the left and frighten them away."

They did as they were told.

The eleven wolves scrambled away in mad fear, hearing the black hunters beat their drums and fleeing the blunt arrows fired towards them. Soon the wolves were back in their cage.

The cage was bolted instantly. The leader, seeing that he was alone on the battlefield, made an impressive leap into the trees, and the hunters almost instantly lost sight of him.

Clue-Clue jumped out of the tree.

"Faster, faster!" she cried. "We can't let him escape from the garden!"

But it was too late. The wolf, as mad as a March hare, fled into the city streets. Now the capital's inhabitants really did see the wolf running down the street with ten black children in hot pursuit. Behind them limped Matthew. There was no way he could keep up with children from the jungle! Sweaty, tired, and almost ready to collapse, Matthew was spotted by an old and kind-hearted woman, who treated him to a roll with fresh butter and a glass of milk.

"Eat, King Matthew, eat," she said. "You are a good king. I'm eighty years old and I have seen various kings. Some were better and some were worse, but I've never seen a king like you. You have even thought about us, the elderly. You gave us a chance to go back to school, which is such a blessing, and you're even paying for it. I have a son far away overseas. He writes to me twice a year. I keep his letters but I can't read them. And I don't want to give them to strangers to read to me, for they may contain some secret, or they might read into them something my son didn't intend. And now I'll be able to see for myself what he's been doing. And our teacher, a very nice woman, said that if I tried really hard, in two months I'd be able to write to him myself."

Matthew drank his milk, kissed the old woman on the hand, thanked her for her kindness and left.

In the meantime, the wolf jumped into the canal and refused to move. Clue-Clue decided to take on the wolf in his den.

"What!?" shouted Matthew. "Over my dead body! This is an underground canal and it's pitch dark in there. You'll either suffocate for want of fresh air or the wolf will tear you to pieces."

But Matthew's arguments fell on deaf ears. Clue-Clue, holding a hunter's knife between her teeth, climbed down into the canal. Even her black friends were frightened, because wild animals are most dangerous in darkness.

Matthew remained on the surface wondering what he should do when he remembered he had an electric torch on him. So without further ado, he lowered himself into the canal. Such a narrow pipe—where could they have gone? He walked cautiously through an underground passage with a vaulted ceiling. He saw water flowing, or rather foul-smelling liquid mud from the gutters. A choking smell filled Matthew's nostrils and made his eyes water.

"Clue-Clue!" shouted Matthew, his voice reverberating from all directions through the canals, which formed a gigantic network under the capital. Matthew had no way of knowing whether Clue-Clue was answering him or not. He switched the torch on and off, unsure whether the battery might go dead. Suddenly, while wading through knee-deep sewage in one underground passage, Matthew heard the muffled sounds of fighting.

He switched on the torch and spied them immediately. Clue-Clue had stabbed the wolf in the throat with her knife, but her hand was trapped in the beast's mouth, impaled on its sharp teeth. Clue-Clue shifted her knife to her left hand and frantically stabbed again. Letting go of her hand, the wolf's muzzle sought her soft belly. If he managed to disembowel her, the fight would be over. There was no time to lose. Matthew hurled himself into the fray, hitting the wolf between the eyes with the torch and momentarily blinding the beast. Taking advantage of his disorientation, Matthew drew his revolver and fired a bullet in the wolf's left eye.

Brave-hearted Clue-Clue fainted and Matthew, fighting to stay on his feet, dragged her as fast as he could towards the entrance, fearing that if he stopped for even a moment, both of them would drown in the sewage. Luckily, the children waiting on the surface had decided to take action. Although Clue-Clue had forbidden them to enter the canal, they could not bear sitting on their hands like a bunch of sissies any longer. No sooner had they stepped into the underground pipe than they spotted a light in the distance. A few minutes later, first Clue-Clue, then Matthew and finally the dead wolf had been brought out into the light of day.

"Look at the mess you've made Matthew," said the sad king. "It's high time you came to your senses, boy. Your reign faces serious threats. It would be regrettable to waste what you've achieved so far. I've come to warn you; but I fear I have come too late. I would have come a week ago, but since the children have been in charge of driving the trains, the railroad service is good for nothing. From the border, I had to travel in wagons reserved for peasants. And perhaps it was just as well because as I rode through various villages and provincial towns, I overheard what your people are saying. The situation couldn't possibly be worse, believe me."

The sad king had left his country in the utmost secrecy with the intention of coming to Matthew's rescue.

"What could have happened that's so bad?" asked Matthew, agitated.

"Oh, there's much that is evil about; you are being cheated and you don't even know it."

"I know everything," protested Matthew, his pride injured. "In case you don't know—I read the newspaper every day. The children are slowly getting accustomed to the changes. But no reform can be introduced without some problems. I know the state is slightly disorganized because of the reforms…"

"Listen, Matthew! The only newspaper you read is your own and it isn't telling you the truth. Try to read some other publications."

The sad king set a parcel of newspapers on the royal desk.

Matthew unpacked them slowly, reading only the headlines that were printed in large block letters. It was enough to know what was written in the articles themselves. The king was stunned by what he read:

King Matthew Goes Crazy
King to Marry African Ape
Rule of Black Devils
Minister-Thief—Spy Escapes from Prison
Two Fortresses Destroyed in Suspicious Blast
No Cannons, No Powder
On the Brink of War
Ministers Whisk Away Crown Jewels
Down with the Tyrant King

"See here!" exclaimed Matthew. "This is a pack of lies. None of this is true. What rule of black devils? Are they referring to the black children who have come to learn our culture? Our language? They are human beings just like us. They might even be more courageous and helpful. When the wolves escaped, it was they who, at their own peril, drove the escaped animals to their cage. Clue-Clue's hand was badly maimed. When there was nobody to sweep chimneys and blazes began, black children became chimney sweeps when white children refused to help. We have cannons and gunpowder. I know that Felix was a newspaper boy, but he was never a thief, and I'm not a tyrant."

"Matthew, getting angry won't help. I'm telling you that things are going badly. Let's go to town and you'll see for yourself."

Matthew dressed like an ordinary boy. The sad king was also wearing casual clothes.

On the way, they passed by the same barracks Matthew and Felix had run by on their way to the station, the night Matthew escaped from the palace with his mind set on joining the war. How happy he had been! How little he had understood and how childish he had been. Since then, he had seen a great deal and had no illusions.

They met an old soldier smoking a pipe near the barracks' gate.

"What is going on in the army?" they asked.

"Nothing much. The children have taken command. They have used up all the ammunition by shooting in the air and have damaged all the big guns. The army's finished and that's all there's to it."

He burst out into tears.

Now they were passing a factory. An elderly worker with a school book on his lap was learning a poem by heart for tomorrow's examination.

"How's it going in the factories?" they asked.

"Come in and see for yourselves. Now everyone can go in."

They went in. All the desks were cluttered with unsigned documents. The main boiler had burst. No machines were working, and only a few boys were hanging about the shop floor.

"What are you doing here?"

"Uh, well, they sent five hundred of us to work here. Most of the boys just walked off, and only thirty of us stayed. We don't know what to do or how to do it. Everything seems to have gone to pieces. All we are capable of is sweeping the floor. Our parents are at school, and staying home is just too boring. It's unpleasant to get paid if you aren't doing anything."

Half the shops in town were closed even though everybody knew the wolves had been recaptured.

They went into one shop where a very kind girl stood behind the counter.

"Could you tell us why so many shops are closed?"

"Because everything has been stolen. There are no police, no troops. Hooligans, looters and muggers loiter in the streets, just waiting for an opportunity to strike. What has not been stolen is now safely tucked away in people's homes."

They looked into the railroad station. Almost at once, they saw a derailed train, most of its carriages destroyed or overturned.

"How did this happen?"

"The switchman went off to play soccer, and the station master went fishing. The engine driver didn't know where the emergency brake was and…one hundred people were killed on the spot."

Matthew bit his lip to keep from crying.

Not far from the station, there was a hospital. Supposedly, the children were caring for the sick. When the doctors had less homework to do, they dropped in for half an hour or so, but it did not help much. The sick moaned and died unattended, and all the children were in tears because they did not know what to do.

"Well, Matthew, should we return to the palace?"

"No, no, I must go to the newspaper headquarters and speak to a certain journalist," answered Matthew quietly.

It was obvious that the blood was boiling in his veins.

"I can't come with you," said the sad king, "because they might recognize me."

"I'll be back soon," answered Matthew, rushing off towards the journalist's office.

The sad king stood there with his arms akimbo, looking on sadly until Matthew disappeared around the corner. As the king returned to the palace, Matthew was traveling at a dead run. He clenched his fists and felt as if the ghost of Henry the Impetuous was speaking to him.

"Just wait until I get hold of you, you son of a gun, you dirty liar, you thief! You will answer for this!"

Matthew barged into the journalist's study. The villain was sitting at his desk, while on his couch lay Felix smoking a cigar.

"So you are here as well!?" exclaimed Matthew. "That's even better. I'll take care of both of you once and for all. What the hell have you done?"

"Please, take a seat, Your Royal Highness," began the journalist in his quiet voice.

Matthew shuddered. Now he was one hundred percent sure that the man was a spy. His heart had suspected it long ago, but now it was undeniably true.

"This is what we do with spies!" exclaimed Matthew, ready to fire his trusty revolver (since the war, Matthew had never left the palace without it), but the spy was faster and caught Matthew's arm. The king managed to fire, but the bullet hit the ceiling.

"Kids should never be given firearms," said the journalist with a malicious smile, squeezing Matthew's arm so hard that the gun dropped from his numb fingers. The journalist caught it in mid-air and locked it away in his desk drawer.

"Now we can talk reasonably. So, what does Your Royal Highness have against us? That I defended Your Royal Highness in my newspaper, that I reassured, that I explained, that I praised Clue-Clue? Is this why Your Royal Highness has accused me of being a spy and attempted to shoot me?!"

"What about this crazy law with the schools?" said Matthew.

"How's that my fault? The children voted in that idea."

"Why didn't your newspaper report that two of our fortresses have been blown up?"

"Such information should be reported, if at all, by the Minister of War. The nation should not have access to such information. This is a military secret."

"And why were you so inquisitive about the forest fire in the country of the foreign king?"

"A journalist must be curious about everything and out of all the information he gathers, he chooses the best material for publication. Your Royal Highness has been reading my newspaper from the word 'go'. Do you find my newspaper well edited or not?"

"Well, well, far too well," laughed Matthew painfully.

The journalist looked Matthew in the eye and asked:

"Does Your Royal Highness still consider me a spy?"

"I... I will call you what you are!" yelled Felix suddenly, jumping off the couch.

The journalist paled visibly, shot a murderous glance at Felix, and before the boys could react, he was already at the door.

"You'll be hearing from me, children–and soon!" he shouted, stumbling recklessly down the stairs.

Suddenly, a car appeared in front of the house. The journalist hopped in and said something to the driver.

"Stop, thief!" yelled Felix out the window.

But it was too late. The car turned the corner and vanished into thin air. Anyway, there was no one to stop it. The handful of onlookers, mostly children, was mostly curious to know what all the fuss was about.

Matthew was finding it hard to come to terms with what had happened when, without warning, Felix threw himself at the king's feet.

"My king, please kill me! All of this is my fault!" roared Felix. "Oh, what have I done?"

"Wait Felix, we will discuss everything in detail, quietly and privately. What's done is done. When threats appear, you have to be quiet and sensible. You need to think not of what has been, but rather about what should be, will be and must be."

Felix wanted to confess at once, but Matthew would not hear of it. There was no time to lose.

"Listen, Felix, all the telephones are out of order. All I've got now is you. Do you know where our ministers live?"

"Who would I be if I didn't know?" boasted Felix. "All of them live on different streets. But I've got strong legs. I was a newspaper boy for two years. You want to summon them, don't you?"

"Yes, at once!"

Matthew looked at his watch.

"How much time do you need?"

"Half an hour."

"OK, then. Tell them to be in the throne room in two hours. Should anyone plead fatigue or illness, remind him that I'm the descendant of Henry the Impetuous."

"They'll come. I know what to tell them!" cried Felix.

He took off his ministerial shoes and his elegant frock coat and medal. On the desk stood a bottle of ink; Felix first smeared it on his trousers, hands and face before trotting away barefoot to summon the ministers. Matthew hurried to the palace to speak to the sad king before the Cabinet meeting.

"Where's the gentleman who talked to me here this morning?" asked Matthew, still panting and puffing when Clue-Clue answered the palace door.

"He went out after leaving a letter on the desk."

Matthew dashed into his study, possessed by a rather nasty feeling. Tearing open the letter, he read:

My dear Matthew! The thing I feared most has happened. That is why I have to leave you. My dear friend, if I didn't know you, I would suggest that you come to my country, but I know that you would not agree. I'm traveling along the northern road. If you need me, a two-hour horseback ride will bring you to the Gold Pheasant Inn where I will dine and wait. If our paths do not cross, remember that I'm your friend. Trust me even if you think that I have betrayed you. Whatever I do, it will be for your own good. I beg you to keep this missive secret. No one, and I mean no one, must know about it. Burn the letter the moment you have read it. Remember: Burn the letter at once! I pity you, my poor child, you lonely orphan. I would very much like to spare you some of the misfortunes that await you. Perhaps you will decide to accompany me after all? Do not fail to burn this letter.

Matthew read the letter quickly, lit a candle and brought it to a corner of the paper. Soon the paper began to smolder and finally burst into a bright flame, only to twist and contort before crumbling into ashes. The flame singed Matthew's fingers, but he paid no attention.

My soul is suffering more than my fingers, he thought.

"Poor, lonely orphan," whispered Matthew, looking at the portraits of his parents hanging in front of his desk.

The small king sighed deeply. He was not going to cry, because in a moment he would have to put on his crown. Red eyes were out of the question. Clue-Clue snuck stealthily into his office and stood before him with so humble an air that Matthew, who wanted only to be left alone, had no heart to bid her to leave.

"What do you want?" he asked the girl quietly.

"The white king is hiding his worries from Clue-Clue. The white king does not want to take black and savage Clue-Clue into his confidence. But Clue-Clue knows and she won't leave the white king in his troubles. A friend in need is a friend indeed."

Clue-Clue said this solemnly with her hands raised towards the sky in the same manner as her father once swore eternal friendship with Matthew.

"What do you know, my dear Clue-Clue?" asked Matthew, deeply moved.

"The white kings envy Matthew his gold. They want to defeat and kill him. The sad king feels sorry for Matthew, but he's weak and afraid of the strong white kings."

"Hold your tongue, Clue-Clue!"

"Clue-Clue will be as silent as a grave, but Clue-Clue saw at a glance that the sad king's an honest man. Matthew might have been betrayed by the letter, but never by Clue-Clue."

"Be quiet, Clue-Clue, no more words!" exclaimed Matthew, swiping the ashes to the floor and trampling them underfoot.

"Clue-Clue swears not to say a word more!"

Their tête-à-tête would have to continue at a later time, for the lackeys returned from school, and, pushing and elbowing each other, barged into the royal study.

Matthew's face flushed with anger:

"What's that noise? How dare you enter the royal study without being ordered to?" he shouted. "Didn't you get enough horsing around at school all morning?"

The Grand Master of Ceremonies turned as red as a beetroot.

"Your Royal Highness, I beg your forgiveness. These poor lads have been deprived of any fun and games since their childhood. They've always been either the children of lackeys and cooks or lackeys and cooks themselves, and they always had to keep quiet. And now, just like madmen or savages…"

"OK, OK, prepare the throne room. There's a meeting in half an hour."

"Oh, I've so much homework for tomorrow," groaned one lackey.

"And I have to draw a map."

"I have six math problems to solve and a whole page…"

"You won't be going to school tomorrow!" interrupted Matthew with a stern face.

They bowed and left quietly. A small scuffle broke out at the door when one lackey pushed another, injuring the latter on the doorknob.

At that moment, Felix darted into the room, sweating profusely, and legs clearly visible through his torn trousers.

"Mission accomplished, they'll be here on time," he reported. Then he began to talk.

The newspapers brought by the sad king were telling the truth. Felix had stolen money and taken bribes. When he stood in for Matthew during audiences, he gave out only some of the parcels, keeping the things he liked for himself. Those who offered him money or gifts were given better parcels. A few of his pals, most notably Tony, acted as regular fences, which meant they took and sold stolen things. But Felix was not a spy. Everything he had done, he had done on the advice of the journalist. It was the journalist who invented Baron von Rauch and the medal for Felix. He pretended to be his friend. He then demanded that Felix forge a document stating that King Matthew had thrown out all of the ministers, taken away the rights of adults and declared that children would rule in their place. When Felix refused, the journalist showed that he meant business. Putting on his coat, the journalist said:

"OK, that's fine; I'll just go and tell the king about the stolen parcels and the bribes."

Felix was so frightened that he agreed. He did not understand how the journalist knew all of his transgressions; at first he reasoned that it was only natural, for a journalist knew everything. But now he realized that the man had been a spy. There was one more thing and it also involved another forged document: an appeal of sorts to children all over the world. Matthew put his hands behind his back, pacing back and forth in his study for a long while.

"You've done many evil things, Felix. But I forgive you."

"What? Forgive? If Your Royal Highness has truly forgiven me, I know what I'll do."

"What's that?"

"I'll tell everything to my father, and he'll give me a beating the likes of which I'll never forget as long as I live."

"Don't do that. What's the use? There are other ways to redeem yourself. Now is the moment of truth. It's sink or swim for me. I need some people I can…hmm…trust. Your quick mind will come in handy."

"The Minister of War has arrived," announced the chamberlain.

Matthew put on his crown—oh, how heavy it was—and entered the throne room.

"Minister of War, tell me what you know. Briefly, quickly and without a lengthy introduction if you please; I just want the gist of it. I think I have a pretty sound grasp of the situation."

"Your Royal Highness, we only have three fortresses (out of five), four hundred cannons (compared to one thousand before the reform) and two hundred thousand usable rifles. We have enough ammunition for ten days of combat (the remains of a three-month supply)."

"How about shoes, rucksacks, biscuits?"

"The supplies are intact, save for the marmalade, which has been completely eaten."

"Is your data precise?"

"Absolutely!"

"Minister, share your thoughts: is war in the air?"

"Your Royal Highness, I don't care about politics."

"How soon can those damaged big guns and rifles be put back into service?"

"Some of them are damaged beyond repair, while others could be repaired quickly, as long as the ovens and boilers in our factories were working normally."

Matthew remembered the factory he had seen and bowed his head. His crown had never weighed so heavily.

"Minister, a word on morale in the army…?"

"Well, morale in the army is declining. Both soldiers and officers are embittered. What hurts them most is that they have been sent to civilian schools. When I was dismissed…"

"This was a forged dismissal; I didn't know anything about it. I never signed it."

The Minister of War frowned.

"When I received that forged dismissal, a visiting delegation demanded that I hand over authority for the military schools. Orders are orders. If you're ordered to go to the civilian school, you go to the civilian school; if they tell you to jump into the fire, you jump into the fire; if you are told to go to hell, you must go to hell."

"What if we do things the old way? Would they forgive the mistakes that we have made?"

The Minister of War drew his sword.

"Your Royal Highness, the entire army, starting with me and down to the last private, stands united with our hero king! We are ready to die for our homeland, for our honor as soldiers."

"That's good. That's very good!"

All is not lost, thought Matthew to himself.

The ministers arrived late and completely breathless, not accustomed to walking. The chamberlain announced that they had been driven to the palace, but they had actually come on foot, for their cars had broken down and anyway, the chauffeurs were busy doing their homework for the following day.

Matthew said, for a start, that the entire mess had been created by the journalist spy. Now a recovery plan was needed. At once they composed a message for the newspaper, announcing that starting the following day children should return to school. If some found out about the order too late, they would be excused for coming late, but come they must. The grownups were to wait until the school recreation bell rang and then return to their regular jobs. The unemployed would be paid benefits for another month and then, if they wanted to, they could go to Bum-Drum's country, who also wanted to have brick houses and schools built in his kingdom. For the time being, both parliaments would be closed. The adult parliament would be reopened first and careful thought given to what to do with the teenagers over fifteen. Once the committee drew up the regulations, the children's parliament would also be opened, but this time the children's wants and wishes would be sent to the adult parliament for consideration. Children could not be allowed to tell adults what to do. Only well-behaved and good pupils would have the right to vote.

The document was signed by the king and all the ministers.

The second appeal was directed to the military. In it, the king reminded the soldiers that the last war had ended in victory for their country.

Our two most important fortresses have been blown up. May the heroic hearts of our soldiers become a fortress for anyone who dares invade our soil—were the last words of the appeal signed by Matthew and the Minister of War.

The Commerce Minister appealed to the craftsmen to repair everything that had been damaged and could be repaired. He called on the shopkeepers to open their shops, for without them the capital had become ugly and sad.

The Minister of Education promised the children that their parliament would be reopened shortly if they were willing to behave in a way befitting patriotic youth.

The Police Prefect promised that policemen would return to their stations first thing the following morning.

"There isn't much more we can do for the moment," said the Prime Minister. "We must wait for the post and telegraph to resume normal operation and learn what's happening both abroad and at home."

"What could have happened?" asked Matthew uneasily, worried at how everything had seemed to go too well. Perhaps the sad king had only wanted to frighten him a bit?

"We don't know what has happened. We just don't know."

Everything went like clockwork the following day. After reading aloud excerpts from the articles covered in that day's newspaper, teachers bid farewell to their pupils and the grownups went home. It took some time before they returned the children's books and exercise books, but by noon, everything was as it used to be. To be quite truthful, everybody was delighted that things had returned to normal once more. The grownups, the children and the teachers rejoiced at the news.

The teachers did not say anything to the children, but they were quite happy because they had dealt with endless problems while the grownups attended school. Among those under the age of thirty, there were many common rogues who treated female teachers as friends, tried to chat them up, were noisy and disrespectful. The elder ones complained that they could not get accustomed to their desks, that the classroom was stuffy and the ink would not write. Granddaddies and grannies mostly slept and paid no attention, and if the headmistress shouted at them, it had absolutely no effect, for they were either hard of hearing or completely deaf. The youths played various pranks on the elderly, who were forever telling on them to the teachers. Anyway, the teachers were quite used to the children. Again the saying 'Better the devil you know than the devil you don't' rang true.

The office employees pretended to be angry at the children for turning everything upside down, but deep down many workers thought that it was just as well because, if an important paper happened to get lost, you could always blame the children. Among the office workers, some kept everything in perfect order and others…not so much.

The situation of Matthew's factories was worse. However, the unemployed were only too willing to help, for they thought that when the owners saw how well they worked, they might be offered a steady job.

As far as law and order was concerned, there were a few minor scuffles, but the police were well-rested and quick to restore order. The thieves, on the other hand, were as meek as mice, for they had had a field day stealing and eating for free, completely unmolested.

So, when—towards evening—the royal limousine cruised through the city streets, it was difficult to see what had happened just the day before.

Matthew was still waiting for news.

In the meantime, Clue-Clue resumed teaching her black brothers and sisters. Sitting in on one lesson, Matthew could not get over how quickly they were learning. After the lesson, Clue-Clue explained to Matthew that she had chosen the brightest children to be centurions and that the remaining nine hundred was not making such progress. Little did poor Clue-Clue know how soon and how ruthlessly their lessons were to be interrupted.

First on the scene as usual was the Prime Minister. Yesterday had been an exception to that rule, for the Minister of War was used to marching, while the Premier was not. The Prime Minister was carrying a bundle of documents under his arm, and his troubled countenance did not bode well.

"What's the news, Prime Minister?"

"It's bad," he sighed. "But it was to be expected. Perhaps it's even better this way."

"What's better? Could you be more specific?"

"War!"

Matthew shivered violently, fear twisting his stomach in knots.

Everybody crowded around the Prime Minister.

"The old king renounced the throne and was succeeded by his eldest son. No sooner had the son put the crown on his head than he ordered the army mobilized and declared war on us. He and his army are presently headed for our capital."

"Has he crossed the border?"

"Yes, two days ago. So far they have covered some forty versts."

They began to read all the telegrams and letters that had come, which took them quite some time. Matthew sat silently, his tired eyes half-closed, and listened attentively. He thought:

Perhaps it is better this way.

The first to speak was the Minister of War:

"I don't know what route the enemy has chosen, but I think he's advancing towards the two destroyed fortresses. If he marches fast, he'll be here in five days. Given the distance, he cannot fail to arrive in ten…"

"I don't understand? Aren't we going to meet them halfway?" exclaimed Matthew, hardly believing his ears.

"That's impossible. The people of the capital must defend themselves. We can send a few small units, but we can't afford to waste more men and rifles. In my opinion, we should let the enemy advance. We'll battle them in the fields not far from the capital. Either we'll defeat the invaders or…"

He left the sentence unfinished.

"Perhaps the two foreign kings could help us," put in the Foreign Minister.

"There won't be time to ask them," answered the Minister of War. "Anyway, politics has never been my strong side."

The Minister of Foreign Affairs made a long speech in which he enumerated the steps which should be taken to make the two kings turn against the first one.

"We can count on the sad king. But he doesn't like to fight and has a small army. Alone, he won't be much help; in fact he didn't even take part in the previous war, but was kept in reserve. He'll probably do the same as the friend of the Oriental kings. It was King Matthew who agreed that the second king should retain priority relations with all the Oriental kings, so he has no reason to fight. But you never know with politicians. He might want some of the black African kings for himself. Who knows?"

Then the Prime Minister took the floor.

"Gentlemen, you may, of course, decide against what I suggest, but here's my suggestion: let's send a note to the enemy, declaring that we have no wish to fight and asking him to inform us precisely what he wants. In my view, all he wants is a contribution. Let me explain. Why did he give us one of his ports and sell us ten ships so cheaply? Because he wanted Bum-Drum to send us gold. We have a lot of money. What would be the harm in giving him, say, half of it?"

Matthew kept silent. He clenched his fists and said nothing.

"Prime Minister," said the Minister of Finance. "I don't think he'll agree. Why should he agree to half of the gold when he could have all of it? Why should he abandon his plans for this war when he intends to win it?"

"Minister of War, I want to know your opinion."

Matthew clenched his fists so tightly that his fingernails cut tiny red moons into his skin. But still he waited.

"I think that we should send the note," said the Minister of War. "If he answers, we will also answer. I'm not much of an expert in diplomacy either… What I do know is that it will cause a delay, which will last a few days, a day at the least. And believe me, in our situation every hour counts. In that time, we will repair one hundred cannons—even fifty would do very nicely—and a few thousand rifles."

"And if he agreed to take half of the gold in exchange for peace?" asked Matthew in a soft voice quite unlike his own.

Silence fell. Everybody looked at the Minister of War, whose face went pale, then red, and then pale again:

"Then we should also agree."

Then he quickly added:

"We cannot win this war on our own, and it's too late to enlist anyone's help."

Matthew closed his eyes and sat like this until the end of the meeting, or should I say Council of War. The ministers even thought that he had fallen asleep. But nothing could have been further from the truth. He did not sleep, and any time he heard the phrase 'We beg the enemy king', his lips quivered.

When he held his pen to sign, he asked only:

"Couldn't we replace 'beg' with some other word?"

So, they had the letter rewritten, and the word 'beg' replaced by the word 'urge'.

We urge you to stop this war.
We urge you to end this disagreement peacefully.
We urge you to cover the cost of this war with half of our gold.

Matthew signed. It was two o'clock in the morning.

Fully dressed, he fell face down on his bed but was unable to fall asleep. At daybreak, he was still awake.

"It's do or die," Matthew whispered.

The son of the old king was in fact leading his army towards the two destroyed fortresses. This was what the Minister of War had foreseen, because it was his 'area of expertise'. But he was moving at a snail's pace and this the minister had not guessed.

The young king had to be very careful and march slowly, digging trenches and hideouts. It was the first war he was to fight on his own and he was terrified of a surprise enemy ambush from the rear. His father had let King Matthew into his territory and had paid dearly thanks to the very same tactic. The young king had to keep his army on its toes. He could not afford to lose the war. Were he to be defeated, everybody would say:

"The old king was better; we want his father instead of the son."

He had to prove that he was a better ruler.

He preferred to advance slowly but surely and, of course, constantly on his guard. There was no need to hurry since Matthew's soldiers were going to school and racking their brains over math problems, and with the children destroying his heavy artillery, Matthew had no means of conducting a war. A clever journalist spy in his employ was working in Matthew's capital to make sure that whatever could go wrong did. Owing to his scheming, everything was falling into place. It was just as well that the children had damaged the railroad network and the telegraph. Matthew would not realize that war had broken out in time to send his troops, and even if he did have time to react, he would never have enough time to raise as many troops as were needed.

That was what the old king's son thought and thus saw no cause for haste. He knew that a forced march would tire his soldiers before the pitched battle on the outskirts of Matthew's capital. It was obvious there would be only one battle.

The young king's army continued to advance and met no resistance along the way. The country folk, still angry with Matthew, and seeing that no one was coming to their defense, greeted the enemy troops as saviors instead of organizing a resistance.

"Back to school children, Little Matt's rule has come to an end…" the young king crowed, certain of his triumph.

Suddenly, on the horizon, an envoy waving a white flag appeared.

Aha! Matthew knows we're at war, thought the young king.

He read the letter from Matthew and collapsed into fits of laughter:

"Well, well, how generous of your king to give me half of his gold. Who would ever reject such a gift?"

"What answer shall I bring to my king?" said the envoy. "If half of the gold is too little, we have more to give. I'm waiting for your reply, Your Majesty."

"Tell your king that I prefer to spank naughty children rather than negotiate with them. Don't bring me any more letters or you might have a nasty accident. Leave! And be quick about it!"

He threw Matthew's letter on the floor and trampled it angrily.

"Your Royal Highness, international law requires that royal correspondence not be left unanswered," said the envoy.

"Fine, I'll answer."

On the reverse side of Matthew's letter, now sadly crumpled and muddy, he scribbled three words:

I'm nobody's fool!

In the meantime, the whole capital had learned about the war and Matthew's letter, and was impatiently waiting for an answer. And some answer it was!

Everybody was seething with anger:

"What a boor! What a cad! Wait till we get our hands on you!"

The city got down to work, building defenses.

"You'll get what's coming to you!"

All the capital's inhabitants stood united behind King Matthew. They had forgotten their grudges and remembered Matthew's merits. All of the newspapers hailed the king as Matthew the Reformer and Matthew the Heroic.

Factories worked around-the-clock. Troops practiced in the streets and squares. Everybody repeated Matthew's words:

"Do or die!"

Every day there was fresh gossip and news—some good, some bad.

The enemy is approaching the capital…
The sad king has promised to help Matt…
Bum-Drum will send all his warriors…

When Clue-Clue and her one thousand black children took to the streets, the city dwellers, carried away by their enthusiasm, showered the girl with flowers and carried her on their shoulders. There were also those who said:

"Although Clue-Clue is very black, she isn't so black that Matthew could not marry her."

Meanwhile the enemy was in fact approaching the capital.

At last the moment of battle was upon them. In the capital, people could hear both heavy artillery and the volley of machine-gun fire. In the evening, people climbed onto roofs for a better view. Some maintained they had seen fire, which was not true.

On the second day, the sound of gunshots was less distinct. Everybody understood what it meant: Matthew had the upper hand and was now chasing the retreating enemy.

On the third day, the battlefield fell silent. The enemy was sure to have escaped, probably fleeing as far as the border.

But soon news came that, although the young king had withdrawn his troops some five versts, he had not been defeated but was now occupying the trenches his men had dug on the way to Matthew's capital.

The battle could have been won, but Matthew was short on gunpowder and heavy guns. What they lacked in equipment, they made up for with determination—the enemy had not bargained on such fierce resistance from the defenders. Nevertheless, Matthew's army had to use gunpowder sparingly to avoid running out of ammunition. It was a pity, but it could not be helped.

Meanwhile the journalist spy, having fled the capital, now joined the young king's forces. The king descended on him like a ton of bricks:

"Why the hell did you tell me that Matthew had neither cannons nor gunpowder? You bloody fool! Had I not been so cautious, I might have already lost the war."

The journalist told him the whole story—how Matthew had finally seen through him, how the king had shot at him, how he had a narrow escape and hid for a week in a damp cellar. Someone must have betrayed them because Matthew had suddenly decided to see for himself what was going on. When Matthew had gone to the city, he knew at once that nothing was functioning as it should and saw one hell of a mess everywhere. The journalist also told the young king about Felix's betrayal.

"Matthew's situation is unenviable—he has too little powder and too few cannons. But on the whole, it's easier to defend yourself than to attack. Moreover, he's within a stone's throw of his capital where everything is close at hand. Our supply lines are long. We won't manage on our own. The friend of the Oriental kings must come to our rescue."

"Whether he does or he doesn't, there'll be little love lost between us. Besides, if he helps us, we'll have to share the gold."

"No getting around that," they both agreed.

Maybe it would have been a better idea to take half the gold and end the war, thought the young king.

The journalist-spy headed at once for the capital of the king who had befriended the Oriental monarchs. Once there, he began trying to convince him to turn against Matthew. But the king was reluctant:

"Matthew has never done anything wrong to me."

However, the spy would not take no for an answer. He said that Matthew was fighting a losing battle. The young king was within a stone's throw of the capital, and if he had managed to cover all that distance by himself, he would certainly win the war. And what then? He would take all the gold for himself. The young king did not need any help; he merely wanted to divide the gold justly to avoid future conflicts.

"First, I want to consult with the sad king. We'll join you together…or not at all."

"How long must I wait for your answer?"

"Three days."

"Good."

The friend of the Oriental kings wrote a letter to the sad king to know his opinion.

He soon received a response: the sad king was gravely ill and therefore unable to write back. At the same time, a letter from Matthew was received by the second king—a request for help in defending against this unjust attack.

See how two-faced this ruler is? He pretended to be my friend, gave me a port and sold me ships. He has destroyed two of my fortresses, taken advantage of the fact that the children damaged our telephone lines and telegraphs and entered our territory with his army. When I asked him what grudge he held against me and whether the port had been just a cruel joke, having offered to pay him half of my gold, the son of the old king sent this impolite response by way of my envoy: "I'm nobody's fool."

Are these the actions of a good king?

Matthew wrote an almost identical letter to the sad king, but in a more cordial tone. The sad king was not truly ill, but he had asked the royal physician to spread this rumor as he was leaving on his secret mission to Matthew's capital. Nobody but the doctor had been allowed to enter his bedroom since.

The doctor did as he was told. Each morning he entered the empty bedroom, pretending to examine the king. He brought various medicines, which he instantly flushed down the toilet, and food which he consumed himself.

When the sad king finally returned from his journey, he was so tired that he went straight to bed. He found it very unpleasant to travel across a country involved in war, even more so because he was traveling incognito and had often been forced to hide.

As soon as the sad king entered his study and read both letters, he said:

"Prepare my royal train; I'm going to the king—the friend of the Oriental kings."

The sad king was hoping to persuade him to go to Matthew's rescue, but he did not know the extent of the journalist-spy's deceit.

"Matt has never done anything wrong to you," intoned the spy sarcastically through clenched teeth, as he was leaving the second king's palace. "I've got three days. Something must be done to make him angry with King Matthew."

The spy had a paper in his breast pocket signed by Felix bearing Matthew's forged signature. It was a fake manifesto to the world's children, which read:

Children, I, King Matthew the First, appeal to you for help in carrying out my reforms. My wish is that you will no longer have to listen to your elders, and I plan to enact laws allowing you to do whatever you please. We children always hear about what we cannot do, that something will not do or is impolite. This is unfair. Why should adults be allowed to do everything, while we are not? They are continually angry and shouting at us, forever in a rage. They even beat us. I want children to enjoy the same rights as adults.

I am king and I know history well. Formerly, peasants, workers, women and black-skinned people had no rights. Now all of these groups have received equal treatment, but not children.

I have already given these rights to the children in my country. The first to follow suit were the children in the country of Queen Campanella. They went on strike. Start likewise a revolution and demand your rights. And if your kings will not agree, overthrow them and choose me. My ambition is to be king of all the children of the world, of all races. I will give you freedom. Help me start a revolution throughout the world.

Signed:
King Matthew the First
Minister Baron von Rauch

The journalist went to the printing house and asked to have a thousand copies of the manifesto run off. Then he scattered the leaflets all over town. Some of them he smeared in mud and hid in his pocket.

Scarcely had the two kings put their heads together to decide how to help Matthew when the journalist arrived.

"Look at what brave King Matthew the First is up to! He's stirring up a children's revolution and wants to become king of the world. Here, I found three such leaflets in the street. Sorry they are so muddy."

As the kings read the manifesto, their worry grew.

"Well, it can't be helped. Matthew has left us no choice. We have to unite against him. He's meddling with our children, which he has absolutely no right to do. The Oriental children are not his either. How could he do such a thing?"

The sad king's eyes filled with tears.

"What has he done? What has come over him? Why would he write such things?"

But what was done was done.

Perhaps it will be better for Matthew if I declare war on him, thought the sad king. They would defeat him without me and then they would have no pity on him, and if I'm involved, I can be of some help to Matthew.

When Matthew was told that the two other kings were against him, he could hardly believe his ears.

"So, I have been betrayed—even by the sad king. What rotten luck! I showed them how to win during the last war. Now I'll show them how to die an honorable death!"

The whole town came out with spades to dig trenches and raise ramparts. They dug three lines of defenses. The first trenches were twenty versts from the outskirts, the second line ten and the third five versts from the toll gates.

"We will retreat step by step."

When the young king learned that the two foreign kings were coming to his rescue and were quite near, he launched an immediate offensive, hoping to beat Matthew on his own. He was partially successful and seized the first trench line. But the second line was stronger: the ditches were far deeper and wider, and there was more barbed wire. Reinforcements arrived just as the young king's troops were about to storm the second line. All three armies joined forces in launching an attack on Matthew's army.

The battle lasted from dawn to dusk. The three enemy armies suffered heavy losses, but Matthew remained strong.

"Perhaps we should surrender?" suggested the sad king, but the other two accused him of cowardice:

"No, we must squash this upstart!"

The following day, the battle raged from the small hours of the morning.

"Ah! They're returning less fire," remarked the enemies, rubbing their hands with glee.

Sure enough, Matthew's troops were shooting sparingly to keep the enemy at bay; the order of the day was 'Save your ammunition and gunpowder'.

"Any suggestions? I've run out of ideas," asked Matthew.

"I think," said the Prime Minister, "that we'll have to ask for a ceasefire again. How can we wage war without gunpowder?"

Clue-Clue attended the Council of War as commander-in-chief of the black regiment. Her unit had not yet taken part in the battle because they were not armed. The black children were expert archers, but at first they could not find the right wood for their bows and arrows, and when at last they found it, they took some time to make their own weapons.

"Listen," said Clue-Clue. "I think that during the night we should withdraw to the third line. Tonight someone will go to the enemy camp and say that Bum-Drum has sent his troops with a compliment of wild beasts. Tomorrow morning we'll release the lions and tigers from their cages and simultaneously open fire. After we've frightened them a bit, we'll ask them if they are ready for peace."

"But isn't that deceitful?" asked Matthew anxiously.

"Not at all, this is called a war stratagem," explained the Minister of Justice.

"So be it," everyone agreed.

Disguised as an enemy soldier and crawling on his stomach, Felix snuck into the enemy camp and began telling everyone on his way about the lions and black soldiers, just like that.

But there were no takers. Nobody was willing to believe Felix; they just laughed and taunted him:

"You must have been dreaming. Silly boy!"

Silly or not, the soldiers still passed on what they had heard, and in this way the message grew increasingly hair-raising, like a game of telephone.

As Felix walked about the camp, the soldiers kept asking him:

"Hey buddy, have you heard the news?"

"What news?" Felix opened his eyes wide.

"They say that Bum-Drum's army and combat lions are coming to Matthew's rescue.

"Well, that's nonsense," Felix replied, wrinkling his nose in disbelief.

"But it's not! People keep hearing the roar of wild beasts."

"Let them roar. I couldn't care less."

"Wait till they tear you to pieces."

"Hey! A lion is nothing but a large pussycat. Why should I be afraid?"

"Look at that hero. You and a lion? You don't even resemble a soldier."

Felix approached a group of soldiers talking excitedly about Bum-Drum who reportedly had sent a ship of venomous snakes. Mission accomplished! Felix did not have to say anything more. He could just listen, laughing up his sleeve, but he was still angry that they had mocked him.

"You'd be better off saying your prayers instead," scolded a young corporal. "That silly laughter of yours could bring down some misfortune on us."

Why did the soldiers believe so quickly?

The soldiers had already been in action for a couple of days. They were tired, stressed out and far away from home, and they had been told that the war would be short and sweet (which was not the case). Under these conditions, the soldiers were even more upset and hence ready to believe whatever they were told.

Upon his return, Felix gave a detailed account of what he had seen and heard in the enemy camp, and the soldiers took heart.

Matthew has been lucky so many times before, so why shouldn't he be lucky once again? they thought.

Silently, under the cover of darkness, Matthew's black African soldiers left their trenches and moved nearer the capital. They carried the cages bearing lions and tigers, accompanied by half of the black warriors. The other half dispersed and was attached in groups of ten to different units so that the enemy would see them everywhere.

The plan was as follows:

"When the enemy opens fire on the deserted trenches and receives no response, they'll launch an attack. When they see that the trenches are empty, the attackers will begin cheering and shouting for joy. They'll be jubilant thinking that Matthew's capital is at their mercy, imagining themselves plundering and looting, drinking and eating as conquerors. And all at once, the black warriors will start to beat their drums, yell like madmen and release the wild beasts on the unsuspecting enemy. There will be panic, tumult and chaos. At that moment, Matthew, at the head of his cavalry, followed by the infantry, will carry out a frontal attack. This will be the terrible final struggle, but in one fell swoop we'll teach them a painful lesson. Once and for all," said Clue-Clue.

"This plan simply can't go wrong," agreed the Minister of War. "People are most afraid when something happens unexpectedly, or when they believe they have won and the tables are turned suddenly."

There were two more important details. Matthew's soldiers were to leave bottles of vodka, wine and beer in the trenches. In order to anger the animals, huge piles of straw, paper and wood were stacked against the backs of the cages. Lit the moment the cage doors opened, the fire would prevent the lions from attacking Matthew's troops.

There were also those who advised releasing a few snakes.

"We'd better leave the snakes alone," said Clue-Clue, "because you never know with snakes; they can be moody and unpredictable. The lions won't let us down."

But the enemy also had a plan.

"Listen," said the young king. "Tomorrow we must capture the capital. Otherwise we are in serious trouble. We are far from home. All our supplies are transported from afar by rail and Matthew is at home. It's very convenient to wage war not far from your capital where all your needs are close at hand. But in big cities, bad news travels faster and it is easy to scare thousands in a matter of minutes. Tomorrow our airplanes will begin bombarding the capital, and its citizens will force Matthew to surrender. Our troops should be deployed in such a way that they won't be able to retreat. Behind them, we will set up machine guns in case they want to pull back. Should anybody try, we will open fire."

"I beg Your Majesty's pardon. Are we going to shoot at our own men?"

"We must capture the city tomorrow. There are no two ways about it," said the young king. "And anyone who tries to escape will be considered a traitor."

It was announced to all the companies that the all-out attack and pitched battle was scheduled for the following morning.

There are three of us, and Matthew is alone—read the order. Matthew has neither cannons nor gunpowder. There is a revolution taking place in his capital. His soldiers refuse to fight. They are ragged and hungry. Tomorrow Matthew will be in prison and we will capture the capital.

The pilots were ordered to take off at daybreak. The airplanes were fuelled up, with all the bombs loaded and ready to fly.

The machine guns were deployed behind the troops.

"Why the machine guns?" asked the soldiers.

"The machine guns are for defense, not offense," the officers explained.

But the soldiers did not like it at all.

Nobody slept that night in either camp. Some cleaned their weapons, others wrote letters home saying goodbye to their nearest and dearest. The absolute silence was only broken occasionally by the sound of crackling campfires or the hooting of owls. In that silence, the soldiers' hearts beat faster than usual.

Dawn.

The sun was just rising when the first cannons opened fire at the empty trenches. The longer the cannonade lasted, the more mirth it produced in Matthew's camp.

"That's it. Waste your cannon balls and powder," the soldiers jeered after each shot.

Matthew stood on a hill, keeping track of events through field glasses.

"Here they are!" said Matthew to himself.

Some were running, the others, more cautious, were crawling on their bellies, at first gingerly and then more bravely. Some were encouraged by the silence in Matthew's trenches; others saw it as a cause for concern.

Suddenly, twenty airplanes took off and headed straight for the capital. Unfortunately, Matthew had no more than five airworthy planes because the children had been so excited to explore the 'iron birds' that they had managed to damage most of them during their short reign.

A fierce air battle broke out in which six enemy airplanes were shot down and all of Matthew's planes either fell or were forced to land.

The beginning of the battle looked exactly as the Council of War had foreseen. The enemy seized the first line of trenches with a roar of triumph:

"They're on the run! Got scared. Got no cannons. Oh! Look! They left in such a hurry that they left booze behind."

Some of them uncorked some of the bottles.

"It's good. Have a drink."

They drank and laughed and were soon thinking only about taking a nap.

"Why leave if it's so nice and cozy in Matthew's trenches?"

But the young king was adamant:

"We must capture the capital today!"

They advanced the cannons and machine guns.

"On my command, unleash hell!"

The soldiers were rather unwilling to attack, for alcohol on an empty stomach had made them very tipsy. But orders are orders. If you can't get out of something, the best thing is to do it at once. So, they picked up steam little by little, first walking and then running to seize the last line of Matthew's defenses.

Suddenly, the cannons boomed and the machine guns rattled. Hundreds of bullets and, quite unexpectedly, a hail of arrows went whistling by their heads.

A wild yell arose in Matthew's camp, accompanied by kettles, drums and reed fifes.

Black warriors began pouring out of the trenches. They were small or maybe it only seemed like that from afar. Perhaps there weren't too many of them, but they were real and not just flights of imagination.

Lions and tigers, dazed and confused by the noise and fire and desperate to escape the heat, rushed forward in terrifying leaps and bounds towards the dumbfounded enemy. Strange as it may seem, the sight of one hundred men killed by gunshot would not have made the same impression as seeing one soldier torn apart by a lion. The enemy soldiers had seen friends shot but never maimed or mauled by a wild beast. A lion's teeth were far more terrifying than a steel bullet…

What came next was simply indescribable. While some of the enemy soldiers ran straight into the barbed wire and dropped their rifles, others were trying to escape and perished under friendly fire. Still others found themselves caught in the crossfire, and not knowing what else to do, fell down helplessly or raised their hands up to the sky as if appealing to a higher power for mercy.

The enemy cavalry, which had helped to defeat Matthew's army, now ran, guns blazing, into the machine gun nests, trampling and injuring the crews.

Smoke, dust and indescribable chaos followed. No one saw anything and no one knew what had happened for an hour or two until the dust cleared.

When historians described the battle years later, each described it differently. There was, however, agreement about one thing; namely, that there had never been a battle like this one in the history of mankind.

The Minister of War was close to tears:

"If only we had ammunition and gunpowder for another two hours."

But you cannot draw water from a stone. There simply wasn't any more.

"Cavalry forward!" Matthew yelled from the back of a gorgeous white steed.

The only thing they could do was take advantage of the panic in enemy ranks and chase their foes, grabing all their supplies and pushing the enemy soldiers so far from the capital that they would never realize that they were not being chased by Bum-Drum's troops, but by a handful of black children and a few dozen wild animals from the zoo. This was how Matthew would ensure victory.

Quite unexpectedly, when Matthew was hurriedly mounting his horse, he looked at the capital, and nearly fell off his steed, thunderstruck.

"No, it can't be. This must be a terrible mistake. I must be seeing things."

But unfortunately, he was not. From all the towers of the capital white flags were waving in the breeze. The capital had surrendered.

Messengers were sent at once with the order:

"Tear those white rags down! Execute the traitors and cowards on the spot."

Alas, it was too late. The enemy had already seen the flags of truce. Initially astounded, they soon regained their composure.

Battle is the kind of experience that can make a person feel intoxicated, but all it takes is a bullet whizzing by your head to sober you up. Fear, hope, despair and desire for revenge can follow one another in quick succession. In the midst of such confusion, soldiers are soon disoriented and strive to think: *What is happening? Is this really happening or is it a bad dream?*

Matthew's big guns were silent; dead lions and tigers lay strewn across the battlefield, riddled with bullets. The white flags fluttering over the capital signaled surrender.

"What does all this mean?" some muttered.

But the young king understood at once.

"Forward!" he shouted.

"Forward!" repeated the officers and rank and file soldiers.

Matthew saw it all, but he was helpless.

The enemy troops were returning, closing ranks and picking up the weapons they had dropped.

The white flags were disappearing. But it was too late. The enemy was approaching, cutting through the barbed wire with special cutters.

"Your Royal Highness," began an old general in a shaky voice.

Matthew knew exactly what to say. He jumped off his horse and, skin as white as a sheet, said slowly and distinctly:

"Follow me, all those who want to die!"

There were few volunteers: Felix, Tony, Clue-Clue and a handful of soldiers.

"Where shall we go?" they asked.

"The building where the lion cages stood is empty. There we will defend ourselves like lions, to the last drop of blood."

"But the building is too small for us." said a young corporal.

"All the better," whispered King Matthew.

They hopped into five nearby cars, taking as many weapons and as much ammunition as they could. They drove off. But before they had gone very far, Matthew turned around and noticed that over their camp a white flag was already waving.

It suddenly occurred to Matthew how ironic fate was. He had ordered his capital to shake off that mark of disgrace and captivity, but now, it was not a city of old men, women and children frightened by a few bombs, but the army, the troops—helpless and powerless in the face of the enemy—throwing themselves on the mercy of the invaders.

"It's just as well that I'm not among them," said Matthew to himself. "Don't cry, Clue-Clue. We'll have a beautiful death, and they'll stop saying that kings wage wars, but only rank and file soldiers die in them."

To die beautifully—that was his only desire. Suddenly, he had a morbid thought: *What kind of funeral will my enemy arrange for me?*

But even this wish of Matthew's was not to be fulfilled. Instead of a minute of suffering, there were hours of humiliation and pain, followed by years of agonizing penance in store for him.

The army had surrendered, and in the entire kingdom, only one place was still free—a square building where a cage of lions once stood.

The enemy tried to storm Matthew's stronghold, but in vain. They sent an envoy, but as soon as he approached the building, waving a white flag as is customary, the besieged defenders dealt him two mortal blows: a bullet to the skull and from Clue-Clue's bow, an arrow that pierced his heart.

"He has killed an envoy."

"He has violated international law."

"He has committed murder."

"This is unheard of!"

"The capital has to be punished for the crime of its king."

But the capital had already declared:

"Matthew is no longer our king."

When the enemy airplanes had begun bombarding the capital, its richest and most eminent citizens called an emergency meeting.

"We have suffered enough under the reign of this unruly child, enough tyranny at the hands of this crazy brat. Should he win once again, it will be far worse than if he's defeated. Who can predict what will come over him? And what about that Felix or what's his name…"

There were those, however, who defended Matthew:

"He's done a lot of good for our country. The mistakes he made were due to lack of experience. But since the boy has a good head on his shoulders, he'll be quick to learn life lessons."

Who knows? Matthew's supporters might have won if a bomb had not fallen in the immediate neighborhood, smashing all the windows in the conference hall.

"Fly the white flag!" shouted someone in desperation.

No one dared to protest against such an open act of treason. What came next is more or less well-known.

They flew those flags of disgrace and surrender, and drew up an act in which the city refused to recognize Matthew as king and declared it would no longer take responsibility for his follies.

"Enough of this comedy!" cried the young king. "We have conquered the entire state and only this henhouse refuses to surrender. General of artillery, bring two cannons here and fire near the hovel. If this obstinate Matthew does not come out, destroy the lair of this wolf cub completely with your next three shots."

"Yes, Your Majesty!"

At that moment, the sad king cried out loudly:

"Wait a moment, Your Royal Highness; don't forget that you're not alone here. There are three armies here and three kings."

The young king bit his lip.

"It's true that there are three of us. But our rights and merits are not the same. I declared war, and my army won the lion's share of the victory."

"Perhaps that's why your soldiers were the first to run away at the sight of lions."

"And then I ordered my soldiers to rally and fight. And they did."

"Because Your Royal Highness knew that we would have hastened to help, had your army been in trouble."

The young king did not answer. It was true. Victory had not been won easily. Half of his troops were dead or wounded, unable to fight. Under such circumstances, he had to be very careful lest the two allies become his enemies.

"So, what do you want to do?" he asked gruffly.

"There's no need to hurry. Holed up in a pavilion for wild animals, Matthew is no threat to us. We'll surround the garden with guards and hunger will soon force Matthew to surrender. In the meantime, we can make up our minds what to do with Matthew when we take him prisoner."

"I think we should shoot him unceremoniously."

"And I think history would never forgive us if we were to touch a single hair on the head of this brave child."

"History will always justify what we do," cried the young king, seething with anger, "and if someone is guilty of so many deaths, so much bloodshed, he's not a child—he's a monster!"

The king who was the friend of the Oriental monarchs sat there without saying a word, and the two kings who were arguing knew all too well that the last word would belong to him because he was very wise.

It would be an unpardonable folly if we made enemies of the black African kings, who are

Matthew's friends, he thought. What's the use of killing the boy? We can exile him to a desert island, and let him rot. We could kill two birds with one stone.

That was what they decided to do.
The agreement that they drew up provided that:

Point One: King Matthew the First should be taken prisoner. He must be taken alive.
Point Two: He should be exiled to a desert island.

Another argument broke out over Point Three. The sad king demanded that Matthew should be allowed to take along ten companions of his own choosing. The young king, however, would not hear of it. Matthew, insisted the latter, should be accompanied by three officers and thirty soldiers—one officer and ten rank and file soldiers from each of the victorious armies.

It took them two full days to reach a compromise.

"OK," said the young king, "I'll agree to ten companions, but they can only join him in exile after one year. We'll tell Matthew he's been sentenced to death and then grant him a last minute reprieve. It's absolutely necessary that his people see him cry and beg for mercy so that stupid nation of his, which so meekly agreed to his rule, understands once and for all that Matthew is by no means the hero they think him to be, but rather an impudent and cowardly brat. Otherwise, in a few years' time, his nation might organize an uprising and demand Matthew's return. Then Matthew will be older and even more dangerous than he's now."

"There is no sense in all this quarrelling," said the king who had befriended the Oriental kings. "In the meantime, Matthew will die of hunger, and our quarrel will be meaningless."

The sad king acceded, and two new points were added to the agreement.

Point Three: Matthew shall be court-martialed and sentenced to death. Then the three kings will grant him a last minute reprieve.
Point Four: Matthew shall spend the first year of his exile alone under armed guard, and after this year, the kings shall allow ten persons willing to live with Matthew in exile to join him on the island.

Further points were negotiated: How many towns each king would take for himself, and how much gold… What should be left in the capital as a free city…and so forth.

Suddenly, an adjutant announced that a gentleman had requested to see the kings. He said it was a matter of the utmost importance. It was a chemist who had invented a special sleeping gas. If they were to use it against Matthew, he would, weakened by hunger, fall asleep, and they could tie him up and shackle him.

"We can test it on animals first," suggested the chemist.

They brought one bottle with gas, put it half a verst from the royal stable and turned on a stream of liquid gas which spread out quickly to form a mist; it covered the whole stable and lasted no more than five minutes.

When they entered the stable, they found all the horses sleeping soundly. Unaware of the test, even the groom, who was having a nap on the hay, was now so fast asleep that they could not wake him up no matter how much they shook him. Even a shot fired from a pistol close to his ear did not rouse him. The boy did not even bat an eyelid. Both the horses and the boy woke up after an hour.

The test proved one hundred percent successful. Little wonder that they decided to use the gas to end the siege immediately.

It was about time because Matthew had not eaten and drunk anything for three days. His handful of comrades-in-arms rationed out what little food and drink they had.

"We must be ready to defend ourselves for a month," he repeated.

Matthew still had not given up hope that the capital would regret what it had done and would put the invaders to the sword.

When Matthew saw some civilians walking around the garden, he thought it was a delegation from the capital and did not give the order to shoot.

But what was this?

A cold liquid hit the window panes with such strength that some of them broke. A fine mist floated into the pavilion. A sweet taste and pungent smell filled their mouths and noses. Matthew could not decide whether he felt good or bad. He grabbed his rifle, suspecting treachery, but his hands seemed to weigh a ton. He struggled to see what was going on.

"Attention!" he shouted, gasping for breath.

Now he could hardly keep his eyes open. The rifle fell out of his hands. Matthew bent down to pick up his weapon but could not stand up.

It was all the same to him.

He forgot where he was…

…and he fell asleep.

It was a rude awakening.

Matthew knew what captivity was. But the first time, no one had known that he was King Matthew the First. Now things were different.

Matthew's wrists and ankles were secured with heavy shackles; the windows of his cell, high on the walls just under the ceiling, were covered with massive bars. The heavy iron door had a tiny round window through which the soldier on duty could observe him.

Now Matthew remembered everything. He lay on his narrow bed thinking:

What should I do?

Matthew was not one of those who brood about their problems and look back at the past. He always thought about what should be done to change things for the better.

In order to know what to do, you have to know what has happened. But Matthew did not know anything.

He was lying on a straw mattress on the bare ground next to the wall. Suddenly, it occurred to him to tap the wall with his fingertips. He half hoped someone would respond, but it was in vain.

"Where's Clue-Clue? What has happened to Felix? What's happening in the capital?"

He heard a prison key grate in the iron door, and two enemy soldiers entered. One stood at the door, and the other put a mug of milk and a roll at the head of Matthew's bed. At first, Matthew thought to overturn the milk, but on second thought he decided not to. After all, he had lost the war; he was a POW, hungry and thirsty, and needed to restore his strength.

Matthew sat up on his mattress, and, carrying his iron chain with difficulty, he reached for the mug. The soldier looked at him impassively.

While eating the roll, Matthew said:

"Your kings are rather on the mean side, aren't they? One roll—that's not too much. When they paid me a visit, I fed them better. And when the old king was my POW, I never stinted on food for him either."

Matthew burst into a fit of laughter.

The soldiers did not utter a word as they had been forbidden to talk to the prisoner. But they reported the incident to the prison governor, who telephoned for further instructions.

An hour later, the soldiers brought Matthew three rolls and three mugs of milk.

"Oh, that's too much. I don't want to take advantage of my benefactors' hospitality. There are three kings. I'll take one from each of them and you can take the fourth for yourselves."

Matthew ate his meal and went to sleep. He slept until midnight and would have slept much longer if he hadn't been woken up.

"The convict formerly known as King Matthew the First will be court-martialed at midnight," read the enemy military prosecutor aloud. The document bore the seals and signatures of the three kings.

"Rise, please!"

"Tell the court to remove my shackles. They're far too heavy and they hurt my ankles."

The shackles did not injure Matthew's legs. They were, if anything, too loose. But Matthew wanted to stand before the court, looking neat and dignified, without struggling with the dangling shackles and chains.

Matthew's request was granted. His heavy iron shackles were replaced with small elegant gold chains.

Matthew entered the courtroom carrying himself proudly. It was the very same room in which not so long ago he had concluded an agreement with his ministers.

He looked around curiously.

The eldest generals of all three kings sat around a long table. To the left the kings themselves were seated. To the right were some civilians dressed in tailcoats and white gloves. Who were they? The gentlemen turned their heads so that he could not see their faces.

The indictment act read as follows:

1. King Matthew issued a proclamation to the children, urging them to rebel and not to listen to their elders.

2. King Matthew attempted to incite a worldwide revolution in order to become king of the world.

3. Matthew shot and killed an envoy that approached him with a white flag. Because at the time Matthew was not the king, he stands trial as a common criminal and should be either hanged or shot.

"What do you say to this?"

"That I issued the proclamation of which you speak is a dirty lie. That I was no longer king when I shot the envoy is another lie. Whether I wanted to become king of the world or not is something known only to me. No one else can know my mind."

"Sirs, please read aloud your resolution," said the presiding judge to the gentlemen in tail-coats and white gloves.

They rose, and one of them began to read. His hands were shaking and he looked as pale as a ghost.

We who have gathered together in the capital during the battle, given the fact that bombs are destroying our town and that the very hall where we have gathered has been bombed, smashing out all the windows—we, citizens of our capital city, want to save our wives and children—and we do not want Matthew to be our king anymore. The capital hereby deprives Matthew of the throne and the crown. We do it with heavy hearts, but we cannot bear this any longer. We are flying white flags as a sign that we are unwilling to wage this war. Therefore, it is not our king who fights this war but Matthew, an ordinary boy who should take responsibility for his own actions. And we are innocent.

"Please sign it." The presiding judge handed Matthew a pen. Matthew took it, thought for a while and wrote at the bottom of the page:

I do not agree with this resolution, which was drafted by a bunch of traitors and cowards who betrayed our country. I am and I will remain King Matthew the First.

Then he read aloud what he had written.

"Gentlemen, judges and generals," said Matthew, turning to his enemies. "If you want to try me, I demand that you address me as King Matthew because I'm the legitimate king, both during my lifetime and after death. If this is not an honest trial, but a cold-blooded attack against a vanquished king, then shame on you as human beings and soldiers. You can say what you please, but don't count on a response from me."

The generals retired to consider Matthew's words. Matthew, on the other hand, whistled a military march under his breath.

The judges returned.

"Does Matthew admit to issuing the manifesto to children all over the world?" asked the presiding judge.

No answer.

"Does Your Royal Highness admit to issuing the manifesto to children all over the world?" asked the presiding judge.

"I do not. I have never issued such an appeal."

"Call in the witness!" ordered the judge.

Who should walk into the courtroom but the journalist-spy? Matthew did not bat an eyelid.

"Here's the witness."

"Yes," said the journalist. "I can testify that Matthew wanted to become the king of all the children in the world."

"Is this true?" asked the judge.

"It is," answered Matthew. "I did want this. I would have become their king. But the signature under the proclamation is false. This spy forged my signature. But it is true that I want to be the king of all the children."

The judges began to examine the signature, nodded their heads, pretended that they could not be sure, that it was impossible to spot the difference.

But now it was all the same, for Matthew had admitted his guilt.

The prosecutor gave a long speech:

"Matthew must be executed; otherwise there will be neither law and order nor peace."

"Does Matthew want someone to speak in his defense?"

No answer.

"Does Your Royal Highness wish for someone to speak in Your defense?" the presiding judge repeated.

"I don't think that will be necessary," answered Matthew. "The hour is so late that it would be a waste of time. We had better go to sleep."

Matthew said this quite cheerfully. He would not reveal what was going on deep down in his soul. He decided to be proud until the end.

The judges retired again. This time they returned with a sentence:

"Execution by firing squad."

"Sign here, please," said the presiding judge.

No response.

"I must ask Your Royal Highness to sign in order to certify that the proceedings were carried out in accordance with the law."

Matthew signed.

At this, one of the gentlemen in tailcoats and white gloves threw himself at the feet of Matthew, and, weeping, he exclaimed:

"My beloved King, forgive me my outrageous treason! Only now do I realize what we have done. I know that had it not been for our pitiful cowardice, it would not be the invaders, but you who would preside over this trial."

Only with difficulty did the soldiers manage to wrench him off the king. What good was such a display? It was too late for regrets.

"I wish you good night, generals and judges," said Matthew proudly, as befitted the king, before leaving the courtroom.

Twenty soldiers with drawn swords accompanied him to his cell. He lay down on his straw mattress at once and pretended to be asleep.

The priest entered his cell and, taking pity on the sleeping boy, said prayers for the condemned without waking him up. After the priest left, Matthew lay still pretending to be asleep, but what he felt and thought about on that night remain a mystery known only to Matthew.

* * *

Now they were leading Matthew.

He was walking down the middle of the road in his gold shackles. The military lined the streets along the route, city folk arrayed behind the cordon.

The day was beautiful. The sun was shining. Hundreds of thousands of inhabitants had taken to the streets to see their king for the last time. Many had tears in their eyes. Had Matthew seen those tears, it would have been easier for him to go to the place of execution.

Those who loved Matthew kept silent, for they were afraid to express their love and respect for him in the presence of the enemy. What would they have said? They were used to cheering "Long live the king!" But what were they to call out as their king was about to be executed?

The hooligans and winos, who at the young king's behest had been given alcohol from Matthew's cellars, were not so conflicted:

"Oh, the king is walking! Not really a full-size king; he looks more like a dwarf! Are you crying Matthew? We'll help you wipe your nose!"

Matthew carried himself proudly, raising his head so that everyone could see his eyes were dry. He frowned slightly hearing those unfriendly slurs, but he continued to look up into the sky and at the sun.

He did not hear what was happening around him. His thoughts were somewhere else:

What has happened to Clue-Clue? Where's Felix? Why did the sad king betray me? What will happen to my country? Will I see my father and mother when a bullet cuts my young life short?

They crossed the entire city before Matthew arrived at the stake on the square where a hole dug for the occasion was already waiting for him. Matthew was pale and quiet as the firing squad loaded their rifles. The soldiers raised their weapons and took aim only to be stopped at the last moment.

Matthew was just as quiet while he listened to the last minute reprieve:

"Instead of execution by firing squad, we hereby exile you to a desert island."

A car pulled up in front of the prisoner to take him back to prison. In a week's time, he would be in exile.

What Matthew did on the island and what became of him, I will let you know as soon as I find out.

www.ingramcontent.com/pod-product-compliance
Lightning Source LLC
LaVergne TN
LVHW081455060526
838201LV00051BA/1802